MOONDROP TO GASCONY

MOONDROP TO GASCONY

ANNE-MARIE WALTERS

FOREWORD BY PROFESSOR M R D FOOT

INTRODUCTION, POSTSCRIPT AND NOTES BY DAVID HEWSON

MOHO BOOKS

Moho Books
Wiltshire, Great Britain

Tel: +44 (0)1730 233870
email: contact@moho-books.com
web site: www.moho-books.com

Moondrop to Gascony originally published by Macmillan & Co Ltd 1946.
This edition published in Great Britain by Moho Books, 2009.

ISBN 978-0-9557208-1-9

British Library Cataloguing in Publication Data
A CIP catalogue record for this book is available from the British Library.

Cover, design and typesetting by Mark Tennent www.tennent.co.uk

Printed in Great Britain by CPI Antony Rowe, Chippenham.

CONTENTS

PREFACE

Writing in the immediate aftermath of World War II, when nerves in France were raw and communities torn apart by acts – and accusations – of collaboration, Anne-Marie Walters largely used pseudonyms to protect those still alive. She even changed the name of the house where she spent most of her time. For this new edition, David Hewson has tracked down the real people behind Anne-Marie's story through interviews with survivors and their children, backed up by documentary evidence from the French and British archives. He presents them here, in addition to biographical details for all the main characters, including Anne-Marie's fellow-SOE agent Claude Arnault and George Starr, head of SOE's WHEELWRIGHT circuit in southwest France. Hewson also fills in the rest of Anne-Marie's own story, from her school days in Geneva and her family's escape to England at the outbreak of war, to why she was sent back to London across the Pyrenees and what happened to her in the post-war years.

In the introduction, postscript and notes, we follow the convention of putting agents' field names in italics and the names of SOE circuits, operations and escape lines in capitals.

In 1947 *Moondrop to Gascony* won the John Llewellyn Rhys Prize. This is awarded to the best work of literature (fiction, non-fiction, poetry or drama) by an author aged 35 or under from the United Kingdom or the Commonwealth.

FOREWORD

BY PROFESSOR M R D FOOT

Anne-Marie Walters had a cosmopolitan upbringing: her mother was French, her father English. She was brought up in Geneva. F P Walters, her father, briefly an Oxford don before the Great War – which he survived – belonged to that then nascent, but always respectable, profession of international civil servant. He rose to be Deputy Secretary-General of the League of Nations, and later wrote its official history. His daughter, bilingual from an early age in French and English, was brought up in the impeccable standards of the old diplomatic corps: a rather odd apprenticeship for her hectic months on the run from the Gestapo among the farmers of Gascony in 1944. She knew how to behave in polite society; the rules she was brought up on turned out not quite useless in the close company of refugee Spanish republican infantry, far-left freebooters, and Gascon vineyard workmen. Once she was stranded in occupied Paris for a week, and was able to take refuge in the flat of a family friend she had not seen for over ten years; the rest of her life in occupied France was a good deal more hectic.

Her parents had taken her with them to England when the world war against Hitler began, and she joined the Women's Auxiliary Air Force (WAAF); whence, after two years' service, she was plucked away into the Special Operations Executive (SOE), one of Great Britain's nine wartime secret services, formed in July 1940 by amalgamating branches of the War Office, Foreign Office and Secret Intelligence Service. She was trained to be a secret agent – SOE specialised in sabotage and subversion behind the enemy's lines – and enjoyed the relaxed atmosphere of its training schools, while learning not to gossip. She was posted to SOE's F Section, of which the main task was to form and arm strong and secure parties of saboteurs, who would make the Germans' rear areas untenable for the enemy whenever the main Allied invasion of France began. They worked quite independently of SOE's RF Section, who acted as liaison between the supporters of General de Gaulle and SOE's supply arrangements, and of several other SOE sections busy in France with such specialist tasks as escape. The details are all set out in the official history. David

Hewson's notes below fill in much of the personal background that she had to leave out.

What makes her book so valuable today is its immediacy. Macmillan first published it in 1946, so that it came on the heels of George Millar's *Maquis* and provided an early, direct account of what life had actually been like for those who lived in active resistance: pretending to be one thing, when on a train or out shopping or bicycling down a lane, while actually being another, a deadly armed enemy of the forces that were oppressing France.

Her training had included learning to parachute, and it was by parachute that she eventually got to France, on 4 January 1944, to act as courier to George Starr, code-named *Hilaire*, one of F Section's brightest stars. His cover was that he was a retired Belgian mining engineer (which helped to cover the Belgian accent of his not very accurate French). He had already been at work for several months, and had reliable saboteurs standing by in four departments of southwestern France, stretching from Périgord to the foothills of the Pyrenees; he badly needed someone to carry messages for him, as he was becoming only too well known to the police of Pétain's regime and, still worse, to the Gestapo.

With what devotion she carried out her tasks will soon appear. She glosses over the indispensable role of Starr's wireless operator, Yvonne Cormeau (*née* Biesterfeld), whom she does not even name. That there were personal frictions within the circuit was not unusual. These led to Anne-Marie's despatch on foot over the Pyrenees just as the moment of liberation was approaching, carrying a message from Starr to London that he did not want to trust to the wireless, maintaining the day-to-day tension of her journey to France and back right up to the end, in one of the outstanding surveys of the real life of a secret agent.

M R D Foot
Nuthampstead
June 2009

INTRODUCTION

It all started in 2003, with the gift of a copy of the 1946 edition of *Moondrop to Gascony*. This inspired me to read some of the books written about the Special Operations Executive (SOE) and its activities in France, especially the southwest and Gascony, where I have lived for 15 years.

This is the countryside of WHEELWRIGHT. Many of Anne-Marie Walters' expeditions on bicycle, or by train and bus, took her remarkably close to where we live. I often find myself wondering whether she would have looked at the same lines of trees (albeit perhaps more slim-waisted in their youth) which provide the summer shade on many of our country roads. The majority of the buildings in Condom and central Toulouse remain largely as she would have seen them. The rolling countryside of Gascony has changed but little, save for the odd intrusions of water-towers, modern communications masts and some new houses strategically placed to take advantage of the spectacular views towards the Pyrenees. Looking at their silhouette, it is all too easy to imagine the heat Anne-Marie encountered when she crossed these mountains during that first week in August, 1944. Today, there are no frontiers, no guards and no enemies.

My appetite was soon whetted to find out more about Anne-Marie and the others who contributed to the success of WHEELWRIGHT. Professor M R D Foot refers to her in the first edition of his *SOE in France*, which became my bible. Philippe de Vomécourt mentions her by name in *Who Lived to See the Day*. But, apart from these two books, and *Inside SOE* by E H Cookridge, I found little about Anne-Marie in print.

The lucky break came in 2006, when I tracked down Mamoulens, the farm near Condom where Anne-Marie spent so much of her time. With the help of the Castagnos family I made contact with her son, Jean-Pierre Comert, who kindly provided a copy of Anne-Marie's death certificate. This was the key to opening her personnel file at The National Archives in Kew, to which few had been given access since 1945. A memorable meeting with Monsieur Pierre Péré at Panjas gave me some clues to local personalities who might be prepared to tell their stories to an expatriate Irishman. Monsieur Jean St-Avit of Vic-Fezensac took me to see the sites of several *parachutages* in the area in which he himself had taken part. He also introduced me to some of his fellow-resistants who had likewise assisted at these midnight receptions.

By now I was quite fascinated by the story of *Moondrop to Gascony*. Above all, I wanted to unravel the pseudonyms which Anne-Marie had justifiably used in 1946 to protect the identities of her friends and others she mentions. It did not take long to appreciate the accuracy of what she had written without the benefit of a diary to refer to. So what if the casualties at the battle of Castelnau-sur-l'Auvignon were not as many as she claimed? The "fog of war" has often affected the accounts of greater battles throughout the ages. And the rest of her story is amazingly well corroborated.

So I gradually began to piece together the details not only of Anne-Marie's life but also the lives of the many people with whom she came in contact. It is the results of these researches that are included in this new edition of *Moondrop to Gascony* in the form of explanatory notes and background information, beginning with the establishment of SOE in southwest France.

The arrival of SOE in southwest France, November 1942

The successful implantation of SOE in southwest France in November 1942, and the subsequent appearance of the WHEELWRIGHT circuit, owes much to fate and to the efforts of three early-day heroes of SOE: Henri Sevenet, Pierre de Vomécourt and Virginia Hall.

Henri Sevenet (*Rodolphe, Barnabé*), born in 1914 and educated in Paris, was called up for military service in 1935. Demobilised in 1937, he spent a further two years in Paris qualifying to be an Inspecteur d'Assurance. Sevenet was recalled to the army in August 1939 and taken prisoner on 18 May 1940, when the Germans invaded. He escaped the same night and made his way on foot to join General Giraud, who had already formed a small group of resistants. Two days later, after Giraud's capture, Sevenet found the general's car abandoned in a wood near Wassigny, in the Aisne. He and three others drove off in it, only to be re-captured the same evening.

By the end of October, Sevenet had escaped yet again. This time he made his way to his home at the Château de Breuil, near Chédigny in the Indre-et-Loire, and then to Lyon. Here he found employment with Citroën as a buyer of raw materials and spare parts. This gave him the authority to visit their branches in Toulouse, Perpignan, Clermont-Ferrand and elsewhere.

Baron Pierre de Vomécourt (*Sylvain*) came from a family which had rendered

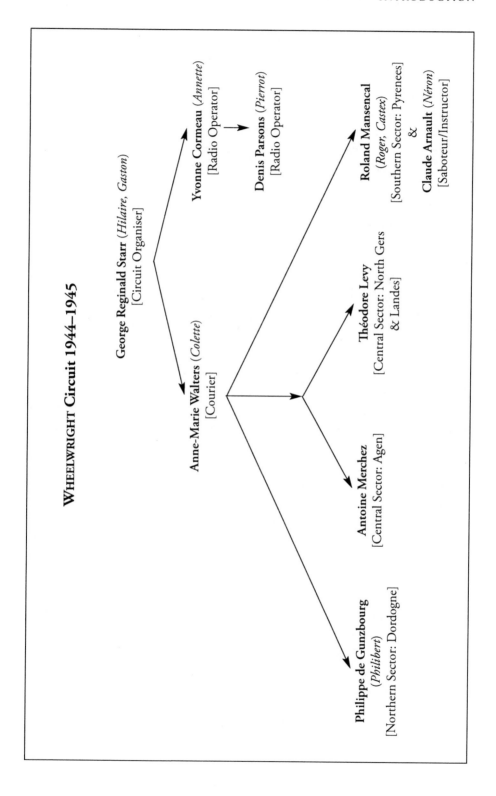

WHEELWRIGHT Circuit 1944–1945

George Reginald Starr (*Hilaire, Gaston*)
[Circuit Organiser]

Yvonne Cormeau (*Annette*)
[Radio Operator]

Denis Parsons (*Pierrot*)
[Radio Operator]

Anne-Marie Walters (*Colette*)
[Courier]

Roland Mansencal
(*Roger, Castex*)
[Southern Sector: Pyrenees]
&
Claude Arnault (*Néron*)
[Saboteur/Instructor]

Théodore Levy
[Central Sector: North Gers
& Landes]

Antoine Merchez
[Central Sector: Agen]

Philippe de Gunzbourg
(*Philibert*)
[Northern Sector: Dordogne]

great service to France over many years. A good shot and a quick thinker, he was attached to a British regiment as French liaison officer, and evacuated from Dunkerque just before the fall of France in June 1940. On arrival in London, he joined the British Army, where he was soon spotted by SOE for work in France; he knew the country, he could speak the language and he had many contacts in both the occupied and unoccupied zones. On 10 May 1941, Pierre de Vomécourt became one of the first SOE agents in France when he parachuted to a "blind" landing – one with no reception committee – not far from his brother Philippe's château at Bas-Soleil, near Limoges. As a Frenchman, Pierre was able to slip back into his normal life without anyone suspecting that, during his absence since June 1940, he had spent several months in England training with SOE.

At their château, Pierre and Philippe (*Gauthier*) were joined by their elder brother, Jean, who had been badly wounded while serving with the Royal Flying Corps in World War I, and was now owner of the Hôtel de la Grande Poste at Pontarlier, in the Doubs. The brothers proceeded to divide France into three regions where they could recruit Frenchmen willing to join the Resistance.

Pierre set up the AUTOGIRO circuit near Paris, where he soon became well established. Jean took charge of eastern France and set up several small but effective Resistance units in place of the escape line he had been running into Switzerland. Philippe took charge of the southern zone from a base at Lyon, where he started to get in touch with his many friends and contacts. In his capacity as an Inspector of Railway Wagons he held an *ausweiss*, which enabled him to travel freely throughout France and support the emerging underground movements and clandestine newspapers with money and supplies. Although SOE normally provided all the funds required for its circuits, the de Vomécourts used a considerable amount of their own money to fund their *réseaux*.

Lyon, the largest town in Vichy France, was also home to **Virginia Hall** (*Marie, Philomène*), the organiser of SOE's HECKLER circuit. Born in 1906 to a wealthy family in Baltimore, Hall enrolled at the Ecole des Sciences Politiques in Paris in 1926. The following year she was accepted by the Konsular Akademie in Vienna, before joining the American Foreign Service. In 1940, she volunteered as an ambulance driver for the French Army but, when the Germans invaded France, escaped to London and worked in the American Embassy as a code clerk for the Military Attaché. It was here that she was discovered by Vera Atkins and quickly recruited by her and Jacques de Guélis to work for SOE's French Section (F Section) who were, at that time, having difficulty finding enough suitable agents to work in France. With her perfect knowledge of French and German and her American citizenship, Hall entered Vichy-controlled France on 23 August 1941, posing as a reporter for the *New York Post*.

Apart from Giliana Gerson, who visited Vichy (using her Chilean passport) for three weeks in June 1941, Virginia Hall was the first permanent woman field agent SOE sent to France. She remained in Lyon for the next 14 months, until forced to flee on foot over the Pyrenees with the help of SOE's VIC escape line when the Germans occupied the whole country in November 1942.[1] During this period she not only worked hard to organise the HECKLER circuit, help Allied airmen escape, provide a courier service for many agents and obtain supplies for clandestine presses and forgers, but also managed to travel and write articles for the *Post* about everyday life in Vichy France[2] – all the while avoiding the Gestapo, who had penetrated some of the Resistance circuits and were already working unofficially in the unoccupied zone.

Shortly after his return to France on 1 April 1942, Pierre de Vomécourt visited Virginia Hall in Lyon. Here he met Henri Sevenet, who had been a childhood friend of the de Vomécourts in Paris. Pierre told Sevenet he was working for the intelligence service and asked whether he would be willing to cooperate. Sevenet agreed at once and was given instructions to form *"groupes d'action"*.

Before Sevenet could start this work, however, he received orders to go to London, which he did, also by crossing the Pyrenees on foot. He arrived in London on 19 July 1942 and soon afterwards attended a shortened SOE training course, at the end of which he was commended "for doing very well indeed on demolition training." By the end of August, Sevenet was back in France, having been dropped by parachute near his home at Chédigny with the following instructions:

1. To operate on targets on the railway line between Tours and Poitiers;
2. To select suitable grounds for the reception of *matériel*;
3. To put himself at the disposal of Philippe de Vomécourt, and to persuade him to return to London.

Sevenet went first to see Philippe at his home near Limoges. Unable to persuade him to leave, he continued to Toulouse and Lyon, where he contacted Brian Stonehouse (*Celestin*), who had been instructed to transmit his signals.[3] Sevenet then began organising his district and selecting suitable dropping grounds in the southwest. These included La Plume, La Réole, Castelnau-sur-l'Auvignon and the race course at Agen.

Through Monsieur Leurquin, the Belgian Consul at Agen, Sevenet made contact with a group of former senior NCOs of the 150e Régiment d'Infanterie, who had been demobilised after the armistice. Among these were Antoine Merchez, Pierre Wallerand, Maurice Dupont (later to win the Military Cross for his exploits leading the DIPLOMAT circuit) and Maurice Rouneau, who had formed the *réseau*

VICTOIRE, which was to become the basis of the WHEELWRIGHT circuit.[4]

At the end of October 1942, Sevenet again went to visit Philippe de Vomécourt, who had received eight new targets, but for which the *réseau* had neither *matériel* or explosives, nor their own radio set and operator. On arrival in Lyon, Sevenet found that three important members of HECKLER (including the radio operator Brian Stonehouse) had been arrested. He therefore decided to travel on to Marseille to collect a radio set for his own use.

About the same time, **George Starr** (*Hilaire*, *Gaston*) set off from Glasgow on a journey which culminated in his building up one of the biggest circuits the British ever had in France (see p22–24 for more on Starr). His original *ordre de mission* was to act as assistant and technical advisor to Sevenet. On arriving in France, however, he heard of the arrests in Lyon and made his way instead to Cannes. Here, he managed to contact Sevenet, who arranged his onward journey to Agen, where Starr took over control of the existing *réseau* VICTOIRE.

At this point Starr was joined by Denise Bloch (*Danielle*), who was originally recruited in July 1942 to work with Sevenet and Stonehouse in the Lyon area. Following the latter's arrest on 24 October 1942, however, Bloch left Lyon and early the next year was sent by Sevenet to act as courier to Starr and WHEELWRIGHT, where she remained until April. Then, after the arrest of Maurice Pertschuk (*Eugène*), Marcus Bloom (*Bishop*) and other members of the PRUNUS circuit in Toulouse on 14 April 1943, and now without an operator, Starr decided to send Bloch over the Pyrenees with Maurice Dupont to take a message to London explaining the gravity of the situation.[5]

Starr now found himself in control of the remnants of two powerful *réseaux*: VICTOIRE and PRUNUS. These he successfully combined to produce WHEELWRIGHT, which continued to thrive and expand until September 1944.

To support Starr in this work, SOE sent Yvonne Cormeau (*Annette*) to be his radio operator in August 1943, followed shortly after by a second operator, Denis Parsons (*Pierrot*). They were joined in January 1944 by Anne-Marie Walters and Claude Arnault.

THE COURIER: ANNE-MARIE WALTERS (1923–1998)

"Then I was sailing through the clear and cold moonlit night, watching gratefully the large canopy over my head and remembering that somehow I had not felt frightened." (*A British Girl Who Went to Join the Maquis*, The *Daily Telegraph*, 14 February 1945.)

Anne-Marie Walters (*Colette*) was born on 16 March 1923 in Geneva, where her father was a rising star in the Secretariat of the League of Nations. Francis Paul Walters, known to all as Frank, was educated at Eton and Oxford, where he was elected a Fellow of University College in 1913,[6] before being commissioned into the Oxfordshire and Buckinghamshire Light Infantry on the outbreak of war. Having been seriously wounded at the battle of Ypres on 25 May 1915, and deemed unfit for further military duties, Frank Walters was appointed Private Secretary to Lord Grey of Fallodon, the recently retired Foreign Secretary. He later held the same position to Lord Robert Cecil, one of the architects of the League of Nations, during the Paris Peace Conference. This experience made Walters an obvious choice to join the Secretariat of the League when it was established in Geneva in 1919. He took up his post in May of that year as personal assistant to Sir Eric Drummond, the first Secretary-General.[7] The following year, Louise Roux-Bourgeois came to work as his secretary. They were married in 1921.

The Walters family settled at 5 chemin des Contamines, on the north side of Lake Geneva, close to where the Palais des Nations was being built. It was a fashionable area, much favoured by diplomatic and other international families. Among the Walters' close neighbours were Sean Lester, later to be the third and last Secretary-General of the League, and his wife Elsie, who had children the same age as Anne-Marie and her younger sister, Cecilia.

Life in Geneva was most agreeable. There were Christmas skiing holidays at Wengen, home of the Downhill Only Club, where Frank Walters, despite his wartime injuries, was a keen member of the curling club. There were summer holidays in a *pension de famille* at La Croix-Valmer, near St-Tropez. Frank Walters' letters of the time mention good fishing and the many international personalities with whom he was in contact.[8]

Anne-Marie began her education at Ecole Guibert in Geneva, before enrolling at the International School (Ecolint) in 1934. Situated south of the lake in the large park of La Grande Boissière, Ecolint had been founded ten years previously by Arthur Sweetser, an American journalist working at the League. It catered to the ever-increasing community of bankers, diplomats and international civil servants coming to live in Geneva, as well as taking local children from all over Switzerland. By the time of Anne-Marie's arrival, the school had grown to more than 400 pupils and was already being used as an 'international finishing school' for children who had begun their education in the US.

Thus, from an early age, Anne-Marie made friends among various different nationalities, many of whose parents were important players on the international scene. Prominent among these were Susie Sweetser, daughter of the school's founder; Dorothy and Patricia Lester; Shirley Nixon, who was also to join the Women's Auxiliary Air Force (WAAF); and Ana Marie Ensesa, who was to provide sustenance and support to Anne-Marie in Barcelona in August 1944.

Anne-Marie played an active role in school life, including editing the Ecolint journal. In a preface dated June 1939 she records that, despite mounting tensions on the world stage, relations among pupils remained as firm as ever:

> *"Cette année l'Ecolint a resserré les nœuds de sa solidarité: plus que jamais elle est demeurée pour ses élèves le centre de la sécurité: les conflits des nations sont restés en dehors de leurs relations amicales. L'Ecolint a été comme un îlot autour duquel se sont déchainés les ambitions et l'orgueil d'aujord'hui."*

It was also during this period that Anne-Marie began to become politically aware. Her father was a liberal and, as Anne-Marie later said, "his whole life had been devoted to the cause of peace." The family often talked about the Civil War in Spain, which greatly affected her. While at school, under the supervision of Thérèse Maurette, pupils were also made very aware of the war and followed the daily progress of Republican Army and the International Brigades. "We all carried out activities in aid of the Spanish Republicans. We collected milk for the children, and collected money in the streets…"

By 1938 the international scene was changing. In March, Austria ceased to be an independent state and on 9 January 1939 Frank Walters wrote to his friend Lord Halifax about "the imminent danger of a fresh and probably fatal crisis within a few weeks – no normal diplomatic action can prevent war."

In May 1940, "the agreeable life" began to recede rapidly. On the outbreak of war, the Swiss authorities asked foreign nationals to consider leaving and Ecolint, although remaining at Geneva throughout the war, decided to set up a branch at the headmistress's summer house in Hendaye, near Biarritz, to accommodate those pupils who were leaving Switzerland.

Following the departure of Joseph Avenol, the then Secretary-General of the League, Frank Walters was left in temporary charge. But on 25 May even he realised the seriousness of the situation and made a quick decision to leave with Louise, Anne-Marie, Cecilia and Micky, the family dog. The furniture was put in storage and two days later the family set off in their Humber car for the safety of Hendaye, via Narbonne, where they spent the night surrounded by large crowds of refugees. Several days later they managed to board a P&O liner at Verdon-sur-Mer, at the mouth of the Gironde, which had been diverted from its return journey from India to collect refugees bound for Britain, but no dogs. The unfortunate Micky had to be abandoned on the quay.

Eight days later the ship reached Glasgow and so the Walters family arrived together in Britain for the first time. Despite the disapproval of her mother, Anne-

Marie, although only 17, volunteered and was accepted in the WAAF,[9] who posted her as a 'plotter' to RAF Fighter Command HQ situated in a former fashionable girls school at Bentley Priory, near Stanmore. Here, all enemy raids were plotted on maps, blackboards and the 'Ops' table by WAAFs receiving instructions through telephone headsets. By means of magnetic 'rakes' they positioned counters of different colours to represent enemy formations.

In June 1942, Anne-Marie wrote to Ecolint that she was

"cantonée près de Londres dans un camp immense. Une semaine sur deux nous travaillons toute la nuit... J'ai certainement appris à être endurcie. Nous menons une vie assez militaire pendant les heures de duty... Pour voir un côté un peu plus gai, nous allons à Londres pendant les heures libres."

A year later, 2001920 Leading Aircraft Woman Walters A M was approached on behalf of SOE: she had the advantages of being a native French speaker, having a French parent and coming from a cosmopolitan background. She was interviewed by Captain Selwyn Jepson – giving as her referees Mr & Mrs Sean Lester – and was accepted for training just as SOE's training system was undergoing a radical change.

Prior to this date, potential recruits were initially sent to a network of top secret 'preliminary schools', where their character and potential for dangerous, clandestine work were assessed over a four-week period without revealing to them too much about SOE's work. Several of these schools were in large country houses which had been requisitioned for the war – thus prompting waggish remarks about the Stately 'Omes of England. The syllabus covered physical training, weapons handling, unarmed combat, elementary demolition, map reading, field craft and basic signalling – in fact, the training all army recruits would normally have received.

The changes introduced at the time of Anne-Marie's arrival produced a much quicker and generally better system of selecting students. In place of preliminary schools, SOE set up a Students' Assessment Board (SAB), based at a country house near Cranleigh in Surrey. Here, candidates were given a wide variety of psychological and practical tests over four days, in complete contrast to the previous system, which had been justifiably criticised as "leisurely". The SAB team consisted of six military testing staff and four Royal Army Medical Corps officers, comprising two psychiatrists and two psychologists. Anne-Marie's SAB report assessed her as "A keen, very intelligent girl with a realistic practical sense. Ample courage, determination and a sense of humour."

And so she was sent by SOE for further training, and enrolled as Ensign F26 in the First Aid Nursing Yeomanry (FANY); all SOE's female recruits were given an honorary commission in the FANY to provide a cover story during training. Anne-Marie's final report at the end of October concluded that "she is well educated, intelligent, quick, practical and cunning. She is active-minded, curious and has plenty of imagination. She is easily the most prolific writer amongst the party, usually to her mother."

So, in November 1943 and now aged 20, Anne-Marie was awaiting her *ordre de mission* from F Section SOE – and the next moon.

THE SABOTAGE INSTRUCTOR: CLAUDE ARNAULT (1923–1986)

Claude Georges Arnault (*Néron*) was born in Haiphong, Vietnam, where his father was employed in the French Colonial Service.

By the time he was 20, Arnault was studying at the French naval academy in Paris. Following the total occupation of France, he decided to leave the country in January 1943 and head for Algeria. With a fellow student he travelled by train to Dax, in southwest France, where he had relations. They then continued by bicycle to St-Jean-Pied-de-Port, a small village in the foothills of the Pyrenees, where a smuggler/*passeur* had agreed to take them on a further eight kilometres to the frontier village of Arnéguy. At Arnéguy, they waited until the frontier guards' backs were turned, then dashed across the road to reach Valcarlos and the relative safety of Spain.

Here, they were advised to give themselves up to the Spanish authorities, who imprisoned them in Pamplona. They were released two weeks later and taken to a hotel, where Arnault lived for two months, awaiting a convoy to Portugal. From there he found a ship to take him to Morocco where, arriving in June, he had the good fortune to meet an American, Colonel Vanderstricht, to whom Arnault explained how he wanted to go back and fight in France. After three months basic training in Morocco, Arnault was sent to England as a potential candidate for SOE.

Arnault passed his Student Assessment Board in early September 1943: "A man of good practical sense and high intelligence. Displays ample alertness and enterprise, and is capable and thorough. Though young, he is mature and has remarkable self-control for his age. A quick, serious and determined man and physically strong and active."

His preliminary training took him to Special Training School (STS) 42 based at Roughwood Park, near Chalfont St Giles, followed by a specialist course at the newly opened STS 40 at Howbury Hall, near Bedford. This school had been set up following serious mistakes made by agents handling the recently introduced S-Phone and similar communications equipment code-named 'Rebecca' and 'Eureka'. To correct these errors, the school ran a concentrated ten-day course on the use and maintenance of these effective new aids to RAF dropping operations. The S-Phone was a long-distance transmitter-receiver, small enough to be strapped to an agent's chest. 'Eureka' was a larger, land-based radar device that relayed information to a travelling set, 'Rebecca', in an aircraft.

By the end of this training, Arnault had a thorough knowledge of explosives and demolitions and also of the latest communications aids, which were to be so useful to him in the months to follow. SOE F Section now considered him ready to be sent as sabotage instructor to Starr and the WHEELWRIGHT circuit to replace Charles Duchalard (*Denis*), who had been sent back to England in October 1943 as unsuitable for the job.

Arnault was dropped with Anne-Marie on 4 January 1944 to a reception committee at the 'Terrain de la Vertu' ground near Gabarret, in the Landes department of southwest France. Until May, he was based in the south of the WHEELWRIGHT area, where he lived with Roland Mansencal (*Roger, Castex*) at Mazères, near Montréjeau, in the Haute-Garonne[10]. He was then sent to the Dordogne to find out whether two men, who had just arrived there and were asking Starr for a rendezvous, were agents or Gestapo. They turned out to be Jacques Poirier (*Nestor*) and his radio operator, whom Arnault had previously met in London.

Although in general Starr forbade the different groups within WHEELWRIGHT to carry out any sabotage work before D-Day, he did give Arnault two important tasks. The first was to stop production at the gunpowder factory in Toulouse. The attack, which took place on the night of 27 March 1944, was partially successful in that it put the plant out of operation for about a month. Then, on 11 May, Arnault attacked the Lorraine-Dietrich factory in Bagnères-de-Bigorre, in the Hautes-Pyrénées, which manufactured parts for tanks and aircraft. This was a complete success. He was able to enter the factory by night with a team of four, arrest the guards, take their keys and destroy all the machines. They then took the train to Tarbes and escaped without difficulty.

Arnault was arrested during his time with WHEELWRIGHT. Returning in a car with a colleague from a liaison visit to the Dordogne, they ran into a group of *miliciens* dressed in French uniforms which they had never seen before, and whom they mistakenly imagined to be in the Resistance. When their papers were found to be unsatisfactory, Arnault and his colleague were interrogated in the nearby Château Ferron, where the Milice had their headquarters[11]. Arnault, claiming that he was simply a cook for the *maquis*, was put in solitary confinement. He started to file through the cell bars but, luckily, on the seventh night, the château was attacked by the RAF following a previous request by field agents. Arnault escaped and, by swimming across the Garonne, was able to rejoin the *maquis* at Losse-Lapeyrade in the Landes.

After D-Day, Arnault was sent to carry out various sabotage operations on the roads and railways in the Dordogne area, as well as the demolition of a petrol depot and an armoured train. He was also responsible for the reception of the JEDBURGH team AMMONIA near Sarlat on 9 June 1944.

After the war, Arnault moved to the USA with his wife, Ghislaine Jeannier, whom he had married in December 1944. They lived in Boston, where he became head of the Berlitz language school. He remarried twice and died at his home in Le Chesnay, near Versailles, on 15 August 1986, with no children to survive him.

Arnault was awarded the Croix de Guerre and the Médaille de la Résistance but there seems to be no record of any decoration being recommended, or awarded, by SOE.

'*LE PATRON*': GEORGE STARR (1904–1980)

George Reginald Starr (*Hilaire*, *Gaston*), one of SOE F Section's most successful, most highly promoted and most decorated officers, was born in London on 6 April 1904. His American father, Alfred, had married and settled in England having originally arrived as accountant of the renowned Barnum and Bailey's Circus, then on a European tour.

On completing his secondary education at Ardingly College in Sussex, at the age of 16 Starr decided that he wanted to become a mining engineer. He spent the next four years working down a coal mine at Madeley Colliery, in Shropshire, to gain the necessary practical experience before enrolling at the Royal School of Mines in London. Three years later saw him well qualified and working in Glasgow for Mather and Coulson, manufacturers and suppliers of mining equipment.

Before long, Starr had been chosen for attachment to their agents in Brussels, from where he visited Poland, Russia and Spain, supervising the installation of equipment in mines. It was during such a visit to Manresa, in Spain, that he met Pilar Canudas Ristol, who was to become his second wife (and who would also work for SOE in Spain throughout the war, controlling the STUTZ line and its three operatives).

By 1939, Starr was back in Belgium working for a mine near Liège, and already in contact with MI5 through the British Military Attaché in Brussels. On the outbreak of war, he was mobilised and attached to the HOPKINSON mission,[12] where he fell under the watchful eye of the future Field Marshal, then Lieutenant Colonel, Gerald Templer, who was GSO I (Intelligence) for the British Expeditionary Force in France and Belgium. Templer's orders were, inter alia, "to ensure that a considerable number of British individuals of both sexes who were engaged in clandestine work in Belgium, Holland and northern France, were evacuated to the UK." Among those chosen was Starr, who reached England as a corporal employed in the carrier-pigeon services branch of the GHQ Liaison Regiment based in St James's Park, London.

By April 1942, Starr had been selected for training by SOE – perhaps an obvious choice, given his knowledge of Europe, foreign languages and his previous connection with MI5. This experience instilled in him the great sense of the importance of tight security which he was to use so successfully in his administration of WHEELWRIGHT.

Starr's strong personality soon became apparent. A training report from July 1942 notes that "he is continually making aggressive contradictions and assertions and is the worst type of know-all, namely one who is often right and can seldom be proved wrong." Unfortunately, this is the only training report to survive on his file.

Starr was commissioned in the General List in July 1942 and accepted by SOE for employment in the field. His *ordre de mission*, dated 12 October 1942, specified:

"You are to act as assistant to *Rodolphe* [Henri Sevenet], who is *Gauthier's* [Philippe de Vomécourt's] personal lieutenant, and you will be a member of *Gauthier's* closed circuit.

You are to instruct *Rodolphe* and his parties in the use of Rebecca and the S-Phone and pass on to them your expert knowledge of explosives and demolitions. You will also instruct the local recruits, as far as you are able to do so, regarding the arms which we can supply.

As *Rodolphe's* assistant you will take your orders from him, but should remember that *Gauthier* is the head of your circuit and is directly responsible to London HQ."

In October 1942, armed with these instructions, Starr left Glasgow on a troopship bound for Gibraltar. From there, his onward journey to southern France was to be in a less glamorous, converted Spanish sardine trawler, known as a *felucca*. Several of these small, 20-ton boats had been acquired by the Royal Navy; commanded and crewed by Polish sailors, they ferried agents between Gibraltar and various isolated landing points on the south coast of France.

Starr set sail from Gibraltar on 29 October 1942 in the *Sea Wolf*, commanded by Lieutenant Jan Buchowski, bound for the *calanque* at Port Miou, a deserted inlet near Cassis, about 25 kilometres southeast of Marseille. As Starr later described it, "then we all went off in this *felucca* which did everything but turn turtle… Six of us, seven or eight crew, wireless operator. No accommodation, packed like sardines."[13] Starr's fellow travellers included Mary Herbert, Odette Sansom, Marie-Thérèse Le Chêne and Marcus Bloom. The latter was on his way to be radio operator for Maurice Pertschuk and the PRUNUS circuit in Toulouse.

Even during the voyage, Starr began to fear that all was not well with the SPRUCE circuit in Lyon: "All the way from Gib I had this feeling that something was wrong with SPRUCE. Radio op on boat had a few calls, and each time I asked if it was for me – I thought they must know something must be wrong, I had the feeling so strongly. When I got to Cannes and spoke to Peter Churchill I asked if he knew anything, and he didn't. He said 'all I can do is to tell you where to go in Marseille and they might know something'."[14]

Starr landed on 3 November, eight days before Germany occupied the whole of France. Due to the quickly changing circumstances already described, he found himself within a month at Agen and in command of the rapidly expanding WHEELWRIGHT circuit.

After Liberation, Starr left France in September 1944, following his celebrated argument with General de Gaulle in Toulouse. He was to return to France, however, in December 1944 to accompany the JUDEX mission on its tour of the WHEELWRIGHT area, when they visited many of the people who had helped the circuit. That same month, Starr's confidential report, written by Brigadier Mockler-Ferryman, described him as "a brave, reliable, hard-working and tactful officer, but inclined to be swayed by the opinion of those around him."

Starr was awarded the Military Cross in 1944 and the DSO, which was published in *The London Gazette* of 21 June 1945. He also received the Légion d'Honneur and the Croix de Guerre.

Following his retirement from SOE in April 1945, Starr was employed by the Supreme Headquarters Allied Expeditionary Force (SHAEF) and by the North German Control Commission as head of production of solid fuels from the German coal mines, then under Allied occupation.

David Hewson
Gers
Summer 2009

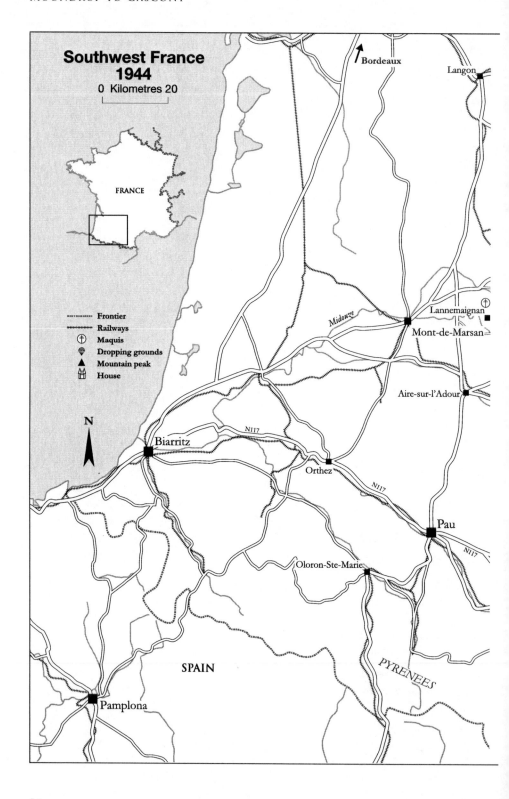

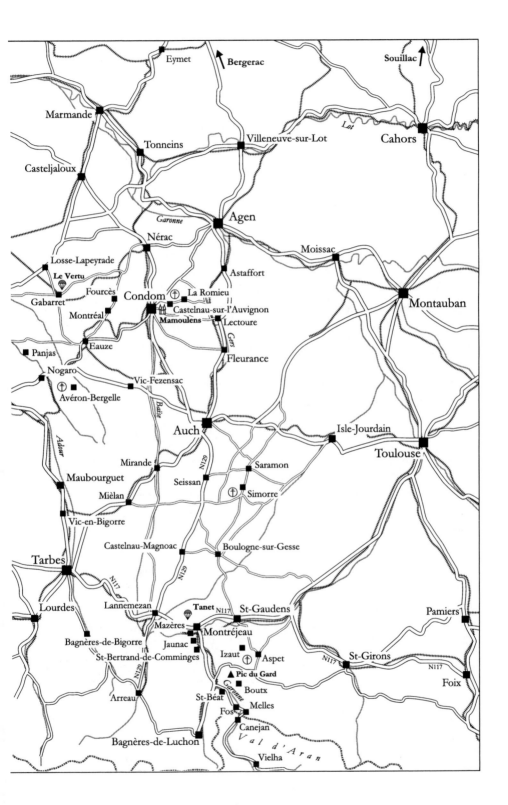

Moondrop to Gascony

Part I

Chapter I

"Come on, Minou, make yourself comfortable," Jean-Claude said.[1] "If you want to sleep, just lean on my shoulder."

As long as he wasn't bored, Jean-Claude was satisfied with everything. Just quietly satisfied. But when he got bored, he sat silently with a vacant look on his face and refused to submit to the most elementary forms of human civility. Trying to argue with Jean-Claude was like attempting to crash head-first through a rubber wall: you bounced right back. This was one of those numerous occasions when he was contented with the impossible: he asked me to make myself comfortable. And without the smallest trace of irony, either. Minou was the nickname he liked giving me.

And all this time, I was tied up like a Christmas parcel in the tight harness of a heavy parachute, sitting on two inches of seat (because that was all the cumbersome parcel on my back allowed me to reach) in the side of a Halifax bomber. I was suffocated by the heat and deafened by the roar of the engines. I simply gave up arguing and gave up Jean-Claude, settled against his shoulder and went to sleep.

I woke up an hour later: Jean-Claude had also fallen asleep and slipped against my arm. His long eyelashes cast childish shadows on his cheeks. The engines still rumbled with a monotonous roar; the noise had become part of me. It caught hold of my head and shoulders and my blood seemed to run rhythmically along my veins. I wondered how the crew managed to keep awake. I looked round and saw the despatcher busily engaged in tightening the straps round the six bundles due to be dropped with us. I shifted Jean-Claude gently and settled him against a bundle of RAF coats: he never stirred. I joined the despatcher just as he was opening the trap.

"What are you doing?" I yelled through the deafening row.

"Leaflets…" he yelled back, pointing to a dozen square parcels on the edge of the hole and turning up the collar of his fur jacket.[2]

The cold wind whistled inside the aircraft. The despatcher cut the strings round the parcels and chucked them out with precise and rapid movements. They hit the slip-stream with a crack. I tightened the scarf around my neck and leaned over the hole. Down below, I could see a city: it looked like a beehive. It also looked very small. The blocks of houses, the straight roads and avenues, the squares and, outside, the neat cutting-out of the land, conveyed a strong impression of design and order.

"Caen…" the sergeant shouted again, in answer to the mute question of my raised eyebrows.

Small puffs of clouds ran past under us in short bursts, hiding the city at broken intervals. In between them I could see black shadows sweeping rapidly across the beehive: heavy clouds were passing in front of the moon. The weather was not improving as we flew further south; it was already poor when we had left England. After all the leaflets had gone, the despatcher started throwing out little cylindrical boxes with tiny parachutes packed on top of them. They whistled as they hit the slip-stream.

"They're pigeons," the sergeant explained after he had closed the trap again. "There's a questionnaire from the BBC in the box with them. The idea is that people answer the questions and let the pigeons fly back home with them. Pretty simple – but I bet half the folks down there eat them. I'm sure I would," he added, with a wink.[3]

Pretty simple, indeed. I wondered how many simple things went on like that that no one knew about. All along, I had ached to keep some sort of a diary of all my activities and new sensations; but that was strictly forbidden, for obvious reasons of security. Now, as I sat down near Jean-Claude again, I wondered how long I would remember my emotions. Maybe I could write them down some day, but what day and when? The past months were very clear and very much of a whole in my memory, although, as soon as we had taken off, their disagreeable moments had receded into a distant unconsciousness.

Could it really be only six months ago that I had had my first interview?[4]

"Do you speak French?" a short and jumpy Captain had asked. His voice was high-pitched and piercing. I had found his cold and bare office after losing myself several times in a labyrinth of corridors inside a large and nondescript block of flats.

"How is it that you speak French so fluently?"

I had explained that I had a French mother and had always lived on the Continent and been brought up like a French girl.

"Are you ready to leave England? Are you ready to do anything we may ask you against the enemy? Can you ride a bicycle?"

I had said yes to everything, although I had no idea what he was getting at.

Three weeks later I had understood, as I began my courses in various super-secret 'schools'; hair-raising cross-examinations, tough soldier's training. If anyone had told me that I would spend the summer of 1943 being timed at assault courses, tapping Morse messages on a dummy key, shooting at moving pieces of cardboard, crawling across the countryside and blowing up mock targets, I would have shrugged my shoulders with disbelief. And then, when I had arrived at the parachute school, I had realized that I never really believed it would happen. And if I *had* jumped, it was only because the boys expected the girls to be scared and to refuse.

"Ha, ha," they had said. "We just can't wait to see you shake like jellyfish and howl with terror on the edge of the hole…" And they had rubbed their hands in anticipation of a good laugh. Only we'd all jumped, and their throats had been as dry as ours when the despatcher had laid a firm hand on our shoulder to warn us that the fatal moment was approaching.

After the jump school, we were sent to a 'security school' where we had learnt the art of being a proper gangster: how to open locks, lie successfully, disguise ourselves and adopt different personalities, how to recognize German uniforms and armament and how to code and decode messages.

We had all had a wonderful time during our weeks of training. Firm and solid friendships were forged in the clean and healthy life of work and exercise and we emerged thoroughly fit and keyed up. My training was over by the end of October.

"You're off by the next moon, the November moon," I had been told at the office in London.

Only things had not run so smoothly: there had been the last six weeks… I had counted without the English end-of-the-year weather. They called it pea-soup in London: heavy clots of yellow fog hanging onto the window-sills and pinning themselves to a standstill on chimney-tops. The city sounds were muffled and the lights were lit at lunchtime, while cars glided like ghosts between the gaslit landmarks of the streets. The office was over-shadowed with depression; the staff officers pointed to the windows in helpless answer to our renewed questions.

"Maybe tomorrow, we can't tell… Ring up or call without fail. But whatever you do, stay at hand and don't go away more than eight hours without leaving a phone number. You're standing by for imminent departure, don't forget…"

As though we could. Tension grew and the sense of looming perils sneaked in. Frightful stories about agents who had been caught roamed about the back-stages of the office. My family was in the process of moving from Oxford to London and I lived in a hotel. Day after day the same routine: reaching the office with a vague hope, and leaving it disappointed; dragging round restaurants, movies and clubs in the company of others, waiting too. It was too difficult inventing stories about your activities to your old friends, so you just didn't see them. As days dragged by, the enthusiasm of the weeks of training dropped and nearly vanished.

I had been over and over my preparations for the 'field'. There were thousands of things to think about. First, clothes:[5] a tailor specially appointed to the office had made a couple of suits and a coat for me. According to the Paris fashions, French women's jackets were at least ten inches longer than in England or the United States. Small details of finishing and lining were also different; nothing was overlooked. I had swiped one of my mother's Parisian *maison de couture* labels and sewn it inside a coat, picked the laundry-marks out of various clothes and rubbed off the names inside my shoes with sandpaper.

Then, make-up and small objects: I had scratched the labels off jars of cream and been given French powder-boxes, nameless tooth-brushes and French tooth-paste; even polish to clean my shoes in case I had to walk straight into a town from a muddy landing field.

To be ready for all the 'in-cases' was an impossibility; the next best thing was to be ready for all the obvious ones.

Two weeks before leaving, I had met Jean-Claude. I had been briefed to be dropped with a Parisian medical student but had not succeeded in contacting him earlier. Somehow, being briefed some weeks before me, Jean-Claude had not been told that he was due to go with a woman: I had some apprehensions about the way he would take it. We bumped into each other in the office doorway; he simply raised his eyebrows.

"I had no idea. But it doesn't matter. I don't really care…"

I didn't know how to take this so I had turned my back and walked out.

I ran into him the next day, by sheer chance, at a French exhibition in Grosvenor House. He was nonchalantly fixing the wires of a microphone.

"Bored…" He dropped the word, without showing the slightest surprise at seeing me.

Jean-Claude was just twenty. He was very tall and very good-looking; his open and childish face had one remarkable feature: large and warm eyes of the purest shade of deep blue. The whole expression of his face rested in them. His full mouth revealed a little weakness, but his calm, serene personality brought about a sensation of security and trust. His new clothes were shabby already.

"Look," he declared, showing cigarette burns in his blue suit. "It looks old like this…"

My family having at last settled in London, I had taken him home. My father was the only one who knew anything of my future destination.

"Be very careful what you say in front of Mother," I had warned Jean-Claude repeatedly. "She thinks we're heading for North Africa…"

He had made a couple of *faux pas*, but caught them up artfully and Mother hadn't noticed anything. He had made himself comfortable at once, and from the depth of an armchair methodically proceeded to contradict everyone. Otherwise he just sat around and said nothing. He had come very often; sometimes he had brought chocolate, handed pieces around and then eaten all the rest. We had both grown very fond of each other: being with Jean-Claude was a relaxation. He was so natural, so unsophisticated, intelligent and alert. When we couldn't be bothered to talk we didn't, but with him silences were never heavy or uncomfortable.

Jean-Claude was going to France as a saboteur and an instructor to various Resistance groups under the orders of a British agent nicknamed 'the *Patron*'.[6] The Patron was an important organiser; he had already been in France eighteen months and his 'circuit' was reputed to be one of the best and safest.[7] I was going as his personal courier and liaison officer. Our 'circuit' was in the southwest of France and comprised roughly the Dordogne, Lot-et-Garonne, Gers, Hautes-Pyrénées and Haute-Garonne departments, and even bits of the bordering ones. Jean-Claude and I were due to be dropped on the edge of the Landes, near the village of Gabarret.[8] We studied the maps for our region to the last detail: reading a Michelin map with care is like getting a mental photograph of every inch of land. We learnt the names of the main streets in the main towns and the hours of trains and buses between them, lying on the floor of the office bathroom: it was the only room we could be spared.

We had rehearsed the story built up round our papers with the greatest care: cover stories were prepared and invented by a specialized staff officer and 'according to the agents' personalities'. I was supposed to be a lady of leisure, born in Cannes and brought up in Switzerland. I had nothing to learn about Switzerland, that part of my cover story was true. But I found maps and postcards of Cannes, learnt the names of the streets, shops and cinemas. Jean-Claude and I stretched that work as far as possible in order to keep ourselves busy and keep our minds off the tension of the long weeks of waiting.

Both of us had been given field names. Mine was Paulette.[9]

"Do you know what they've found for me?" Jean-Claude fumed. "Néron… Yes, Néron. I'm sure they simply want to make a fool of me. There's an obvious connection between Néron and Claudius…"

Poor Jean-Claude, it was a tough war for him. Later, however, we called him by his real name. Néron simply remained his code-name for radio messages.

That morning, December 16th, when I least expected it, someone had rung through and told me to report within an hour. I had horrible indigestion from a meal I had eaten at a Belgian club a couple of days before. Outside, the fog was thicker and yellower than ever; the houses on the other side of Queen's Gate were invisible. I collected my last small objects in a frantic hurry. My cases had gone to the aerodrome to be packed at the beginning of the month. All I took with me was to be carried in my pockets.

At the office I had received part of my equipment. My papers: a ration card, a clothing card and an identity card, all made in England to the exact image of French ones. I was given money: 99,000 francs and 1,000 in small cash, and a little gun, a Czech .32. I was the only woman in a group of twenty-two men briefed to leave the same night. The tall Colonel had appeared.[10]

"Here's a little souvenir from us all," he had said, his mouth twitching a little, "and the very best of luck to you children…" I had received a silver powder compact and the others a silver pencil. The Colonel kissed me good-bye and shook everyone's hands. It was very moving and very final.

"*Merde*…" said everyone as we walked away. No one was supposed to say "good luck"; it brought bad luck. "*Merde*" was the only wish of good fortune allowed.

We had driven more than a hundred miles across the country. The fog was not so thick outside London, but still very much there. No one had spoken. The car had rolled silently along the edgeless road: I wondered at the choice of weather. We might have left long ago, if we were to go off on a foggy night anyway…

We arrived at the 'departure school', a large house in central England, at four in the afternoon.[11] A pompous Captain greeted us with a chart and pencil in his hand.

"I'm afraid I have bad news for you. Everyone has been scrapped off for tonight, except Hairdresser and Milkmaid…" Hairdresser and Milkmaid were the code-names Jean-Claude and I had been given for the trip. The RAF knew us under no other names.

The others had looked at us angrily.

"Why should these two go off? They're the youngest…"

"Well? Aren't we the most important?" Jean-Claude had declared airily.

We were led to a small hut where we received our last bits of equipment: a green-and-brown camouflaged parachute suit with long trouser-legs and dozens of zip-fasteners and pockets, a flashlight and spare batteries, a knife and a compass, a small flask filled with rum; even a sharp spade, tucked into a leg pocket, in case we had to bury our parachute ourselves.

At five we were treated to a gargantuan meal of eggs, steaks and oranges tenderly prepared by sweet-voiced women in khaki.

"You'll even have some wine…" we had been told with a you-lucky-people tone. "White Chablis…" The white Chablis had turned out to be of a curious dirty-water colour and had finished upsetting my stomach completely.

Then we had been inspected a last time, making sure our shoes were not wrapped up with the morning's *News Chronicle* and that we didn't retain London theatre tickets in the corner of pockets. At six we had left; the others had waved on the steps:

"Bye… We'll see you at breakfast tomorrow; you'll never get there with this weather. You'll have *eggs*, don't forget…"

The fog closed down visibly as we drove to the aerodrome. We dressed in small huts[12] reserved for 'operational personnel', which made me feel very important. The jump-suit was about fifteen times my size, but everything was straightened out by the time I was tied up in the straps of the parachute. My ankles were bandaged tightly by an RAF sergeant, as I was jumping in low, walking shoes.

As we climbed into the car taking us to the plane, and sat uncomfortably in the back, I remarked with great satisfaction that I wasn't frightened in the slightest. I had always expected to be, but now that I was at last faced with the realisation of all my past imaginings, I was nearly disappointed to find myself calm and unconcerned. Jean-Claude and I shook hands with the crew and chatted below the wings of the heavy Halifax. Someone nudged me: "There's a General to see you off…" I never saw the General but I shook hands with lots of people I had never seen before. They patted me on the back and I wondered if they were jealous. Then our cumbersome persons had been pulled from the inside and pushed from the outside through the narrow door of the plane and we had taken off at about 8.30pm.

At this point in my thoughts the despatcher came in from the nose of the aircraft to warn me that we were approaching our dropping point. I woke Jean-Claude up. All three of us ate sandwiches and drank coffee out of a thermos before getting ready. The sergeant kept making encouraging signs to me, the keep-your-chin-up and thumbs-up sort of business. He tightened my straps until I felt like a hunchback in a strait-jacket, banged with his closed fists on the 'chute's closing apparatus to make sure it would not come undone and hooked our static lines: I watched him closely as he stuck the safety-pin through the hook. I sat next to the hole and Jean-Claude sat facing me, on my right. The despatcher opened the aperture and the wind rushed in, cold and damp.

I looked down: slowly, very slowly, my throat dried up and the usual cold wave preceding a jump began running up and down my back. So I sang to myself. I always sing to myself when I'm scared.

Down below, I couldn't see a thing but black emptiness and specks of grey fog or cloud flitting by. We sat and sat and we grew colder and colder. Then my mind went numb and I stopped thinking altogether. After half an hour of this morbid and silent wait, the despatcher stood up and closed the trap, motioning us back to the front of the bomber.

"Too much fog," he declared. "The pilot can't see a thing. He thinks he's seen some lights but he's lost them. We've been circling your dropping point for more than thirty minutes. It's no good calling the attention of the Germans to this area: we're going home now."

"Minou, are you ready to jump blind?" Jean-Claude said quickly.

I nodded in answer and he urged the despatcher to ask the pilot to drop us anywhere in the vicinity of the field. The sergeant argued nearly three minutes on the interphone.

"Absolutely nothing doing," was the reply. "The skipper doesn't want to get in a jam. You never know, there might be a bust-up down there, and wouldn't it be a good job if you landed straight in the hands of the Germans?"

We were powerless. Jean-Claude eyed the trap from the corner of his eye. I knew he was considering making a dash for it. But it was useless.

"We knew it would be like this before we started," the sergeant continued. "Those damned chairbornes back home think they know everything. The fellows who fly ought to have something to say. Only hope we can get home with all this muck around…"

I was a little stupefied. And both Jean-Claude and I were mad because of the fuss made over a simple journey. My shoulders ached from the tight straps: we took our parachutes off as soon as we'd crossed the French coast again.

After what seemed like endless hours, Jean-Claude nudged me and pointed to his watch. It was 4am. We had been flying nearly eight hours and the crew was scheduled back at 3am.

"Why aren't we there yet?" I shouted to the sergeant. "Go in front and see for yourself," he shouted back.

We were flying in clear moonlight, and the night was very pure. But below lay a thick white floor of clouds. Not a break to be seen anywhere. Small specks of yellow light were reflected like peas on the heavy mass.

"Searchlights trying to help us," the pilot shouted through the increased din. "Trying to find a landing base…difficult…ground fog."

The despatcher ordered us to put our parachutes on again.

"You may have to bale out. Never know… We only have fifty minutes of petrol left…"

I had much more apprehension at the idea of baling out over England than jumping over occupied France. I looked at Jean-Claude: he was so calm that I began to feel annoyed. It was very disagreeable not to be on the interphone and follow what was going on.

We flew another forty-five minutes. Then all at once we went down fast and turned steeply, then climbed again. I began to feel a little sick.

Three members of the crew came and sat next to us. The despatcher told me to hang on to the side of the bomber and to put my feet up on the opposite side.

"We might make a bumpy landing and you'd get thrown about..."

Jean-Claude caught hold of my arm with a tight grip. For a second the thought that we might crash whipped through my mind. But I decided immediately that nothing like that could happen to *me*...

"Jean-Claude, what do *you* think?"

"Don't worry..." he calmly replied.

"Darn you," I thought, "don't tell me what to do. Just what's going to happen..."

Again, drop, drop, and once more up again. I felt sicker.

"No, no reason to be scared..." I thought. "Only I wish I knew what's going on." Then I stopped caring. Jean-Claude dug his nails into my arm.

The third time we did not pick up. Instead we went down and down until suddenly I heard a noise: breaking wood. Then everything went black. Huge masses of twisted steel whirled around me as I was pushed head-first into a depth of rolling metal and wet earth.

"I'm still conscious...I'm still conscious..." was the only thought that ran through my mind.

Suddenly it all stopped. I lay on my back facing a large hole in the fuselage. Earth filled my mouth. The silence hit me like a pain after the long hours in the deafening row of the four engines. It was only interrupted by a swishing noise in the distance: one of the engines gasping out its last breath of life. Petrol poured over my head freely from a neatly cut white pipe. I was soon soaked; the smell filled my nostrils. I had only one arm free. Then I saw a flame overhead.

"Oh God!... I'm going to be burnt alive..."

For the first time terror shot through me. I believe I shouted something. I made a tremendous effort to get myself out; my parachute was caught, the straps dug deep into my shoulders. Before I could move I'd have to climb out of the harness.

But the flame went out – the nearest thing to one of God's miracles that I shall ever see. I was left weak and dry-mouthed but with an energy I didn't think I possessed. All this had lasted only a few seconds. I looked around for Jean-Claude.

"Don't worry," he said. He was sitting in a mass of wrecked metal. "If we haven't burnt or blown up *yet*, it means that we're not going to..."

"My God..." I suddenly remembered the supplies we were carrying for the Resistance; more than a ton of high explosive, ammunition and detonators.

"I'm absolutely okay," Jean-Claude went on, "but my feet are caught, and I can't get out."

"Well, break your ankles or tear yourself out; never mind, but GET OUT!" I shouted. I expected the whole thing to blow up any minute. Also he was too calm; I couldn't bear it.

I extricated myself after getting free of my parachute harness, and climbed out of the fuselage. As soon as I was in the open I felt reassured. I stood on shattered pine branches. All over the place trees were torn out of the earth and pieces of metal lay smouldering. Nothing remained of the nose of the aircraft but shattered pieces of steel; the wings were torn off; I couldn't see the tail at all. I wondered where the crew was.

I handed my knife to Jean-Claude who started cutting his shoes off methodically. A tottering figure approached from the back of the smouldering wreck, groaning softly. "I'm the rear gunner... My arm..." Then he fainted, just as he reached me. There was blood all over his side. I sat him up against a pine branch and poured some of my rum down his throat: it revived him.

"Where *is* the tail?" I asked.

"Up in the trees, over there," he said, pointing with his chin. It looked like a furious eagle, in a pine tree, fifty yards away.

The sky was full of the sound of aircraft trying to land. The floodlit runway (obviously very near us), and the rockets shot into the sky at regular intervals, lit up every grain of fog; there was an air of satanic unreality in this red-and-yellow scene of littered trees and wrecked steel. The atmosphere reeked of petrol.

Just as people approached Jean-Claude got out. All three of us started walking towards their voices, the rear gunner leaning heavily on me. Ground crews joined us.

"What the hell is this woman doing in this mess?" I heard one of them say. Jean-Claude and I looked at each other: it was going to be difficult to explain. We decided to say we were journalists, but it was doubtful whether anyone would believe us; our jump-suits and arms and the scattered containers would give us away.

As we reached the truck, I felt something warm run down my back. It was blood. It appeared I had a cut in my head. My hair was thick with earth and blood; it made an awful mess. The gunner sat in front and I climbed behind with Jean-Claude.

"I'm glad, I'm so glad we came out of it. Oh God, I'm so glad!..." he kept repeating. He put his arms around me and rubbed his head against my shoulder.

"Minou, please try not to think about it. It's all over now, don't think about it."

"I'm going to murder you, if you don't shut up," I thought.

There we were: driving on the edge of a floodlit runway. Planes landing near, the noise of engines, engines and noise all over the place. Smells of petrol all over the place. Lights, red, green and yellow lights. Flares and rockets in the sky. Hot blood running down my back. And the close memory, the vision of the plunge into darkness and wet earth; the terror, sharp as a knife; the rear gunner and his torn arm. All this a few minutes ago, as close as a burning pain – and all Jean-Claude could say: "Don't think about it. Please, Minou, don't think…"

I sat stiff and I hated him. I hated him so much that I couldn't tell him. I wanted to cry and I could not. All I asked for was peace and silence, all by myself in a dark corner. And to think of it over and over again until it was out of my system.

At last we reached the infirmary. Jean-Claude had sensed my antagonism and kept silent. The MO was rushing around busily: six planes had crashed that morning and many men were hurt. They sat about the white room looking very pale and raised weary eyebrows at the dishevelled figure I must have been in my torn fur coat. My legs wobbled. I sat away from Jean-Claude.

After a while the MO cut some of my hair and washed and stitched the cut, which was a superficial one. I asked to see the crew of our Halifax. I found three of them in bed in the next room. All were badly injured.

"What's happened to the others?" I asked the despatcher.

He smiled and shook his head. They were all dead. The bodies of the pilot and the engineer were not even found in the wreckage. Four missing… My head swayed, I had to sit down.

"We knew it, we all knew it," the radio operator said. "The skipper went and told the CO he didn't want to go. 'Do what you're told,' the CO told him. We'd done twenty-one missions together… And he cut the contact too…"

"Yes. That saved us from fire," the despatcher continued. "We had no more petrol left – fifty yards from the runway, we were… We asked base to let us bale you two out. But they wouldn't. Security, I suppose. It's my fourth crash," he added with a painful smile.

It was all a nightmare. I could still see the smile of the pilot showing me the searchlights and assuring me that we'd soon be home. Only a few hours ago we were all shaking hands and they were smiling gaily, never telling me they had asked not to go.[13]

CHAPTER II

After a breakfast of greasy bacon and greasy fried bread on a greasy plate, and tea and tinned milk, we were driven to London in the CO's own car. Jean-Claude's face was scratched and bruised and I had a large white bandage around my head: the mere sight of it made me feel sick, so I concealed it under a turban.

"I hope the people who saw us off yesterday aren't back from the departure school..." Jean-Claude mumbled. But they were.

"Ah, ah, what did we tell you? Did you get the *eggs*?" they asked. But their triumphant smiles froze as they caught sight of Jean-Claude's bruises and my bandage. Somehow, the office had been told that we had baled out in Kent; when they heard of the crash they called a doctor, gave us whisky and insisted on taking us everywhere in large cars. We begged to be allowed to start off again the same night: I knew I would be scared if I were given time to think things over. But our plea remained ignored and we were informed that we had had a nervous shock and ought to rest a few days.

The fog clung over London more than ever and New Year dragged past miserably. The British press led a war of nerves on the Germans with a Second-Front-any-minute-now campaign which nearly drove me to despair: I was convinced I'd never be in France before D-Day... I saw little of Jean-Claude; his very presence irritated me to tears.

On January 3rd, at last, we started out again. It was a brilliant night, the first one for weeks. The aerodrome was bustling with activity as planes took off for every part of occupied Europe, trying to catch up with the delays caused by the fog. Our car followed a Lancaster just about to take off. She swung her tail in a graceful curve as she reached the runway, marked all the way along with blazing orange lamps: she stood still for a while, like a runner waiting for the signal to go, then all at once quivered violently and raced off, quickly merging into the black night. I followed the red, green and yellow lights.

"Soon you'll be in one of those..." And I felt frankly scared. Gone my beautiful assurance of the first day: now I was conscious of the risks and perils we might run into. The prevailing smell of petrol brought back the clear memory of my first contact with bone-melting terror. Ignorance is sometimes a blessed thing. Jean-Claude and I chatted with the crew. The pilot drew me under the wings of the Halifax. He was a tall, fair Scotsman; his cap was thrown back over his neck and his uniform patched with pieces of leather.[1]

"Look, here are your containers…" They were attached to the bomb-racks and marked with black 15's in a white circle to indicate the number dropped. "This is the first time I'm taking parachutists, you know," he said with a smile.

I told him briefly about our first trip. He put a hand on my shoulder.

"I give you my word that you'll get there safely," he said, and wrinkled his nose in affectionate reassurance.

I suddenly felt a warm confidence creep over me. He had understood that I was frightened, and I was in safe hands.

We took off at 9pm. Right away, I tensed up again and remained on the look-out for alarming details: smells of burnt rubber, smells of petrol and turpentine.

"This kite is all new," the despatcher explained patiently. "It's her first operational trip. But I assure you she's a baby and much faster than the one you went in last time. This is a new model…"

We were greeted by light flak over the French coast and bumped a bit as blast hit the underwings. Jean-Claude slept again. I couldn't: I tried to read a book of Maupassant's stories which I had scrounged at the departure school. It took a tremendous effort to concentrate and I had to read my sentences five times over to understand them. Why was Jean-Claude so calm? His unabashed serenity was like a red cloth to a bull to me, and my irritation only gained in weight during the journey.

The despatcher sat on a pack of leaflets with his legs dangling down. He looked no older than a high-school kid, singing little tunes to himself all the way, and keeping me informed with unfailing good-humour:

"Over the Channel now… Crossed the French coast… Over the Loire… Soon there…"

But over Angoulême the Halifax suddenly broke into a steep climb: I slipped to the floor and caught on to the seat. Jean-Claude lost his balance and woke up. I pulled myself up to the small, circular windows where I caught a lop-sided view of Angoulême, white and shining in the moonlight. But a few seconds later it had disappeared and all I could see was a star-freckled sky. The despatcher ran to the nose of the plane. Both Jean-Claude and I were slipping backwards and forwards and sideways as the Halifax kept turning sharply and steeply. Suddenly we dropped, diving faster and faster. My muscles stiffened into a tight knot as renewed terror flashed through me.

"Oh, my God, no… Not *again*…"

Then all at once we flew straight again. I sat collapsed and weak. The despatcher returned.

"It was nothing," he shouted, "only an enemy fighter. He'd taken to chasing us. But the skipper knows his job; he never fails. He shook him off easily… That's evasive action for you!"

Jean-Claude went back to sleep. Outside, the night was beautifully clear. Soon we would be in France, soon it would all be over. We were flying very low and I could clearly see the trees and their shadows below the long wings. I kept my nose glued to the window. We had been flying nearly three hours when the despatcher woke Jean-Claude and told us to get ready.

Once more he tightened our straps, hooked our static lines and opened the trap. He crouched on his knees near me.

"See those packages on the other side?" he yelled. "The one on the left will go first, and you go immediately after the second."

Jean-Claude was after me, immediately followed by four more packages: the whole operation would amount to a quick stick of containers, men and packages.

The cold wind gushed inside, stiffening the skin of my face. I looked down: below I could see trees and white roads smoothly running by. At intervals I caught sight of the shadow of the Halifax gliding steadfastly along the fields and skipping over trees and houses. We sat twenty minutes in silence on the edge of the hole. The little sergeant listened intently on the interphone.

"No contact yet…" he growled. I had a vision of a third journey and more endless anxiety. This time, I would jump blind before the despatcher had time to close the trap again. I looked up and met Jean-Claude's eyes. He had guessed what was in my mind and nodded imperceptibly in agreement. Happen what may… Suddenly the sergeant uttered a loud yell and raised his hand.

"Okay – got 'em! ACTION STATIONS!" A wave of insensitiveness ran through my body, making me immune from fright. I wriggled to the extreme edge, Jean-Claude close behind. The next second the engines slowed up and the Halifax quivered, the containers flashed by under the hole in a swishing of opening silk. Then it was the packages, the loud "Go!…" right in my ear, the drop, the swirl of the slip-stream as it hit me and cut my breath. The silence crashed around in a rolling vision of earth and sky, while the body of the Halifax loomed enormous over me.

I looked up: my rigging lines were twisted, not allowing the canopy to be properly opened – I was dropping too fast. Jean-Claude was nowhere to be seen. I kicked and kicked until the parachute opened completely, and sailed down the cold and brilliant night.

I read a book once, called *Sweet Death*. Death, it explained, is only painful to those who watch it. Once the mind is resigned to the idea, dying becomes something of a pleasure. I thought it was nonsense. Now I changed my mind: dying must be very similar to jumping. On the edge of the hole, faced with the inevitability of the jump, the mind takes a resolution over the body bigger than any human instinct. The body is no longer of any concern: I actually did not mind whether the parachute opened or not, as I pushed myself out into space.

And a strange pleasure arises from this total physical unconcern, this total victory of the mind over the body.[2]

During the descent, however, this feeling recedes and the body takes over again, making you preciously aware of the beat of life. And you are left a little weak and warm with inner satisfaction.

I was so engrossed with my rigging lines that I forgot to watch the ground until a soft thump brought me back to it. I found myself sitting in the water of a marshy field.[3] There, under my hand, lay the soil of France, soft and friendly. I could hardly believe it. How I had romanticised this moment and how I had waited for it!… In the distance I caught sight of the black Halifax, silhouetted against the sky. Just as she flew over a line of trees, she wiggled her wings in a last friendly farewell. Gone, the last link with Britain and daily safety.

It was very cold and not a sound could be heard. I jumped to my feet and proceeded to fold my parachute. I sank in mud and water as I ran to the top of the canopy to pull and straighten it out. Things had to be done quickly and silently. I cocked my gun and left it at 'safety'. We had been warned of the possibility of the Germans attacking fields during dropping operations. From the gruesome stories that roamed about the office, this seemed to happen more often than not.

A few seconds later I heard voices and stooped to the ground.

"I wonder where they can be? I thought I saw one dropping around here, but it might've been a container."

They were good French voices; the words came out low and sharp in the clear night. I got up and waved to a black figure who rushed to me.

"Hello, welcome, welcome," the man said, nearly shaking my arm off. "But this must be Mademoiselle Paulette. We've been waiting for you for so long… How are you? Are you all right? My goodness, what a ridiculous way to come back to France!…"

He had a round, young face, and a round beret pulled right over his ears. A few minutes later, Jean-Claude arrived from the other side carrying his parachute and followed by three other men. He was soaked up to the waist.

"I thought you were making straight for the canal, Mademoiselle Paulette," a short man with a strong German accent declared. "Didn't you see it?"[4]

"No, I didn't even notice the ground. And I wanted to so much…"

"Well, you landed less than fifty yards from the canal. Fine mess if you'd gone straight in: it's more than eight feet deep! Anyway, please let me introduce myself. I'm Scharks,[5] the chief of the reception party."

"And I'm Morel,"[6] said the man with the round beret who had greeted me. We all shook hands over again.

"Wonderful pilot you had," Scharks declared, jumping about. "This is the best *parachutage* I've seen: twenty-three parachutes all in one go. Only two parcels are off the field, but we'll find them easily."[7]

"Why did we take so long to contact you?" said Jean-Claude.

"I don't know. I think you must've been flying a little off your course because we heard you in the distance and as soon as your pilot caught sight of our lights he flew over and dropped his stuff. The whole thing took no longer than three or four minutes, which is absolutely terrific. I've never…"

"Come on, Scharks, don't talk so much," Morel interrupted. "These children must be cold and hungry and they're soaked. Take them to the farm while I see to the collecting of the material and packages."

We followed Scharks across the wide, open field. I tripped and sank in muddy patches of earth and water. The men had high rubber boots on; silent shapes moved about, bent under the weight of the heavy containers. We passed a cart pulled by two oxen.[8]

"To carry the containers," Scharks explained. "It's too much for men to carry such weights right across the field."

Scharks was an Alsatian. His brother had worked with our chief, the Patron, for over a year. He had been caught by the Gestapo in October '43 and within twenty-four hours Scharks had taken his place and begun to carry on his work.

"This way," he said, showing us through a narrow path on the edge of the forest. We walked nearly an hour through the trees. The Landes were an ideal place for *parachutages*: the woods stretched for miles and miles with occasional wide clearings. It was impossible for the Germans to keep a watch on them.

The moon grinned behind the trees and the pines smelt good. Small, thorny plants grew by the path and pricked my ankles: I was grateful for them, for they brought the realisation that I wasn't dreaming. The night was wide and quiet and the earth hard and steady beneath my feet after the noisy insecurity of the plane.

At last we reached a small and decrepit farm in a clearing.[9] We had to climb over straw and manure to get to the door, and bend our heads to get through it. The farmer and his wife, both old and bent, dragged chairs to the wide fireplace and retired to a corner where they sat side by side, watching us, their hands crossed on their laps, too shy to talk. Scharks threw armfuls of wood on the fire and tall flames sprang up, licking the black sides of the chimney.

"You'd better put those *sabots* on and dry your shoes," Scharks declared, full of helpful attention. When I retrieved my shoes from in front of the fire a couple of hours later, they were bent in two and cracked like cardboard. Scharks talked and talked about locomotives that had been blown up the day before, and stations that were due to blow up the next day, as though Jean-Claude and I had been working with him for the last year. He rushed around preparing food and coffee. At the first taste of the latter I gulped and made a wry face.

"Ah," he exclaimed, "I've been waiting for this moment. That's '*café Pétain*'; and that's the only coffee you'll be drinking until the Americans bring us some…"

The concoction was black and that is the nearest it got to coffee. It tasted of something between dishwater and roasted acorns.

Soon after, Morel came in, followed by the rest of the reception party. Morel was a tall, strong-looking man with a proud and open face. Later I found that this air of nobility and dignity is common to all the peasants of Gascony.

"The Patron," he said, "spent the whole of last night on the field: your message came over the BBC two days ago. He slept today and I don't think that he knew it had come over again."

We had removed our jump-suits and distributed small objects as souvenirs to the numerous people around. For months after, young men would come and shake hands with me. "Don't you remember me?" they would say. "I was in your reception party…"

Their words bounced and sang; their southern accent was new to my ears. It struck me for the first time that my way of speaking would mark me out as a stranger to the region… I was hot in the face in front of the fire, but cold in the back as people walked in and out allowing gusts of frozen night to slip in. I became very sleepy, made a pile of our jump-suits in a corner, and fell asleep on top of them.

Jean-Claude woke me up at dawn; the packages had been found and the men had gone home. We set out across frozen fields, Morel leading: a soft, pale-blue sky promised a sunny day, the smell of the Landes pines came out sharply in the cold morning. We trudged along an endless track until we reached Gabarret.

"My wife has prepared a hot soup for you," Morel said. "She must be waiting for us now. You can wash and tidy yourselves up a little too, if you want."

We followed him docilely. His wife greeted us on the doorstep and, after shaking our hands half a dozen times, showed us into the kitchen. Everything was shining and spotlessly clean in her house, from the blue, starched apron around her waist to the brass cauldron in which the soup was boiling.

"I'll show you to my room, where you can wash," she said. "You can have some of the soap I've made myself; it's much better than the one you buy. It's easy to make when you live so near to Landes, because you can get hold of a lot of resin."

I wondered what the soap you buy was like, as I vainly tried to get a little lather out of the voluminous piece she produced. We sat round the table covered with a blue-and-white oil-cloth. Every detail struck me as something that I had forgotten about in the long years of war in England: the smoking onion soup bowl in the middle of the table; the two bottles of wine – just plain ordinary bottles with plain ordinary wine; Morel cutting large chunks of bread with a penknife that he pulled out of his pocket and wiped against the top of the loaf; the double coffee-pot warming up in the ashes of the fire; and the good smell of wax and floor polish.

Jean-Claude sat with a glum look on his face and answered Morel's enthusiastic questions with grumpy monosyllables. He was in one of his infuriating, unresponsive moods. I tried to drown his bad manners in a flow of words.

Morel was a carpenter and owned a small, closed truck. "One of my workmen[10] will drive you to Condom this morning," he said. "He was in your reception party last night and will know where to take you. The Patron wants you to meet a number of people on the way; amongst others, the grocer[11] in Fourcès and the baker in Montréal. They are friends of mine and the Resistance chiefs in their villages."

We started out in the middle of the morning. Wherever we stopped we were greeted like movie stars, invariably dragged into the shops' back-rooms and pressed to drink wine and liqueurs. Nothing could make people understand that I wasn't used to so much alcohol; they were hurt if I refused. It's a wonder I wasn't drunk by the time I reached Condom.

The feeling of exhilaration continued to daze me all along the drive. I had forgotten so many things: how every kilometre was marked with a stone painted red on top for the big roads and yellow for the secondary ones, how the name of every village and town was posted up a few hundred yards before you reached it. And how warm and bright the winter sun could be; its rays played on the frozen windows of the car and transformed the patches of snow and hoar-frost-covered fields into thousands of blinding sparkles. For the first time in many months I was conscious of the smell of the sun, the noises of the morning, the heart-beats of the road and the life of every piece of stone, sun-ray or stick. I wanted to cry and laugh all at once. Suddenly Jean-Claude touched my shoulder softly, and leant towards me.

"Minou," he said, putting my tumultuous emotions into words, "*c'est quand même bon, la France.*"

CHAPTER III

At lunch-time we arrived in Condom, where I was to meet my chief. All along the way I tossed and turned cover stories in my head expecting to meet German road blocks at every bend. In point of fact we only passed a few peaceful farmers following their cow-driven carts with a slow and swaying walk. We had dropped Jean-Claude at Fourcès, a small village on the way; he had orders to stop there and start instruction on small groups in the vicinity.

All along the road the driver worried about his tyres.

"We thought you'd bring some from England with you," he kept repeating. "We'd counted on them for so long..."

I had a vision of myself swinging under my parachute with a couple of Goodrich tyres round my waist. His own, as a matter of fact, were reduced to a few shreds and it was a wonder to me they lasted more than a mile.

Condom is typical of the old cities of Gascony. It was very white and brilliant in the midday sun as I first saw it. The deep arches of a thirteenth-century monastery mark two sides of the central square; the cobbled streets are narrow and the houses high, to stop the hot summer sun from burning and bleaching everything around. After the miserable weeks in the London fog, the light, very pure and somehow soft, struck me like a musical note. On the promenade, the trees threw their bare arms to the bluest sky I'd seen for years. The smell was sharp and new.

Morel's driver led me to a painter's shop in the main street. As I followed him in I felt that everyone noticed and commented upon me and I wanted to crawl along the walls; somehow, it would have seemed more natural to climb on the roof and come down the chimney to my host's kitchen. I was just in time for lunch. There again, the warmth of the reception awaiting me was highly embarrassing. As I later discovered, the right to be part of the Resistance and to shelter anything clandestine was an honour to almost everyone I met. I found this slightly disconcerting, as I had expected to find myself having to pour thanks and gratitude over all who gave me hospitality.

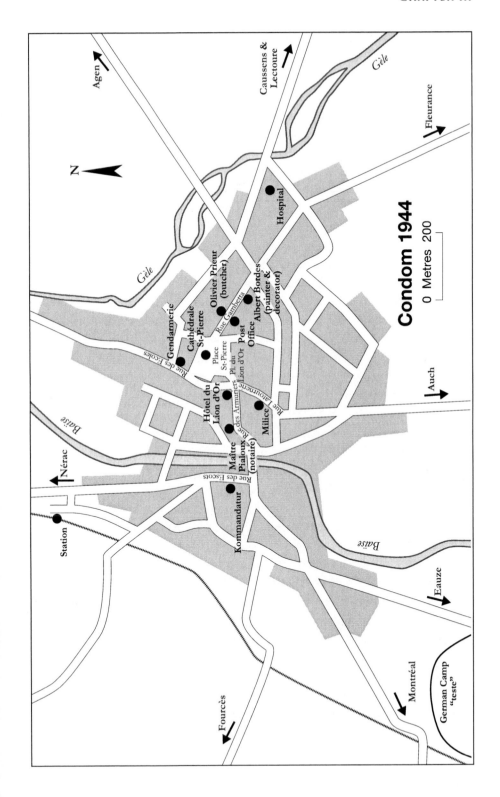

Condom 1944

0 Metres 200

The painter, Monsieur Laroche, was like a figure of the early twenties, with large, drooping moustaches, no collar and an overwhelming *bonhomie*.[1] He showed me to the kitchen in the back-shop where his wife rushed chairs and glasses to the table. She was just like her husband; her hair was tied on top of her head in a neat little bun and her high-cheeked, Mongolian face vanished in a thousand wrinkles when she smiled. I could easily imagine her, at twenty, posing for a picture, her right foot forward, her neck stiff in a high collar and her hands modestly folded on her stomach. She was all in a bustle.

"My daughters, Mademoiselle Paulette," she said, as three girls walked into the room. "They are just back from work... Please sit down... Please have a glass of wine... Are you tired? Are you hungry?.. Lunch will be ready in just a second..." I couldn't stop her nervous flow of words. The three daughters stood awkward and embarrassed in the middle of the kitchen.

"This is Gilberte, this is Andrée and this is Suzanne," she went on with a triumphant gleam in her eye. They were all neatly dressed in simple and well-cut clothes. Gilberte, the eldest, was obviously the responsible element in the house, always busy, always working and pushing people around. Andrée was very pretty, with soft, hazel eyes and brown hair curling gracefully over her shoulders. Suzanne just sat and giggled. She was later very useful to me with dressmakers and various details important to women. But she never stopped giggling.

"My son Robert is in bed," Madame Laroche went on, busily frying potatoes. "He had a motor-cycle accident the other day; he crashed into a truck, tearing along at his usual crazy speed. Fortunately, he only succeeded in twisting his knee rather badly. He spent the whole of yesterday raving with fury because he couldn't attend your *parachutage*. You'll meet him after lunch."

We all sat down to my first complete meal in France, spread on the best cloth, eaten on the best plates, with the best knives and forks. It was an orgy of steak, onions, ham and cakes. But it was only later that I discovered that all this was the fruit of painful saving and well above the means of the Laroche family. Questions about England were shot at me right and left, especially about the invasion. Wherever I went during the following months, people expected me to know all the plans of the Allies and to announce the exact day of the landing.

"Well, you come from England, don't you?" they would say.

I had an awful time trying to convince them that life was not easy there just because coffee and bread were not rationed... I told gruesome tales of bombing and got desperately muddled when I tried to prove, figures in hand, that clothes rationing gave headaches to British women and were insufficient to their needs.

"Yes, but you can buy wool, can't you? And material that is made of *real* textile, and shoes for the children? And bread isn't rationed, and coffee isn't rationed..."

Always the same thing. So I went on with stories of millions of men ready for war, of endless convoys of tanks and guns on their way to embarkation ports, of planes zooming about the skies and bombers thundering over the Channel on their way to Germany. I emerged from that meal completely exhausted and feeling a little sick; it had ended with more of the nauseating Pétain coffee which Madame Laroche insisted on improving by pouring *eau-de-vie* into it.

After lunch I was led upstairs to meet Robert. Robert was a large, dishevelled figure under his enormous yellow eiderdown. He talked and talked and talked, but I understood nothing of it, which was highly embarrassing. His speech was a mixture of French and patois poured forth at a fantastic speed: all the words telescoped into one another. Four or five young men walked in with berets tipped on the back of their heads. They all talked at once.

"When are THEY coming? And what does it feel like to jump out of a plane?" I began my story over again; God knows how many more times I had to tell it during the months that followed.

"Stay here while I go and get Suzanne's bed ready for you," Madame Laroche declared. "You must be very tired. I'll put the *moine* in for you and you'll be comfortable..."

With this she walked out, leaving everyone laughing at my horrified expression.

"A monk? I don't want a monk in my bed..."

"Okay, don't worry. It isn't a real one, you'll see," Robert Laroche assured me.

Half an hour later I lifted the blankets of Suzanne's bed in tense wonder at the large lump underneath. I found the *moine*: a wooden affair, somewhat reminiscent of a *luge* upside-down, on which lay an earthenware bowl filled with smouldering ashes. The bed was like a warm oven: the sort of place one dreams about on cold and windy winter nights.

It was 2pm by then. I opened the window wide. The warm sun and cold air poured in, brightening the colour of the artificial flowers on the table and catching the brass ornaments hanging on the walls. How very unreal everything still was!

"I'm in France. This *is* France," I thought. And to make the real state of things become a part of me, I rubbed my hands on the window-sill until they burnt. Now I have to look after myself, I'm alone. And if I don't, God only knows the things that might happen. I would stop being, altogether. I don't mind that so much, as long as it isn't a painful process. I thought of the small pill I had been given before I left. The little lieutenant who had handed it to me was nervous; he was not so sure he was doing the right thing.

"If you put it in your mouth, you must bite hard..." he had said. Bite hard, that was all; after that I would never think again. The idea that I would stop thinking seemed impossible to grasp: to stop seeing or hearing, yes, but not to stop having ideas. And then, all at once, I felt that nothing could ever happen to me. I looked around for 'escape ways', faithful to the nearness of my training, and sank into the soft bed after having planned a sprint through the back garden and over the neighbouring wall in case anything happened.

I was shaken by Madame Laroche a few hours later. "Wake up, Mademoiselle Paulette, the Patron is here."

I sat up feeling sleepy and stupid, my hair falling all over my face. A little man with a leather cap hiding his ears walked in with springy steps. The sun was down.

"Hello, brrr… It's cold motor-cycling about at this hour," he said, removing his cap.

He was practically bald with a little moustache (the moustache was an irregular ornament, being shaved off when he visited certain parts of the region) and about forty-five. He had a sly look, his eyes quickly avoiding yours when he spoke. He appeared to be in a frayed state of nerves as he bounced about the room and spoke in broken sentences. He spoke French with a strong foreign accent, not specifically English, but undefinable to German ears in the mix-up of regional accents.

"There are a few things I must get straight with you, before we go on to anything else," he declared. "First, I am very strict on discipline. Of course anyone may make a mistake, but I don't forgive people who make the same mistake twice. To put things plainly, you have to do what I tell you and we'll get on all right. If you don't, I shall have to shoot you. It may mean the lives of many families if you let yourself be caught. The second thing is that if you *are* caught, I am afraid we can do nothing for you. So don't expect anything…"

I felt intensely ridiculous in my blue pyjamas and hot in the back of the neck. Yet somehow this crude introduction was not wholly unnatural considering the situation: I had trained myself to expect so many unexpected things that nothing could find me unprepared. The Patron went on:

"I'll give you a short general lecture now; but don't worry, you'll learn things as you go on. The main thing to remember is, always to profit by a lesson. Also, you have been taught many things in England: let them become a part of you but don't go out of your way to put them into practice. For instance, cover stories are practically useless. If the Germans make a thorough enquiry about you, no cover story will hold. I have a few personal rules of my own: whenever it is humanly possible I avoid establishing a contact with someone I don't know by sight, or without someone who can identify him. Passwords are poisonous traps."

He fumbled for a cigarette; he couldn't spend five minutes without smoking. His fingers were stained with nicotine. He had small hands with pointed finger-tips. They all seemed to have been broken below the nail where the skin went up in a bump.

"Mind *you* never smoke in public: women smoke so little here that you would be picked out right away.

"In a few days we shall go on a trip together," he went on. "I want to present you personally to my regional chiefs and from then on you will be my only link with them. You already know Scharks: he's a good man. As he commands this sector, I see him myself very often. In fact you will soon find that you know more about our distant sectors than the one right round you. Now – tomorrow I shall take you to Nasoulens[2], a farm about eight kilometres from here. You will stay there for a while. It's only two or three kilometres from where I live and it'll be easy for me to come and see you whenever I want."

He walked about the room for a while, puffing hard at his cigarette and looking at my suitcases and the clothes lying on a chair.

"Show me your papers…"

I handed him the identity card and the clothes and food cards.

"These two are excellent," he declared after looking the latter over and putting them up to the light. "It's a good idea to carry them all together, but when you get other identity papers, take care not to carry cards with different names. It's quite a common mistake."

I saw him frown as he inspected the identity documents closely. He shook his head.

"No good," he said at last. "London makes mistakes sometimes.[3] This card shows that you've crossed the demarcation line illegally last year. It has the wrong stamp on it. Have a photograph taken tomorrow and I'll have a new one ready for you in a few days."

He left me on this. It seemed monstrous that I should stay any time at all without papers. The future loomed new and exciting, uncertainly shaded by the various impressions the Patron had created. I had expected this first encounter to bring a sense of security, now I wasn't so sure.

The next day I walked self-consciously about Condom with Suzanne. I imagined I stuck out like a sore thumb when a policeman calmly ambled in my direction, his *képi* on his neck and sun-rays playing with his buttons. He did not pay the slightest attention to me but, nevertheless, I felt that I had played a masterful piece of acting, looking perfectly calm and casual.

It took me nearly three weeks to shake off this form of self-consciousness and to get over the idea that I had 'British agent' written all over my face. The close study of maps and city plans with Jean-Claude brought about the sensation that I was as obvious as if I were trying to walk unseen on the plan itself.

In the afternoon the Patron arrived.

"Privat[4] will take you to Nasoulens in his car," he declared. Privat was one of the Condom butchers. "He bought a bicycle for you a couple of months ago; you'll find it waiting up there. Start walking outside the town and Privat will catch you up. In small towns like Condom the story that Privat has a new girl would get round like wildfire if you were seen driving with him."

Suzanne accompanied me on the road. Condom is in the hollow of a small valley, so we started going uphill right after the last houses. I could see that future bicycle runs meant hours of solid climbing. Privat caught me up in a screeching of tyres and brakes and I climbed up by his side. His beret was cocked cheekily on one ear and he greeted me with a smile and a wink.

"Well, Mademoiselle Paulette, how does it feel to be here now? We've been waiting for you for such a long time. We're a good crowd here; so is the Patron, although he seems a little rough at first. I'm sure you'll like it with us."

"I'm sure I will, and it would just be too bad if I didn't, wouldn't it?" He laughed with good humour.

"Have you seen your new bicycle?" he went on. "I found it when I was in Toulouse some time ago, complete with tyres, for a small matter of 7000 francs… You can only find things like that in the black market, you know. I'm proud of my catch and I bet you'll be pleased."

Privat and I chatted gaily as we roared up the hill. I soon discovered that Privat was reputed to be the most reckless driver in the neighbourhood, and when French drivers start being reckless it is always something of a miracle to me that they don't have accidents every time they go out. We passed the Patron laboriously puffing his way up on a *vélo-moteur*, a small 3 or 4hp motor-cycle very popular in the Resistance. He waved and disappeared in the storm of dust Privat aroused behind him. At one point we swung to the left and jolted along a muddy white road, very characteristic of French country roads.

"That is Nasoulens, over there…" Privat said, pointing to a neat little house down a curve in the hills. It had a red-tiled roof. "You're very lucky; it's all new and clean. The farmers are friends of mine and I suggested to the Patron that you should live there. They have been told that you are a Parisian student recovering from pneumonia. As a matter of fact, they know that you belong to the Resistance, but they don't know what you're doing or where you come from."

I knew the pneumonia line would stand a good chance: I coughed pitifully, still choked by the remains of the London fog. But how long would I be able to lie to people I lived with? Cover stories had been hammered so much into my head that the Patron's words had been without effect. Privat waved to black figures working in the fields and they started running towards the house.

We stopped in the back yard. Two dogs sprang out of the farm, barking and furiously showing their teeth.

"Fany, Sirrou… come here. Down; DOWN…" shouted a little old lady chasing out of the house behind them. She had a square face wrinkled by the sun and years, and waved her arms, smoothed her apron and bounced about in a panic.

"*Mon Dieu, Mon Dieu,* I'm all alone, all alone. I'll go and call my daughter. What can I do with no one here, what can I do? But gracious me, please come in," she went on, obviously in a terrific muddle. Privat laughed and attempted to calm her down while I walked around looking at my new home. It had brown shutters and white-painted windows, white-and-red-checked curtains, flower-beds at the front and bamboo bushes at the back. This looked like an exceptional sort of place. Sirrou sniffed at my feet while Fany lay across the door ignoring the fuss and determined to keep us out.

The farmer's wife came running around the corner, soon followed by her husband strolling calmly with his hands in his pockets.

"Hello," waved Privat, "here's your new farm-hand. Paulette, this is Odilla and this is Henri Cérensac. But where's André?.. Their son," he added.[5]

"He's coming. We're pruning the vines and he's finishing his row." Monsieur Cérensac turned to me.

"Well, well, Mademoiselle Paulette, we're glad to see you. We've been waiting for you for more than a month now. Why were you so long in coming?" I bit the word "fog" off my lips. "But come inside, and let's all have a glass of wine. Fany, scram…"

He put his arm around my shoulder and we stepped in. A cloud of indifference settled over me: this business of getting used to new faces and new ways so often in such a short time was tiring.

A soft light poured in through the pink glass of the hall door. The floor, covered with red and white tiles; and the kitchen, furnished with new wood fittings, shone with tender care: a smell of wax hung in the wooden staircase. Madame Cérensac took some glasses out of the cupboard, wiped them vigorously with precise and dexterous movements and filled them with white wine. She smiled at me.

"I hope you don't mind my mother; she gets terribly fussed whenever anything unusual occurs and forgets all the rules of politeness…"

Her mother, still rushing around, appeared unaware that she was the subject of conversation. She was always like this, being shouted at and seemingly unaware of it.

"I'll show you to your room," Odilla Cérensac went on. But at this point the dogs barked again and we heard the approaching puffs of the Patron's *vélo-moteur*. He took his heavy *canadienne* off and handed cigarettes around. *Canadiennes* are short, waterproof jackets, lined with thick lamb's wool. Two seconds later André came in, completing what was to be my future family, very tall and very sunburnt:

like Robert Laroche, he spoke so indistinctly that it was more than a month before I could understand what he was talking about. He was hard-working and honest but had no patience; sometimes he shouted so loudly at his grandmother that I wanted to run out of the room.

"You two must be nearly the same age," said Madame Cérensac. "How old are you, Paulette?"

"Twenty. I shall be twenty-one in two months' time."

"Well, you're a month older than André then…"

"What a household this is going to be," Cérensac interrupted, throwing his hands to the ceiling. "My son already does what he wants and Paulette doesn't look as though she'll be very different. We'll have to be firm, Odilla."

"Why, but it's very simple," said the Patron. "If you can't control her, just throw her out; she can sleep under a bush…"

"No, not on your life. Poor little thing, she looks pale and thin and she has a cough like a dog's bark. I'd feel responsible," Cérensac retorted with a wink in my direction.

At this point the Poor Little Thing wondered what her father would think if he had heard that. His words still rang in her ear: "The thing that worries me is that you will arrive in France obviously strong and healthy and will be noticed as such in a crowd of thin and tired people…"

It was 4pm by then. The sun was going down behind the hills and the wine and brandy I had swallowed brought warmth to my chest and sweet torpors to my brain. I was in the middle of the Armagnac country and within a few weeks the special brand of cognac became part of my daily meal, like it was to the country people. I went out for a little fresh air. Odilla Cérensac followed me.

"I'm afraid this is still very primitive," she declared, somewhat embarrassed. "We haven't any form of convenience here. The bushes behind the hen-house are the best place…"

It took me a few seconds to realize what she meant… During the first weeks that followed, I spent precious time making thorough reconnaissances of my chosen emplacements before using them, making dead sure no one would fall upon me at the wrong moment. Later on, I became so used to it that I didn't care what happened.

"I'll be back tomorrow to see how you get on," the Patron declared, pulling his *canadienne* on.

"All right, all right," Cérensac cut in, laying a protecting hand on my shoulder. "Don't worry, we can very well do without you. She'll be all right here, and soon fatter, too…"

Henri Cérensac was a typical Gascon, with dark, shiny eyes which he kept well protected with a beret tipped low over his forehead; he walked very erect, his head thrown back with a proud consciousness of the value of his race. Dignity and honesty were written all over his open, clean-cut face. His wife was the same; her eyes twinkled and smiled continually. She was extremely efficient and exact in everything she did. I never knew her to be wrong in anything she asserted, to misunderstand anyone's emotions or not to succeed in whatever she undertook.

She showed me to my room.

"You'll be careful, won't you? The house has just been built and we've only lived in it eighteen months. No one has slept in your room yet."

It was a pretty room, obviously the best in the house. A yellow eiderdown, frilly curtains, new furniture and, again, the clean, good smell of wax. I started to unpack right away. It was the first time I had opened my cases in over six weeks and I joyfully pulled out a number of things that I had forgotten about. What was my life here going to be like? I had always lived in a town and been used to some form of continuous mental activity. Suddenly I felt very lonely and very tired. I wondered if my father had been told that I had arrived safely or whether he was still worrying about me...

At 6.30 everyone sat around a bowl of smoking soup. Dinner was always early as the men returned tired and hungry from long days of work in the fields.

"Tell us about Paris and what life there is like, especially what it costs," said Madame Cérensac, cheerfully making conversation.

"This is where my troubles start..." I thought. I invented and made up stories, racking my brains to remember what I'd heard on the BBC or read in London's French paper, *France*,[6] about life in occupied Paris. I made a number of *faux pas* and saved my face as best I could by explaining that I was too poor to have much to do with the black market and consequently knew little of the price of things. I also reverted frequently to the ah-I-can't-tell-you-*that* airs which the whole family discreetly understood. They were alert and quick-witted and took little time to understand that Paris and my past were things I did not wish to talk about. To my intense relief they changed the subject and never came back to it. A month or so later, I told them the truth: sheltering a parachutist was a grave risk and I thought that it wasn't fair to keep them in the dark. They smiled and took it without concern.

After dinner Madame Cérensac put the *moines* in the beds. I went straight up to mine while Cérensac stayed in the kitchen reading a book carefully bound with newspaper. He always read for an hour or two on winter nights; in the summer he worked. The old grandmother, who had insisted on going to bed last ever since her daughter had been married, slept in her chair, her chin on her chest, her glasses on the tip of her nose and the Parish weekly magazine opened on her lap. André had gone to Caussens, a little village that Privat and I had crossed on the way up.

"He goes to Caussens three times a week," Madame Cérensac informed me. "He sees his girl and brings back the bread."

"You've got luck on your side," Jean-Claude and I had been told after we had returned unhurt from the crash. As I slipped between the warm sheets and watched the dying glow of the *moine's* smouldering ashes, I thought that Nasoulens was going to be my second piece of luck. Outside, Fany barked at some distant noise and, somewhere far, Sirrou echoed with a long and plaintive call.

CHAPTER IV

Ispent the next day just roaming about the farm, trying to convince myself I wasn't bored. Pork *pâté* in earthenware jars and a loaf four feet long lay on the table beside a bottle of wine when I went down: that was breakfast and I didn't dare refuse it. Later on I got half a litre of milk from the neighbouring farm every morning and indulged in *café-au-lait*.

"You'll need same *sabots*: I'll buy you a pair on Saturday in Condom," Madame Cérensac declared. "Saturday is market day; we all go down. And I'll cut an apron for you out of one of my mother's old nightgowns: I dye them and they're very useful…"

I went all over Nasoulens during the morning: the cow-shed, the barn, the hen-houses, the pigsty. I hate pigs. They look like fat women on high heels. One day one of them got free and ran round the house, its large ears flapping about in the wind and its uncontrollable tail wiggling all over its bouncing behind. But I think that I hate geese even more. Only now do I appreciate the expression 'as stupid as a goose'. Three of them walked perpetually round and round the hen-house, looking superior and hissing with outstretched necks at the person who brought them their food. I had a tough fight with the gander once; he pinched a bit off my hind part.

The neighbours always know everything, often more about you than you do yourself; so, after we had discussed it, Cérensac casually told people that I was the daughter of an old friend of his, a sergeant in the Francs-Tireurs during the last war.[1] The tale went down well in the neighbourhood and I was soon considered a member of the family.

At lunchtime we ate an enormous meal, two or three different meat dishes, and I thought of the dreary stews and the boiled cabbage I had eaten during two years in the WAAF, of the starving children in Paris, and the undernourished factory workers: I was slowly getting used to incongruity.

In the afternoon the Patron came. He brought new good advice, my papers and a beret, saying that I had to watch my local colour and be like everybody else.

"You'd better not do your hair swept up across the back like this. Women in little country towns round here wear it very high in front and down at the back… But I'm sure you'll soon notice details that men would miss. Your clothes aren't very suitable for this region either. I'll get you some and give you a few black-market contacts."

I explained that I had been briefed to go to the north of France and live in Paris at first, and how my clothes were designed for that.

"You're better here," he replied.

He went on to tell me that he had been begging London to send him a courier for months.

"I've had to go everywhere myself all this time. Four or five months ago the Boches put a heavy price on my head and it's been getting more difficult every day. The other day I came on a Gestapo barrage. I had a transmitter set in the back of my Simca car and my *canadienne* thrown over it; fortunately they didn't search the car – I don't know why though, because they were actually pulling the floor-boards out of two trucks they'd stopped by the side of the road. Somehow, I have a nondescript face."

Indeed his appearance was highly unimpressive. Like everybody else, a beret pulled low over his forehead over-shadowed his sallow face; the skin was tight over his cheeks and the thin lips above a pointed and irresolute chin often trembled with weariness. He told me how he had been caught by the Gestapo and tortured for a month two years before. His teeth had been pulled out one by one. High-tension current was shot through him by means of electric gadgets attached around his arms, legs and kidneys. He had been beaten until his body was raw, but eventually released for lack of evidence. He never looked me once in the eyes while he told me all this. But he showed me scars on his arms and legs, scars that were not healed yet.[2]

"How is your bicycle?" he went on.

I had been for a ride in the morning and it had worked well; though shining and new, it was very much what everybody called 'of nowadays'. The handle-bars and all parts that are usually chromium were simply covered with silver paint. Within one week they were rusted. In spite of that it lasted until it was blown to bits in a *maquis* fight.

"Now – on Sunday, I'll come and fetch you and we'll drive to a farm about 30 kilometres away where you'll meet VanderBock; he's my right-hand contact in Agen and a very good man.[3] Monday, you'll go to Agen and he'll introduce you to my regional chief for the Lot-et-Garonne. After that you'll join me and I'll take you on an introductory tour."

We stopped talking shop as Cérensac walked into the warm kitchen; we had more wine and more armagnac before the Patron left.

On the Saturday, the whole family (minus the grandmother) cleaned up and prepared to go to Condom; we had lunch at 10am and started out shortly after. André, all smart and brilliantined, was the first one ready, soon followed by his father who made fun of his perfumed hair-grease. Common sense was the prevailing quality in the household: André shrugged his shoulders, completely unconcerned. Madame Cérensac looked far smarter than I, in a neat navy-blue dress and coat. We all rode down the hill in a file, shopping baskets dangling on our handle-bars.

The main square of Condom was a bustle of sunshine and busy housewives. The men sat in the cafés playing *belote*[4] while their womenfolk argued endlessly over the price of vegetables and the latest scandals: Saturday was gossip's day of glory. The young people, clad in their Sunday best, walked solemnly about the streets. The town breathed of a clean quality of well-earned pleasure. I bought some books; poor books, but all the Germans allowed to the 'inferior' French population.

I met the Patron in the square once, but he looked away; so it was obvious we were not to know each other in Condom.

I paid a visit to the Laroches and later joined Madame Cérensac, weighed down under bulging shopping bags. Her husband, a wooden box under his left arm, caught us up on the way home.

"Guess what I've got in there," he said, pointing to the box. But, too impatient to wait for my answer, "Oysters… Odilla makes a wonderful garlic sauce to eat with them. She's the best cook in the region…" Which turned out to be no exaggeration either.

Sunday dragged along in anticipation of my first outing into the world. We had an even more enormous lunch than the day before: Sunday was always a feast from which I emerged dopy and sleepy. Madame Cérensac, in a clean apron and with flour up to her elbows, baked a *pastis*, a large Gascon pastry filled with armagnac-sodden apples and cooked in a special oven, under wood ashes.

In the afternoon the Patron took me to meet VanderBock, a fat hearty Belgian who worshipped him. He slapped me on the back.

"My daughter Marie is just about your age; you'll meet her tomorrow," he said.[5] "Her husband is in England in the Free French Air Force." He and the Patron went on to an interminable discussion about people and places I knew nothing about.

"By the way," said the Patron, "take this as a general rule. All 'tractions' running on petrol are owned by the Gestapo. So watch out for them…" 'Traction' is short for front-drive Citroën.

"I'll expect you off the Condom bus tomorrow morning," VanderBock said when we left. "You'll find my shop just beside the Garage Agenais."

I hardly slept that night. I simply couldn't imagine what things would be like and how they would fit in with all I had been told to expect in London. I had never seen a Boche in uniform. I wondered about the Gestapo, 'la Georgette', as they called it in the region; – and the tortures. But then, those were things that could happen to other people – but not to me. The Patron had taken my pill away and thrown it into the fire. Jean-Claude had told him I had it. Later we had a row about it: Jean-Claude put on the air of a righteous martyr, but deep down I agreed that he was right.

I was to catch the 7am bus the next morning, so I got up at five; it was roughly an hour's ride to Condom. Madame Cérensac wrapped a chunk of bread and a little *pâté* in a towel. "You'll be hungry later," she declared.

It was as black as ink when I stepped out. Grey clouds ran in heavy, pressed masses along the sky; the last glow of the setting moon fringed them with a sinister silveriness. The wind, an icy wind, blew with gloomy, lingering gusts. The trees somehow looked depraved, edging the long road. It rained.

So I started singing to myself and suddenly remembered that I always sang to myself when I was scared. I had sung all the way down on my first parachute jump and had felt self-conscious on landing in case anyone had heard me. I wondered, as I sang, what was the value of omens and instincts; whether something was telling me not to go to Agen, or whether I was just scared because this was my first trip. Later I learnt to know the difference between an instinct of danger and fright. People don't get caught right away, I told myself now. And then I remembered all the stories I had been told about agents jumping right on top of police stations[6] and even into German camps, or being picked up within twenty-four hours of arriving, in barrages or snap-controls.

There was no point in worrying like this, so I forced myself to think of something else. I thought of how happy I was to be in France at last, how much I'd yearned for it. Later on it became a habit: I would always think of how happy I was to be in France when I cycled to catch the morning bus. What would some of my friends say if they knew? Rain ran down my face; the road was wet and shining; not a sound was to be heard except for the grinding of my pedals. I pulled my beret right down over my ears.

Condom still slept on. The only sign of life was the distant sound of the *gazogène* warming up in the cold square. '*Faire les gaz*', they called it. I left my bicycle against the Laroches' door.

I sat next to two *gendarmes* on the bus, feeling I was pulling off a particularly well-calculated 'coup'. Each of them had a bag on his lap, out of which emerged the neck of a bottle of wine; they rolled cigarettes and talked. Everybody talked, arguing about seats (there were always about ten times more people than the bus could carry) and about the price of things. I decided that food and the price of things was the main subject of conversation in France. Eventually, after two or three false starts, the bus moved off, half an hour late.

It left packed to bursting point. The conductor made his way through the vociferations, treading on toes and flattening people on top of one another, completely unmoved and disinterested.

"Agen?" he said to me, and without waiting for my answer punched a ticket.

"*Please…*" I replied, and then my answer resounded in my ears. God, I'd said "please" in English. I looked round in dismay and misery, nevertheless not forgetting to stick to my casual air. But no one had heard; they were too busy arguing and yelling at one another. Or sleeping. I sat there, furious with myself. What a lousy agent I was making, on my first trip too. And I'd repeatedly been told about that in England: "Be careful not to answer 'come in' when someone knocks at your door…" That was the same sort of thing, one of those silly details that lead you straight to a prison cell. Never again – and I never did either.

In Agen the bus stopped outside the railway station. There was no control at the bus stop, as I had been led to believe, so I started to walk down the main street to the Garage Agenais.

Then I saw my first German. I think I shall remember him to my dying day. He was horribly ugly: quite like I had expected a Boche to be. Tall and lanky, he looked as though he'd had a fat, protruding stomach in better days, a stomach which had died down to nothing; his pants were bunched up round his waist in a sloppy fashion while his short jacket flapped loosely over them. His hideous army cap sat crooked over one ear; he dragged his feet wearily behind him and his ears stuck out. He carried a yellow attaché-case and glanced at me with a half-witted expression.

"Ah, if you knew…" I thought, and felt very superior. And for the first time I experienced real anger at the idea that such a specimen should claim to belong to a master race. After he'd passed, I felt I had got over an important step in getting-accustomed-to-things.

VanderBock sold accessories for automobiles. A shock awaited me when I reached his shop. Three petrol-driven tractions were parked in front of the door, right on the pavement. Four men in civilian clothes and closely shaven walked about near them. They were well dressed, in grey double-breasted suits: obviously the Gestapo. One of them wore black glasses and had a scar right across his left cheek. They were talking to a beautiful woman leaning nonchalantly against VanderBock's window. She looked like a Hollywood movie star with long, golden hair waving down to her shoulders, a mink coat which she had slung casually over her shoulders and fashionable, thick wooden-soled shoes. They all spoke German.

"Right on the first day," I thought. "What on earth do I do now?" I passed VanderBock's shop without even looking inside and stepped into the first shop I saw. It was a grocer's.

"What does Mademoiselle want?" asked a fat woman behind her counter.

For a brief second I wondered what on earth one buys in a grocer's.

"Shoe polish…" I replied, illuminated.

"I'm afraid this is all I have," she said, producing a revolting-looking black tube. But I felt very happy with it and walked out clutching it. At this moment VanderBock arrived.

"Why didn't you come in?" he said.

"Well, I thought those tractions in front of your shop meant that the Gestapo was arresting you."

"Of course, I should've told you… They often come and use the garage next door. They're around all day."

He led me to his flat, above the shop, where I met his daughter Marie. Marie was a rather pretty girl with fair hair and too much make-up. I decided immediately that the Agen accent was the worst in the region. She worked in the shop with her father and was one of those perpetually busy people, weighed down with worries and the responsibility of her whole family.

"My husband has been gone eighteen months now," she told me. "He had to hide in a farm to avoid being deported to Germany for forced labour. He didn't want to leave, but I persuaded him to go to England. I found an escape route for him through the Pyrenees."

"How did you do that?"

"Well, it was much easier for me to run about than it was for him. So I took a train to Luchon: I had to slip between two German inspectors checking permits at the door of the station there. Luchon is in the forbidden zone edging the Spanish border and you need a special permit to enter it," she explained. "Then I contacted an old *gendarme* I knew there, and he took me to the mountains where, together, we found an abandoned *télépherique* trail. It was only four hours' walk to the border by that way. He left a week later. I heard from him when he was in Morocco, on his way to London, but nothing since."

"Now look, I want to know more about those Gestapo people hanging round your shop this morning," I told Marie.

"Ah, yes. They're very dangerous characters; we know them all. But the worst one of the lot is the woman."

"The woman? Do you mean the mink coat?"

"Yes. She's at the head of the Gestapo in Agen. The last chief was killed by the Resistance a couple of months ago. This is why we still have a curfew at 8pm; also, they shot quite a number of political prisoners in reprisal. She took his place, and she's worse than he was. As a matter of fact," she added, lowering her voice so that no one in the house should hear, "she's a specialist in tortures inflicted on men. I've been told that men are strapped to a couch and that she shuts herself up in their cell – she always gets her information: apparently they never fail to talk after they've been through her hands."

"But surely something should be done about getting rid of her?"

"You have no idea how well protected she is. And don't forget that we have a curfew after eight; the Gestapo Headquarters are patrolled and watched, even from a distance.[7] But just a little patience, the Resistance here has a programme in store for her, as soon as the invasion comes…"

I felt cold sweat pouring down my back after Marie had finished telling me about it.

"But then, the local Gestapo here have done worse. They caught a boy of seventeen yesterday afternoon; he screamed and cried all night. But after dawn broke this morning, he wasn't heard any more. It gives you a nasty sensation at night, you know. I think I shall have to move Mother to the country for a while; she's growing more and more restless."

After lunch, when I met the rest of the family, Marie and I walked along the quays of the Garonne and went window-shopping in the main street. I discarded my beret; it was all right in a small town like Condom, but in Agen women wore high, complicated hair styles and even more complicated ear-rings. I bought a pair; they pinched and hurt my ears and it took me weeks to get used to them.

Then VanderBock and Marie introduced me to Cyprien, chief of the Lot-et-Garonne sector.[8] Cyprien was the sort of man who would not get used to the idea that he had to grow old. He was greying at the temples and pretty pleased with his appearance: I caught him casting swift and indulgent glances at himself in shop windows. He usually went about in a brown-leather jacket and a soft felt hat pulled over one eye: the Gestapo had classed him as 'Enemy No. 1' in Agen, and his description with those garments was placarded all over the police stations, but nothing would induce him to change them. I always felt a little uncomfortable in the company of this provincial beau.

"What a pleasure to meet you, Mademoiselle Paulette," he began right away. "Why doesn't London always send us young ladies like you – we'd do a lot of good work here, I'm sure… But you must be thirsty. Why don't you come and have an *apéritif* with me in my favourite little café near the station?"

"Why, thank you very much, but as a matter of fact I'm *not* thirsty. And there is not much point in going to cafés unnecessarily."

He looked at me with a little pity, as though I was being over-cautious and dull. "Well, you'll change your mind pretty quickly, you'll see. Maybe another time."

"Maybe…"

He went on to give me his various addresses in the region and a number of other details. He was intelligent and efficient, but an individualist; his ways, his tricks and his people were the best everywhere. In later days Cyprien never failed to invite me for an *apéritif*, but I never accepted once.

That night I slept in a room near the station. It belonged to a pal of Marie's, a football star who obviously stuck his hair down with fantastic amounts of hair-grease. The sheets were filthy, so was the room. I laid a towel over the pillow and slept very uncomfortably. There was no water to wash with in the morning.

I took the train at six. The Patron was waiting for me at the small country station of Lectoure. We drove to Seissan, a village on the Auch–Lannemezan road. He had chosen the house of a Communist, Monsieur Chénier,[9] for a rendezvous with Roger, the chief of the Pyrenees sector.[10]

"I have excellent papers," the Patron told me as we drove along. "They're absolutely real *carte de travail* (workmen's card) and *permis de circuler* (road licence). I run about so much that I can't afford not to have as near to perfect papers as possible; as it is, my description is in every police station. Fortunately, I have useful contacts at the Auch Prefecture: of course I can't use them too often, but I'll get you similar papers because you'll need them as much as I do."

We arrived at Chénier's just in time for lunch and immediately embarked on a heated discussion. He called us the IS – or Intelligence Service. The Patron jumped up.

"I tell you we have nothing to do with the IS. We're plain soldiers; our work is secret, of course, but then so is anything to do with the invasion. Our job here is to prepare the way for Allied military operations from a purely military aspect. Arms and instruction. That's all we do…"

Chénier had obviously been told that thousands of times: I couldn't quite make out if he was trying to annoy the Patron or if he never believed him. He had a habit of passing his fingers through his grey hair, then tucking his thumbs in his belt and pulling his trousers up.

"You and your invasion," he went on, shrugging his shoulders. "You make me laugh. You know as well as I do that the policy of the Anglo-Americans is to let the Russians fight and annihilate half the German armies… Then, after most of the Germans are killed, after half the population of France has died in concentration camps and of starvation, the Anglo-Americans will land. And there won't be anybody to stop them. And they'll wave flags and say they are the big victors…"

I caught a malicious gleam in his eye as I was about to burst out in protest, so I said nothing.

"For goodness' sake shut up, Alfred," broke in Madame Chénier. She was much younger than her husband; she had disappeared when we arrived and soon returned in a see-I-follow-the-Paris-fashion dress, all gathers and folds about the shoulders and waist. "Whenever he starts this sort of talk it ends in a row, and finally it is I who have to go around making apologetic calls on the offended neighbours. I'm sick and tired of it. Let's have some green Chartreuse. I found a bottle of it the other day."

"Nobody asked you to go and apologise to the neighbours," said Chénier indignantly.

The Patron hadn't seen the gleam. "Now look here," he exclaimed, "we're all Allies. You must admit that nothing would be more completely disastrous than a failure. The day the Allies are ready to invade they'll do it, and then you'll see. I can assure you that they are just as anxious to see the war finished as you are. We all admire the Russians as much as you do, but we are also conscious of our worth, of what we can do, and of our responsibilities. Ask Paulette what they are doing in England now…"

Roger arrived in the middle of the afternoon. He was grumpy. Roger was perpetually grumpy, grousing at the weather, at the long trip he'd had to do on his bicycle, cursing the *parachutages* that didn't come, always having arguments with his fellow-resisters. But he was very honest and very straight and also very kind-hearted. I disliked him very much at first, possibly because he complained to the Patron that I was too young for a courier. He was prejudiced against all young people because he'd had an awful time a few months before with a young agent who spent his time running after women and who would rather jump out of windows than walk down stairs.[11] Later, however, we became good friends.

We spent the night at Seissan. I slept in the daughter's room, all pink satin and white organdie and little pink bows, and rabbits painted on the foot of the bed and beads hanging from the lamp-shades. As soon as I was in bed a strong smell of perfume tickled my nostrils; I became so curious that I got up again and had a look round. And then I found what it was: Madame Chénier perfumed the chamber-pot. Delighted with my discovery, I fell asleep in a delicate cloud of Chanel No. 5.

Chénier kept the stocks of his clothes shop in the back of his house; he was a great help to the Patron when Allied airmen had to be equipped. I acquired a cycling jacket with a long zip-fastener and an overall for the farm, and the following afternoon the Patron and I returned to Nasoulens.

Chapter V

"You'll go to Agen tomorrow, Paulette," said the Patron. He had just received a number of messages from London. "VanderBock will give you details of how to contact Colomiers.[1] He is my man in the south Dordogne sector. He is very efficient. He will give you the position on the map of a number of fields that he has been looking for. You will give him messages for each of them and bring the coded pin-points back to me. I take it that London showed you how to do that?"

Satisfied with my answer, he went on:

"You'll probably have to go there by car. It's a long way. If VanderBock can't arrange it you'll have to go by train, and you won't be back for some days. Be careful to have a cover story ready when you leave Agen."

Marie greeted me the next day with a kiss on both cheeks. Her father had a car ready for me within two hours and came straggling in followed by a tall young man with curly black hair and a long, sharp nose: l'Asperge.[2] When l'Asperge smiled, the corners of his mouth went up and I thought of Punch. He was absolutely filthy with the charcoal on which he ran his 'traction'.

"Okay," he said. "I'm ready to start. If anyone stops us, you're my girl and you're just taking a little trip with me. See? I carry sacks of paper to Bergerac. But we mustn't give our exact destination."

L'Asperge was another of those reckless drivers. His 'gazo' worked well, which is unusual for a 'gazo', but he had to stop every fifty kilometres or so to put in more charcoal. We arrived at Eymet at lunchtime, a pretty and prosperous-looking village in south Dordogne, surrounded by orchards. I went in alone and asked a little girl, returning from school with her books under her arm, where the Lantrets lived.[3] Without a word she took my hand and led me along the street. "Over there…" she said, and pointed to a house down a small lane. Her pigtails waved in the wind as she went on her way.

Few things are more difficult than bringing passwords into a normal conversation. The Lantrets were wine-merchants. They frowned at the sight of a stranger walking in at lunchtime, and their look clearly implied that I could well have waited until it was over. I gave the password right away to an aristocratic-looking woman who rose to meet me and identified herself as Madame Lantret.

"Have you received the forty-eight bottles of Montbazillac?"

She looked startled, replied that she had, and beckoned me to walk in.

"I'm Paulette," I told her, "and I've come to see Colomiers."

Her face changed at this announcement. She had been expecting my visit for a month, she told me. I was ushered into the dining-room and presented to the rest of the family; to Madame Lantret's mother, who was nearly blind through having made too much lace; to the mother of Madame Lantret's mother, who was ninety-two and didn't know there was a war on.

"You're Bernard's fiancée. Ah!" she said to me.

Bernard was the son. His face went pink.

"Don't listen to her. She's so old she doesn't know what she's saying. For some reason she is convinced that I'm engaged."

Bernard was only seventeen: he was short and tough, his hair cut close, *en brosse*, according to the best *maquis* fashion. A month before, he had rendered nine locomotives useless by sabotaging the oil-pipes; he had carried out this operation all by himself, one night. After D-Day, although so young, he became one of the dashing figures of the Dordogne *maquis*, always in the front line and leading men twice his age.

We spent the whole afternoon chasing Colomiers. He worked full time for the Resistance and was continually running round on his bicycle. We were sent from house to house where it was expected that the people might be expected to know where he was expected to be. At one moment we stopped the car some five hundred yards from a large farm and Bernard and I walked back to it. An old man in a leather jerkin stood still to watch us go by. He annoyed me. Then he annoyed me even more when I saw that he was standing in the middle of the road to watch us. Bernard frowned.

"Everybody's like that in this beastly place. Always poking their noses into other people's business. Why the hell should he want to know where we are going?"

At the farm we were told that Colomiers was very probably at Campsegret, a small village over thirty kilometres away. Then I put my foot in it.

"There's an old fox out there who has been watching us. He looked very inquisitive and I think you'd better look out for him."

"Yes, I know..." replied one of the women. "He's my father."

From Campsegret we went to Bergerac and from Bergerac back to Campsegret before we contacted Colomiers. I was very bad-tempered by then. L'Asperge was getting worried because night was coming and he wouldn't have enough charcoal to go back to Agen. Also we had to return before the curfew.

Colomiers was a tall man in the middle thirties. He was a Jew. Two years before he'd had a chance of going to the United States, but he had preferred to stay in France. The Gestapo had been chasing him ever since, both as a Jew and as a Resistance chief, but he never faltered in the execution of his task.

Darkness was falling fast as we talked in an unlit room. Colomiers sat on a blue sofa with yellow stripes. He was dressed in a high-necked sweater and riding breeches with stockings up to the knees. He spoke slowly and distinctly, a pure and literary French. He looked tired, his eyes were puffed; he stroked his knee continually with a long-fingered, white hand. The atmosphere was slightly strained.

"I've been going on for too long," he told me. "I'm weary. I haven't had news of my wife for two years. But I like working for the Patron. I would like to go to England, rest for a while and come back. But I would do it only if the Patron sent me, and the invasion seems so near that it isn't worth while. So I simply go on and on…"

Colomiers had had a narrow escape a few months earlier. He, the Patron, Cyprien, Schark's brother[4] and a few others were holding a war conference in a château near Agen.[5] The Gestapo heard that Cyprien, their Enemy No. 1, would be there and arrived in strength at the end of it. The Patron had left the château a quarter of an hour before, declaring that he had a nasty feeling in the pit of his stomach. Cyprien's wife opened the door and began to argue loudly with the Gestapo men, thus warning the others and giving them time to get away. Cyprien escaped through the roof. But Colomiers, absorbed in quiet, philosophical thoughts, came calmly down the stairs, blissfully unaware of what was going on, and found himself face to face with five Gestapo men.

"Hey you – are you Cyprien?" shouted one of them.

"No, I'm afraid I'm not," Colomiers replied with a polite nod. Without batting an eyelid he picked up his coat and hat and stepped out. Then ran for his life.

A second after his exit: "*Lieber Gott*, but that was Colomiers…" yelled one of the Gestapo men. But it was too late. Schark's brother was the only one caught and nothing more was ever heard of him.

Colomiers and I agreed on the messages and parachuting fields and decided on fixed dates for our next meetings. It was quite dark when I stepped out and l'Asperge growled:

"Now that's a fine thing. Just look at this weather. We'll get back to Agen after the curfew, *if* we get in at all."

A heavy fog had settled over the countryside while I talked with Colomiers. Fortunately l'Asperge had succeeded in getting hold of more charcoal and we started out, leaving Bernard to get back to Eymet his own way. L'Asperge and I hardly spoke all the way home. The road was visible only up to thirty yards in front of the car; he drove terribly fast, winding up hills at sixty miles an hour. I shut my eyes at every corner in the hope of not seeing the crash. But I had counted without l'Asperge, who knew the road and his car like the back of his hand. The night was very still and very thick and its monotony broken only by the swiftly-gone vision of white poles indicating road bends.

We arrived outside Agen shortly before 9pm. L'Asperge stopped the car and climbed out.

"Wait here," he said. "I'll go and see if the Boches have set up a road block. In that case we would have to avoid the town and I would take you to my mother's house where you could stay the night. But if the road is free we'll drive into Agen without lights and cut the engine before reaching VanderBock's place."

It sounded like a merry party. I was all for his mother's house. But then, there was also something dramatically adventurous in the silent drive across a Boche-infested city. The fog closed in even thicker and the silence weighed heavily. L'Asperge was away ten minutes.

"No road block," he said, climbing back into the car. "I'd rather go in if you don't mind, because if we go to my mother's house, it means that I have to get up early to be in Agen in time for work tomorrow morning."

I was thankful that my companion knew the town so well: I was as blind as a bat when we drove in. The car slid like a ghost past the German Soldatenheim (rest centre) and came to a stop in front of VanderBock's shop. We had to ring nearly ten minutes before Marie opened the door.

"Confound you couple of idiots," she fulminated, after the door was closed. "We all thought it was the Gestapo. Mother is nearly having a fit upstairs. What the hell do you think you're doing coming in at this time? This is good enough to get us all caught. What you don't know is that a German soldier was killed in the rue Alsace-Lorraine this afternoon. The Boches took six hostages in the street and they are patrolling the town tonight."

The corners of l'Asperge's mouth went up; he grinned and pushed a black curl off his forehead.

"Good… We had 'em," he gloated.

"Enough of this," grumbled Marie. "Don't ever do it again. Paulette can sleep with me; she can't go out again now. As for you, you big telegraph pole, you can manage for yourself…" With this she pushed l'Asperge out.

I took the bus to Condom the next evening. It was already dark when I started cycling up the hill to Nasoulens. After a while I climbed off the bicycle and pushed it. Again this feeling of being very small and very alone in a big world came over me. Small fears like those one has as a child crept up my spine: I imagined animals jumping out of the dark, rustling bushes and slimy things following me on the long, empty road. Then the incongruity of it all struck me – only a few weeks before, I was crawling down mountainsides with a tommy-gun on my back, making mock attacks on tunnels and trains in the pouring rain, jumping out of aeroplanes and playing at the tough paratrooper… And now I had shivers down my back imagining wild animals lurking in quiet little bushes edging a quiet French road.

I reached Nasoulens with a sigh of relief. Already the feeling that I was back to something safe and warm was growing over me. Later on I would always feel a little pang of excitement riding up the hill. The farm became a haven of rest and relaxation and the affectionate welcome of the Cérensacs a necessary part of my life.

"Why, Petite," Cérensac cried (from that day he always called me "Petite"), "we were worried. We thought you'd be back yesterday. What happened?"

I told him about my trip while his wife prepared the dinner. He shook his head.

"I don't like all this. You must not go running about after the curfew again; it's dangerous, and a silly way to be picked up."

A couple of days later my cough had become worse and I went to bed with a high temperature. The Patron came to see me with a large piece of parachuted chocolate and a tin of tea. I was so hot and flushed that he became alarmed and called a doctor. He also warned London, to my great annoyance.

Dr. Driziers came late the same evening on his *vélo-moteur*.[6] I liked him at once; he was young, sharp and efficient, with a professional manner. He never accepted any money from poor people or from the Resistance. He prescribed drastic treatments; Odilla and Henri Cérensac looked after me as though I had been their own daughter, getting up three or four times a night to see how I was and to carry out Dr. Driziers' orders. I was up and about four days later.

While I was ill, Jean-Claude passed through Condom on his way to Tarbes. He was going to work with Roger in the Pyrenees sector. Robert Laroche accompanied him. Later on, he said to me:

"What's wrong with Jean-Claude? He sat and sat and never said a word to us. We could hardly get him to answer with anything but mumbles. In the end I thought I'd hit him…"

I tried to explain that Jean-Claude was shy and never talked much anyway. But Robert shook his head doubtfully.

I was furious with Jean-Claude. I knew what he would say to me: "I simply did not feel like talking. Why should I do things I don't want? Why should I be a hypocrite?" And all the arguing in the world would not convince him that he ought to make an effort to be amiable to people who went out of their way to feed him and make him feel at home. I still had not forgiven him for the night of the crash. We had a violent discussion the next time I saw him and I came out the loser. Jean-Claude was an impossible person to argue with; somehow he always turned out to be right. And then he was stubborn as a mule. Which is probably why he was so successful. Because he was stubborn, but always right.

CHAPTER VI

During the week that followed my illness the Patron came almost every day. He kept me well informed with stories of the 'circuit'. It was then that I got a clear view of what my life would be like during the months to follow. At the Patron's entire disposal; to carry money, messages, orders or anything that had to be passed around; to impose his authority over his regional delegates; to carry out liaison missions; also to entertain him when he was bored. The Patron came practically every day during the spring: I had to leave my books or whatever I was doing at the sound of his *vélo-moteur*, sit in the kitchen or in the garden, and chat with him. Talking has never been a difficult proposition for me, but I often wished for more independence.

The great subject of conversation in the region at that time was the breaking open of the prison at Eysse in the Lot-et-Garonne, where nearly sixty political prisoners had been set free.[1] It appeared that a party of prisoners had succeeded in tying up their guards and had opened the gates to freedom to a number of their friends. Arms had been smuggled through to them by various means. It was a success dearly paid for: a fortnight later, Darnand, chief of the Milice, came to Eysse and had a number of patriots executed in reprisal.

Three days after the event, the Patron arrived with his business air.

"I've just heard that there is one of our people in this group of escaped prisoners. His name is Major H—.[2] He has fourteen men with him whom he wants to get to England. Some worked with him before he was caught and others helped him to get out, so he is sticking by them. Tomorrow you will go to Agen and fix their transport with Cyprien. Then you will go to Tarbes and fix about their passage over the Pyrenees with Roger."

"Don't you think it would be better if I went to Tarbes first? It would be easier if I could tell Cyprien when the guides will be ready to take them across."

"Do as you think best," the Patron replied. "But for goodness' sake be quick. These men are hidden not very far from the prison camp and the Gestapo and the Milice are combing every house to find them."

The next morning (I could only leave in the mornings because of the buses from Condom) I took a bus to Auch, and from there another one to Tarbes. It was a hateful journey: three hours' travelling from Auch to Tarbes, standing up in a mass of people compressed to bursting point – women fainting, children crying and everyone arguing at once. At every stop an angry crowd had to be pushed off. It was dreadfully cold. I had put my fur coat aside, thinking that it would look odd in Condom. But when I reached Tarbes, I was so numb with cold that I promised myself not to mind local colour and wear it in future.

Roger did not live in Tarbes. He had told me to go straight to his nephew's house when I came. His nephew, Raymond Mautrens, owned an electrician's shop;[3] he expected me. Roger had given him my description. I was doubtful about such a vague introduction, however, remembering my instructions on security. But things turned out for the best: Roger, in Tarbes for the day, was standing on the doorstep when I arrived.

"Ha," he barked, in his usual growly way. "You look English in that coat." It was a plain grey swagger coat: I had a suit made of the same material, thinking the combination would be useful for travelling. I shrugged my shoulders, but his remark bore fruit. The next time I wore my swagger coat I felt English all the day, so I discarded it for good.

We went upstairs and had lunch with Raymond Mautrens and his wife Janine.[4] They had two daughters.[5] Maryse, the eldest, was two years old and in the process of having the measles. Her little face was red and puffed, the corners of her mouth drooped tragically, and the household was in a continuous state of panic in case three-months-old Francine should catch the measles too.

"We'll have to take the train for Montréjeau at 3pm," Roger said. "I live just outside in the village of Mazères. I shall have to spend the afternoon running about trying to contact guides. Fifteen men… The Patron stops at nothing, does he? What in the name of God does he think I can do with *fifteen* men until they start? Just make them vanish in the air, like this?" he went on, flicking his fingers angrily. "Within two hours the whole neighbourhood will know about them. And it's not so simple to persuade guides to go off now: the snow is deep in the mountains, there are frequent avalanches, and they have to dig a path inch by inch on the track they will follow before they start out with a party. And they'll want good money too. Fifteen men…"

I remembered that the Patron had told me how Roger fussed and fumed over everything but got things done better than anyone else. "Also," he had concluded, "you know where you stand with him." So I let the storm pass. Occasionally Raymond Mautrens winked at me – his uncle's vociferations always amused him. He was a slightly fat young man with a college-boy look and mentality. Janine, his wife, was much more mature and quiet; she had no sense of humour and little gaiety, but her steady and intelligent personality counter-balanced the general muddle prevailing round her husband.

Roger and I took the train after lunch and arrived at Montréjeau a couple of hours later. We walked back along the line for some five hundred yards, climbed down the embankment, and started walking to Mazères, three kilometres through the fields.

"This system has the double advantage of being quicker and saving us from possible snap-controls at the station door," Roger informed me.

"You'll find Jean-Claude at my house," he went on. "I guess you'll enjoy speaking your jargon, together."

"What jargon?" I asked.

"Why, English of course."

"Whatever makes you think that I speak English with Jean-Claude?"

"Well, if you're English, and Jean-Claude is English, I suppose that you *speak* English together."

"But Jean-Claude isn't English. He's French."

"He told me he was English," Roger shouted, "and I suppose he knows what he's saying."

I knew Jean-Claude would be furious when he heard that I had given his little game away. Indeed, he was. "You ought to learn to shut your trap," he said to me. "If I told them I was English it's because I have more authority that way." But, though Roger grumbled the whole time, he never talked out of his turn and no one ever knew that Jean-Claude wasn't English.

We went out for a walk together while Roger chased after guides and fixed rendezvous and 'safe houses'. The country was lovely but somehow depressing. Mazères is at the foot of the Pyrenees and the great mountains come down in gentle slopes to the flat Lannemezan plateau. The first hills were dark green in the winter air, but, far above, the peaks, covered with snow, were hardly visible on the clouded sky. I shuddered at the thought of the long and strenuous climb the weakened escapees had before them. High-tension electric wires hanging from gruesome-looking pylons crossed the wind-swept plateau in all directions. Electric power is one of the main resources of the region.

Jean-Claude and I argued angrily all the afternoon. It was all my fault because I was still irritated with him; and then it was a comfort to relax, after having been obliged to be amiable and sociable with the many people I had met in the past weeks. Once more Jean-Claude proved one of his infuriating points to me.

"It all just shows, Minou," he said. "If you'd been like me and not bothered to talk to people you didn't *feel* like talking to, you wouldn't be such a pest now…"

Roger came back at nightfall. He was exhausted. "I've cycled forty-five kilometres. It was the hell of a business contacting the guides; they were holding a war conference in the mountains. They are leaving tomorrow with a party of thirty-five American pilots and airmen. They won't be back for four or five days, *if* they come back. They agreed to take your fifteen men across in a fortnight's time. This is the best I can do. The other guide working for us was caught by the Gestapo six weeks ago. I don't know anyone else I can trust."

He had supper with us and went off to Montréjeau. His name was amongst the first on the Luchon Gestapo's list: for three months now he had not slept at home. His wife Miette, small and fair-haired, prepared my bed.[6]

"You will have to take the 5.20am train if you want to be back in Condom for lunch: it means getting up at four. Why don't you go later?"

"I can't. I must tell the Patron right away that the guides can't take those escapees yet. He'll have to decide on some way to get them out of the Lot-et-Garonne."

Miette smiled kindly. She was a helpful and hospitable little person. She had a mania: cats. There were cats all over the house, mainly Siamese: Domino, Fouffi, Méou and la Mine. Méou, her favourite, had a habit of hanging down her back with his claws dug into her shoulders and his hind legs rocking to and fro. He and la Mine slept on her pillow at night. Fortunately Jean-Claude loved cats: the poor animals would have had a miserable time otherwise.

"Since Jean-Claude has been here," Miette told me sadly, "all my rabbits have disappeared; they used to run freely about the garden until he started chasing them. Now they've all gone. As for my hens, you should see them when he comes into the garden; they all fly off and run like mad to the neighbour's garden. He takes them as a target-for javelin practice."

"I hate hens," Jean-Claude told me later. "They're stupid animals and they make a disgusting noise…"

Everybody was asleep when I left the house the next morning. It was pitch dark and terribly cold. I nearly got lost three times on the way to the station and caught the train by the skin of my teeth. It was a workmen's train to Toulouse: most of them slept in the dark carriage, a handkerchief tied around their neck and a cap pulled low over their ears. Just before getting in they awoke, pulled a snack of bread, *pâté* and red wine out of their haversacks, and immediately began a heated discussion.

In Toulouse I had an hour to wait before catching the *micheline* (rail car) to Auch, so I sat in the buffet. I had a careful look at what people round me were eating: asking for something which had disappeared for years was a common mistake. Everyone seemed to have brought their own food, so I asked for coffee.

"We've only got saccharine to take with it," the waiter busily replied.

"Okay, I'll have it anyway."

A few months later my tactics were different. It would be something like this: Big, big smile. "Now come on, you must have a little sugar somewhere?"

"Ah, Mademoiselle, we don't get much, you know."

More smiles. "Well, surely you'll have a little for me, won't you?"

And with the help of an extra five francs it usually worked. Anyway the coffee was so dreadful that I never asked for it unless I had to for the look of the thing.

Back at Nasoulens, I cycled to the Patron's house. He decided to park the escapees in the region.

"Do you remember how to contact the grocer at Fourcès?" he said to me. I thought I did: Jean-Claude and I had stopped there on our way to Condom on the morning we arrived.

"Well, go to Agen and see Cyprien tomorrow. He must have things ready to move at a moment's notice. Try and bring the men to Fourcès in the evening; meanwhile I'll go and warn the grocer and give him a chance to prepare safe houses for them."

As I cycled down to Condom at 5.30 the next morning I discovered a friendly myth. On the top of the first hill there was a barn. Next to the barn there was a pine tree. The two things, blacker than the dark sky on which they were silhouetted, took the shape of a Halifax. From then on, I looked forward to my Halifax whenever I started out early. When the nights grew shorter it became a barn and a pine tree again. And I missed it.

The Agen bus driver and I had become friends.[7] He would greet me with a smile when I arrived and took to keeping me a place on the seat next to him. It was a great help in view of the crowds fighting to climb in. The only drawback was that I would find my seat burning, while my nose froze because of a hole in the window just in front of me. I never knew his name and he never knew mine. But I think that he had understood.

"Where do you go in Agen?" he asked me one day.

"I go to the market, and I go shopping, and I stay with friends at the Garage Agenais," I lied.

That day, when we reached Agen, he stopped a few yards before the Garage Agenais.

"Hurry up and get out," he said. "I'm not really supposed to stop here – and I've heard that the Boches are inspecting papers at the bus stop…" he added, lowering his voice. I thanked him and jumped out. From then on, he always dropped me there, although he invariably had arguments with other people wanting to get off too.

"No, nothing doing," I'd hear him yell. "I don't care what you say… And I don't owe anybody any explanations."

And the heavy bus would move off with its load of angry people while he waved and winked at me.

Cyprien had everything ready as the Patron had anticipated. But things looked bad. We had a conference in VanderBock's shop.

"A trainload of SS arrived yesterday. It appears that they want to eliminate the Resistance in the district. It's all the fault of the Communists," said Cyprien, hitting his knee. "They have too much courage and not enough common sense. Hardly a day goes by without a German soldier being shot dead by one of them in full daylight. It's no use at all; it irritates the Boches into taking reprisals far more costly to us than the death of a plain soldier is to them."

"Yes, all this is very well," VanderBock cut in, "but what are you going to do about it? I've heard at the Gendarmerie that they are going to set up road blocks at all the entrances of the town."

"Is there no way of getting to Fourcès without going through Agen?" I asked.

"No, none whatsoever. You have to cross the Garonne and the bridges will probably all be guarded," VanderBock replied.

"Well," said Cyprien, "the only thing we can do is to get through the town before they set up the barrages... In other words race them to it. The most serious drawback is that I only have a 'gazo' truck. If I could have had a petrol-driven one, we might have a chance if the Germans start to chase us. As it is, you have to hold your thumbs. Now, Paulette, this might be dangerous. Maybe you'd better start cycling out now and meet the truck on the road near Nérac. What do you think?"

Nérac, the birthplace of Henry IV, is more than halfway between Agen and Fourcès.

Deep down, in the pit of my stomach, something was shouting "road to Nérac". But this was my first chance of showing that I was not afraid. Although I *was*, I did not want the others to know it.

"Not at all," I told Cyprien, "of course I'll go with them. Vague meetings on empty roads never work out properly. Anyway, the Patron told me to accompany them."

"As a matter of fact," Cyprien said with a smile, "I believe it will be a good thing. You might cheer them up a little; they're in a wretched state of nerves. And a woman might make them forget the dangers on the road..."

Every day brought some new aspects of a courier's job. But then I knew that women were Cyprien's weak point.

"All right," Cyprien went on. "I'll go off in the truck in half an hour and collect the boys. They're in a number of farms in the vicinity of Villeneuve-sur-Lot. L'Asperge will come with me and bring them here: there is no point in my coming back with them. Anyway, I've got things to do over there. They'll arrive in Agen about four this afternoon. VanderBock, you'd better go up the Villeneuve road to meet them and stop them if there is a barrage. I'm afraid in that case they will have to spend the night in the woods. They cannot stay where they are any longer: the Boches and the Milice are closing their net and you can't ask too much of the people sheltering them. You, Paulette, l'Asperge will pick you up near the canal at the beginning of the cours de Belgique. As for you, Marie, you'd better go to the bridge on the Nérac road and see if there's a barrage there."

"All that's fine," I said, "but what do we do if there is a barrage?"

"You'll have Thévenin, a *gendarme* who works for us, in the car.[8] He can bluff you through better than anyone else. Otherwise, you'll have to make a dash for it."

Everything worked as scheduled. Cyprien was an efficient man when it came to operational organisation. I accompanied VanderBock up the Villeneuve road; there was no control. But we saw two truckloads of SS heading towards Montauban, on the road to Toulouse. They looked fit, healthy and clean in their green uniforms with the two black SS on the collar and appeared arrogantly Aryan, looking down at us from the height of their truck. I understood what it meant to hate the Germans.

"You may just make it," VanderBock said comfortingly. "But don't think you are safe when you have crossed the Garonne and are out of Agen. They've been observed going all over the place and you might have trouble crossing the Baïse."

"We'll be all right, I'm sure…" I suddenly felt very confident.

We saw the truck coming from a distance. L'Asperge was driving carefully. Thévenin, the *gendarme,* had a merry, pink face. Three anxious faces appeared in the opening of a sliding door behind the driver.

"Get back," said Thévenin. "We're approaching Agen and you must be careful."

The faces disappeared.

"I'll cycle back," I told him, "and you can follow in ten minutes. If you see me coming back again, it means that the Boches have arrived. If you don't, drive straight through and pick me up."

No Germans. Fifteen minutes later the truck stopped on the cours de Belgique and I climbed in. L'Asperge loaded four bags of charcoal and my bicycle onto the roof.

"You'd better get in the back with them. Might just as well have as few people in front as possible."

I slipped through the sliding door to the back.[9] A stifling smell caught my throat: there was not a breath of air there. And not a sound: fifteen men, piled on top of one another, in a space of 5ft by 7, had been sitting there for more than three hours. Someone made a little room for me beside the door. After a while I got used to the semi-darkness and saw that everyone was looking at me with anxiety, expecting me to say something. Some were biting their lips.

"Don't worry," I whispered. "It isn't very far and we'll soon be there."

"Somebody told us the Germans had set road blocks outside the town," my fair-haired neighbour whispered back.

"No, they may do it some time, but they haven't yet." And I hoped I was telling the truth.

We started off right away. I could see the road ahead through a slit in the boards. Half a kilometre before the Garonne bridge I caught sight of Marie riding her bicycle towards us at top speed.

"There are no Germans," she said when l'Asperge had stopped. "But instead there's a barrage of French police; they're searching cars and they told me that German sentries would replace them at six."

Thévenin waved his hand in the air. "That's fine, I can deal with the *gendarmes* very well."

"Okay, don't waste time. Goodbye…"

The tension around me was terrific. It began to get hold of me. The lack of air brought beads of sweat to my forehead. It was about half-past five and the sun, which had shone brilliantly all day, was disappearing behind the hills. Thévenin had been right. He knew all the *gendarmes* on the barrage and we stopped only two minutes. Over the bridge everyone relaxed and Thévenin opened the sliding door.

"You must be choked in there…"

My fair-haired neighbour introduced himself:

"I'm Major H— and these are my friends.[10] We've all been together at Eysse for many months. We hope to stick together till we get to Spain."

"Yes," said another. "I've known him for eighteen months now. We've all been prisoners for eighteen months except for five who have been in two years."

"We were made to break stones all day long and work fourteen hours a day. They are going to deport the whole camp to Germany; that's why we decided to try and get out at all costs," a third said.

"The last few days have been awful," Major H— went on. "Of the sixty who escaped, they've already caught thirty-two. They searched the house I was in, a farm near Villeneuve, and I had to hide between the floorboards in the attic. The farmers got awfully nervous after that: so did I, hiding in the top floor all the day… I heard you were parachuted. Is that true?"

"Yes, I was…" Major H— brightened up a little.

"Is old Colonel B— still about? And do you know B.P. and Vera and Joan?[11]

I came here in 1942. I don't suppose many of the old lot can be left."

I told him all I could think of about my training, about the jump school.

"Do you mean Quicksilver is still there? My God, what riotous parties we had with him! And You-Lucky-People too..?"

The conversation became general, although kept on a low tone. Everyone relaxed a little. The men all looked very thin and very white. It was obvious that their nerves were badly shaken and that they needed a rest cure and healthy nourishment for a while. I wondered how they would stand the long and exhausting walk in the heavy snow and cold mountains.

"Damn, damn, damn…" l'Asperge said suddenly. "This confounded car is absolutely no good. I can't climb this hill with such a heavy load. To hell with '*gazos*'."

So we all had to get out and help push the car up the hill. The men kept their guns and Stens with them.

"Won't it be fun if this happens in a town…" said Major H— with a sour grin. It did too – the '*gazo*' slowed down dangerously as it climbed the hill in the middle of Nérac. But l'Asperge saved the situation by getting rapidly in and out of the first gear and advancing five yards at a time. Everybody heaved a sigh of relief at the top. But too soon…

Outside Nérac you cross the Baïse on a narrow suspension bridge. As we approached it we saw black figures moving at one end.

"Watch out… The Milice," Thévenin said quickly.

The sliding door had been closed again before Nérac, but we all heard him.

"We'll have to crash it," l'Asperge growled under his breath. "I hope to God this car doesn't let me down. Never again with a '*gazo*'."

There was a hysterical stillness in the air around me. My heart was beating fast and I hoped no one could hear it. I tried to bring all my anxiety down to my hands by digging my nails into my palms. Behind me, one of the men caught hold of my shoulder and gripped it until I thought I would scream; he was completely unaware of his gesture and later did not remember it. Sweat was rolling down everybody's face. That is what captivity does to people.

I saw l'Asperge put the car into first and slow down to a stop at a gesture from one of the *miliciens*.

"French police," said Thévenin.

"Have you a movement order?"

"Here it is…" Thévenin's chief[12] worked with us too and had given him one.

"What are you carrying?" the *milicien* went on.

The nails dug deeper into my shoulder; I had a bruise after. I couldn't even hear the men breathing. Except one; he sounded like a steam-engine.

"We have twenty-four sacks of charcoal inside…"

"I'd like to inspect."

"You saw my movement order and I have no time to waste," said Thévenin.

The *milicien* stepped back to consult his friends. Thévenin looked at l'Asperge and made a small movement of the head. The '*gazo*' moved off at once, trembling all over from the effort asked from it.

"Stop, STOP…" the *miliciens* all yelled at once. "Lie flat…" said Thévenin through the door. We all expected them to shoot right away. But they must have been caught by surprise or muddled with their rifles. We were already off the bridge when we heard a few shots.

"The dirty double-crossing swine…" said one of the men.

"Boy, that was a neat job," Major H— muttered. I felt weak; it had been the same sort of emotion I had experienced when the fighter had chased our Halifax: shut up in a closed and narrow space, depending on events out of my control.

A quarter of an hour later we approached Fourcès.

"Stop here," I told l'Asperge. "I'll go forward on my bicycle while you wait. I want to see if everything is all right and where we are to take them to."

The night had fallen by then and it had become colder. We were on the side of a narrow road four kilometres from Fourcès.

"How long will you be gone?" said Major H—. "We can't stand all this much longer, you know…"

"Not much more than half an hour."

"Please be quick. We're waiting anxiously," said one of the others.

I had a sensation of deliverance as I cycled at top speed to Fourcès. The grocer threw his arms to the ceiling.

"I've nearly been going silly with worry the whole afternoon. I didn't know which way you'd come in: there were fifty *miliciens* here and forty more in Montréal on some sort of manoeuvres. I visualised you all landing right into them and hopelessly trapped. Do you know when they left?"

"…"

"You'd never guess. Twenty-five minutes ago…"

Never a dull moment. It was amazing that we had not met them on the road; they couldn't be the ones who had stopped us at Nérac – they would not have had time to get there. My streak of luck was still following me.

An hour later my fifteen companions were all parked in the barn of a lonely farm on top of a hill: no one could approach it without being seen. We all shook hands warmly and sat around an enormous supper. A whole ham and four loaves of four feet each vanished in a matter of minutes. The reaction from the tense days the boys had just been through showed itself by a ravenous hunger.[13]

I spent the night at Fourcès and cycled back to Nasoulens the next morning. The Patron came.

"You need not have been there at all," he said, after hearing my story. "I don't want you to run unnecessary risks... It would bring awful trouble to us if you were caught... Anyway, I'm glad it's over."

Which was a bit of a cold shower.

CHAPTER VII

I went back to Montréjeau a day or two later and fixed all the details of the passage of the Eysse escapees. Privat, the butcher from Condom who had taken me up to Nasoulens on the first day, was to drive them there with his friend Robert Laroche. Privat had his own source of petrol; he bought it in Agen on the black market for 5 francs a litre. His light truck was a precious asset to us: it was closed, very fast and very powerful. The Patron gave me a contact in Auch, where I collected blank road licences ready stamped and signed; the spaces were filled in as the occasion required. Some of them were temporary, others were permanent; the latter could be used until their number had been taken down at some control or other.

Privat and Robert left for the Pyrenees armed to the teeth.

"Don't worry," Privat told the boys. "First, the Captain of the Gendarmerie[1] has given me all the details about road blocks and snap-controls on the way, and we'll avoid them. Then we are tough guys; we'll fight 'em off if they try to stop us." With this he opened a wooden box full of hand grenades.

"They'd better not get in our way with these…" he added with a broad grin. "But take care; they're armed, the detonators are in."

The escapees, who had rested and relaxed during the past days, were in a greatly improved state of mind and felt much stronger. We had decided that I should meet them on the road between Lannemezan and Montréjeau. We bumped down steep little country roads to reach Roger's house by the back and avoid being seen by the people of Mazères.

Jean-Claude had found a new hobby; he was sticking up a stamp collection. I found him sorting the stamps out with the help of a magnifying glass.

"Shut the door…" he shouted without turning his head. "The draught is upsetting all my work."

Miette gave up a month's ration of sugar and coffee to prepare a meal. She wouldn't have shared her last crust: she would have given it whole. But we waited hours before it was ready because Miette was incredibly slow in everything she did. After dinner she inspected everyone.

"I see they will need gloves and jumpers and scarves," she said. "And what do you think you're doing, Major H—, with this thin jacket?"

"Well, er – what's wrong with it?"

"Nothing, except that you'll die of cold in the mountains. Do you realise that you will walk probably as much as four days in deep snow, that you will sleep in the forests, that you will climb up to eight or nine thousand feet? I'll get you a couple of warm sweaters."

Miette, followed by her cats, always knew what to do in difficult moments. The Gestapo had already visited her house twice, with the obvious intention of finding compromising things and arresting Roger and her. Both times he was away and she received them; when they left, it was with apologies and excuses, lifting their hats and clicking their heels. And Miette had laughed softly to herself after the door was closed. There was a shop in Montréjeau where she could get everything she wanted, at fantastic black-market prices of course; there she would be able to clothe all the boys adequately for their long climb.

After warm handshakes all round and the usual formula of good luck, I returned home with Robert and Privat. On the way up the bumpy road, Robert yelled:

"Stop, for heaven's sake – what about those loaded grenades? They're jumping about like anything; they might go off…"

"No, they won't," Privat retorted. "But we'll take the detonator out if it makes you happier."

They had a complete arsenal in the back of the truck. Robert unscrewed the grenades one after the other and handed them to me.

"I know nothing about these murderous objects and I don't want to blow up for nothing…" Privat and I laughed.

"Don't laugh too soon, Paulette," he interrupted angrily. "We still have all the drive back with Privat, and we're lucky if we get to Condom…"

As soon as we started off again, I saw what he meant. The brakes were defective, and on the rare occasions when Privat wanted to slow down, the car zigzagged across the road while passers-by threw themselves in ditches and flew up trees. We drove seventy-five miles in under an hour and a half: Robert never took his eyes off the road or his crisped hands off the window ledge.

"This is the last time I go in any car with you, Privat," he yelled, pale in the face and wobbly at the knees, after we had arrived. "Good grief, how we didn't kill a dozen people apart from all the chickens scattered on the road, is beyond my imagination! Whenever I go with you I say 'never again', but this time it is for good."

I strongly agreed with this. Inside his house, we both collapsed on kitchen chairs and sought comfort in a few armagnacs. This was an opportunity that Suzanne did not miss; she giggled for hours and hours.

After this I spent a few quiet days on the farm. The moments spent with the Cérensacs became part of a wholesome happiness. I learnt new things: how to prune and graft the vine, how to lay the grafted shoots in sand; then later how to take them out, soak them in the pond and classify them. I learnt about the poultry with Odilla: I had no idea of the amount of time and work they involved. I often followed Cérensac as he cleaned his cow-shed in the evenings.

"I'm proud of my cows," he used to say. "But I wish I could feed them better. I can't get the manure for my fields, so their fodder is poor and insufficient."

I used to sit on the ladder leading to the hayloft, watch him work and listen to him. The proximity of nature was new to me and I began to love the smells of the farm: smells of animals in the cycle of existence, smells of honest sweat, smells of a clean life. Smells, too, of the cherry trees in blossom and the red-velvet rose bushes flowering throughout the summer; smells of the damp earth in the quietness of dawn, and of the sun-warmed grass at nightfall. The dogs lay in front of the house, blinking at the sun, while the cat, Missou, curled femininely in a corner of the window-sill.

I was too lazy to go working in the fields very often. Also it bored me. I often watched André and Henri Cérensac as they led or followed their cows on the endless uneventful trek backwards and forwards across the fields. Working like this from early morning to late evening, peasants must either not think at all or become philosophers. The Cérensacs belonged to the philosophers. They knew how to take life as it came to them and to enjoy it through the satisfactory accomplishment of their work. For twenty years they saved *sou* after *sou* to be able to build a new farm; to be able to offer a modern home to their son, so that he should not be attracted to the comforts and glamour of city life. Nasoulens was an achievement: the house was pretty, the animals well cared-for and happy, the corn grew high and thick, the vines rich and prosperous. The profits were small, but they lived well on the produce of the farm.

I was happy at Nasoulens. After a while I mentioned weakly something about going away.

"Whatever for?" said Odilla.

"Well, for security. I don't want you to get into trouble, and people in the neighbourhood might start talking and give the *miliciens* something to think about." There were three *miliciens*, the only ones in the district, in a small village nearby.

"I don't want to hear any more nonsense from you, Petite," Cérensac said. "This is your home and you will stay here; unless you're unhappy with us…"

A little later I made a different sort of request, trying to make them accept some remuneration for my board and lodging and generally all they were doing for me. But Henri Cérensac's eyebrows met in a thick black line.

"What the hell do you think I am? Accept money from the Resistance? That would be the day…"

At first I feared that Cérensac's stubbornness might deprive me of my perfect independence: but that was before I had understood their way of life. When I wanted to do absolutely nothing but lie in the grass and read or doze off, I was never afflicted with martyrised glances from overworked victims. And when I wanted to help it was taken for granted without fuss. It was not only total freedom that I appreciated so much at Nasoulens, but the feeling of total freedom.

At the beginning of March, the apple trees began to bloom and the leaves poked their pale, and velvety little noses out of their buds. The sun was already hot and the air had a strong and intoxicating smell of spring. I was sent to Agen to accompany a French police inspector to Roger's house and see that he should get over the Pyrenees as soon as possible.

"He worked for the Resistance in Paris and Grenoble," said the Patron, "but he had to leave both places because the Gestapo was hot on his trail. Now their net is again closing around him in Agen, and it's a matter of days, if not of hours, before he is caught there. So the best thing is to send him to England for a while. He's becoming more of a danger than an asset to us."

The Patron was generous: to all the people who crossed the Pyrenees with his help he gave 20,000 francs. With this they had some chance of getting across Spain without being interned. I left early the next morning as usual: a pale white line edged the top of the hills and gave a pearl-grey tone to the trees and fields. The illusion of the Halifax no longer existed; it was now a black barn and a black tree against a soft sky.

I stayed a couple of days in Agen waiting for François de Tranches, the police inspector, to equip himself.[2] I spent my time walking by the edge of the Garonne and arguing with Marie. She used to clutch my arm in a very woman-to-woman and confidence-for-confidence manner.

"My little Paulette," she said, "what a shame to use so much energy in coming here when anybody might have done your work…"

Nothing could aggravate me more.

"Listen, Marie, if you haven't been told, there is no reason why you should understand it. In fact I had trouble with it myself at first. It's a plain question of military rule. In England people are working night and day to prepare the invasion. The Resistance is doing the same here, but its action wouldn't be of any use if it wasn't in liaison with the Allied High Command. This is why we're here, or rather, that's what the Patron is doing. He needed a courier. It was natural that London should send him one of their own people. It's just like a regiment: they will only send one of their own men on liaison missions, even though other people might know the way better. It's a question of security."

"But as far as that goes, I think my father and I have proved that we can be trusted?"

"Of course you have. *We* know that. But London has only our word for it, and from their point of view we might make a mistake. You may know a good deal of what I carry around, but there is also a lot that you don't know about. There are details of sabotage operations, details of orders for D-Day, which if they got into the hands of the Germans would not only blow up the Resistance in the whole region, but also endanger the success of the invasion, if not mess it up altogether. Then there is the question of money. I carry large sums to various of our people. If this got known, it would be said that they work for money, or that they keep the money for themselves. It's quite natural that you should remember that your neighbour has received fifty thousand francs, but in a few months I shall be gone and will have forgotten all about it. That's a question of discretion. Then, there's a question of authority. It is doubtful whether old and experienced men would accept orders brought by a twenty-year-old girl, if she didn't have the authority of London behind her."

Marie threw me a slanting look, shining with pity. I had to make an effort to keep my temper.

"That's not all. There are other details that amount to an important total. Let's say all the reasons I've just mentioned were to be ruled out, and you were doing my work. The whole district, maybe the whole of Agen, knows you are working in the shop with your father. If you were to go away several times a week, sometimes for a few days, sometimes at five minutes' notice, everyone would notice it. All the bus drivers know you. The railwaymen know you, the police know you. If they were to become suspicious, which they would do very quickly, they could make a complete plan of your destinations and activities with the greatest of ease. And all the people you meet or who visit you would be on the list of suspects too. Isn't that right?" She was kicking small stones with the tip of her shoe and had let go of my arm.

"Yes," she said. "But you don't race about as much as all that."

"No, I don't. I race about *more* than that. When I'm not in Agen, I may be in Condom, in Auch, in Toulouse, in Tarbes or Montréjeau. One day I am sent to

Auch to collect blank and stamped travel permits. The next I go to Tarbes to take some money to the man who works there. The third I cycle to take a message to the radio operator. Then I'm off for three days to Tarbes and Montréjeau, where I have to wait for a reply from Jean-Claude or someone else. You don't realize that mine is a full-time job, and that for you, it would mean quitting your job completely, disappearing, bringing suspicion on your father, giving up your means of existence, etc., etc." I was getting bored with my speech.

Marie skipped on one foot, caught hold of my arm again and smiled sweetly. "My little Paulette," she said, "don't let me upset you. I know you are happy doing your work as a courier, so just go on."

The evening before we left, François de Tranches appeared to introduce himself. He was equipped to go to the North Pole – skiing trousers, heavy sweaters and boots; he was a thorough and precise young man in everything he did. He looked honest, straight and cheerful. I liked him at once.

On the way to the station the next morning, he confessed to a certain discomfort.

"One thing that worries me is that I am travelling with two identity cards and my gun."

"But why?"

"Well, you see, for the moment I'm only suspect to the Gestapo. I need a false card to show them. On the other hand, if we come on to a French police control, I have my inspector's card with the right to carry arms."

We sat together in a cold unlighted carriage, crammed to bursting point. François spoke softly:

"You have no idea how tired I am. I've been working all these past months for people who cared only for themselves: the security of their people was the last thing they thought about. It is so sweet of you to take me with you like this and to bother about me. It's such a wonderful feeling to have someone looking after you."

"But I've got nothing to do with it. You know that I was sent to see you off…"

"I know. And you will tell the Patron how much I appreciate his kindness. But I don't suppose he was the one who suggested you should bring some sandwiches for me…"

We went on a little longer with our guarded conversation until François dropped asleep. I felt uncomfortable: I was getting Gestapo-conscious. This had been creeping over me for some time, but from that day it became a habit. At first I tried to fight it off. But it was as well not to relax at any time.

A few hours later we sat in an empty compartment in the fast train from Toulouse to Montréjeau. We sat facing each other near the wide window. The day had no colour; it was cold and cloudy. A hideous blue plush covered the seat.

François talked about his experiences. He was telling me about an escape he had made through a sewer in Paris. I refused a cigarette and thought of the microphones: London had warned us about them. The Germans stuck microphones under tables and seats in unexpected places and recorded conversations. But this was ridiculous; they couldn't place them in –

"Papers, please…"

A close-cropped man had walked into the compartment from nowhere. The ticket collector is usually announced by a wave of movement passing along the carriage. Nothing of that, this time: suddenly the man was at the door, his eyes hard on us. As he opened it he seemed to be looking personally at both of us simultaneously. He wore a grey raincoat and spoke with a strong German accent. He belonged to the Gestapo. His appearance and question had come so fast that I could not recall my immediate reaction to them. I thought he had heard our conversation. My brain worked coldly and very clearly at that moment, and I always had this strong consciousness of acting naturally.

The man put out his hand to me. I gave him my papers: his eyes did not look down at my hand but remained fixed on my face.

"What's your name?" he asked rapidly.

"Marie-Françoise Périer."

"Where were you born?"

"Paris."

"Where are you going?"

"Montréjeau."

"What for?"

"I'm going to stay with my sister-in-law for a few days."

"What are you going to do there?"

"Well, I've been operated on a few weeks ago and I would like to recuperate in a place where I can get milk and butter. Also I need a change of air," I replied coyly.

He whipped round to François.

"Are you two together?"

There was no getting away from it; we shared a railway ticket.

"Yes, we are," François said.

"Going to stay together?"

"Yes."

He shrugged his shoulders and studied François' civilian papers. He looked at them closely for a long while. I felt uncomfortable in the silence and looked at François. A cold wave ran down my back; he was becoming pale. Horribly pale. The colour left his face slowly in a horizontal line going up from his chin to his forehead. "Don't, don't think about that revolver," I wanted to cry to him. "If that man looks at you now, we're done…"

I picked up my bag and fumbled in it to find my handkerchief. The Gestapo agent looked at me as he handed his papers back to François. His eyes shone with the icy blueness of the sea on stormy days; the thin line of his lips dropped cruelly at the corners. He walked out without another word. I wanted to lean back and close my eyes.

"Shh… Don't move," said François. With a quick movement he slipped his hand in his back pocket and dropped his gun behind the seat. He looked straight out of the window; his face was blank and serene. A silent figure went by in the corridor. It stopped in front of the door for a second. Then it glided off again. François went on looking half-witted.

"They always do that," he said softly. "If you get away with the first one of them and want to relax, you get picked up by the next. You'll see that yet a third will pass by."

He was right. A third man with a soft felt hat and a raincoat walked casually along the corridor three or four minutes later, smoking a cigarette.

"My brother was caught like that," François went on. "He said to a friend of his, 'My God, that was a narrow one…' and the next moment he was tapped on the shoulder by a second Gestapo agent following the first. It's a clever trick."

"But François, you should've seen yourself. You went as pale as a sheet while he looked at your papers."

"I suddenly thought of my revolver. And when I pulled my identity card out, I saw that my inspector's card was right under it, and that the red and blue line was sure to catch his eye. Fortunately, he talked so much to you that I had a chance to close my wallet without his noticing it. It was very careless of me not to watch where I put it this morning. Wasn't it a nasty moment?"

"Yes. And this is my first direct encounter with the Gestapo. And I hope the last." But it wasn't.

At Mazères I found Miette alone. Roger was in Tarbes for a few days and Jean-Claude was out.

"Monsieur de Tranches can stay here until Roger comes back," she said. "Nobody will know he's here if he doesn't go out." François showed every sign of being happy where he was. He had found books. Miette belonged to a family of teachers and possessed a big library.

Jean-Claude's room was in an appalling mess; clothes strewn all over the floor, books piled dangerously high on the mantelpiece, paint-boxes, drawings and stamps scattered on the table.

"Why don't you push him around a little, Miette?" I asked.

"You sound as though you'd never tried to make Jean-Claude do something he doesn't want to do. I've given up long ago… From time to time, I clean the place up myself. But what infuriates me is *this*," she added, pouncing on the bedside table.

He had left his gun lying on it.

"And *this*…" Bits of rubberised fabric lay on the floor by the fireplace. Rubberised fabric is a waterproof material used to cover charges and keep the detonators and primers from getting damp. It was parachuted to the Resistance, and was as incriminating as any arms.

It began pouring with rain. When Jean-Claude came back he was soaked to the skin; his hair stuck to his forehead and raindrops ran down his cheeks. He looked rather angelic and for the first time I began to think I could forgive his lack of understanding after the crash. He took his shoes off and walked about in his socks, leaving wet marks all over the floor; his raincoat, dripping from a peg, made an enormous puddle in the hall.

"See what I mean?" Miette said desperately, throwing her arms to the ceiling. "But I am so fond of him, in spite of the trouble he gives me, that I haven't the heart to scold him."

Jean-Claude heard the last words as he walked in.

"If you don't," he said calmly, "it's only because you know that it wouldn't make any difference."

"Minou," he went on, "I'm glad you're here. I have twelve people coming here tonight for instruction. I don't know why I asked so many at a time: I can't cope with that number and do it properly. So you'll take charge of six."

"Don't be silly, Néron…"

"And don't call me Néron," he shouted. "It makes people laugh and it diminishes my authority."

"As though you *could* have any authority, anyway…" The next minute we were fighting hard, hitting and kicking each other. Miette's cries brought François running to the kitchen, and they separated us, not without getting a few scratches. We all laughed around a bowl of steaming coffee prepared by Miette. Later she got used to these battles, a good cure for knotted nerves.

"But seriously, Jean-Claude, you don't expect me to instruct grown men, do you?"

"Of course I do. We've had the same training and you know as much as I do. Anyway, they'll like it."

But they didn't. And I felt very unhappy. The tall neighbour, Picolet,[3] was a tough hunter and found it very distasteful to be taught how to handle a Colt by a woman. I couldn't induce him to hold his arm in the right position and I swore never to be put in such an embarrassing situation again. François, much amused, helped me out by asking a lot of questions on a subject he knew more about than I ever would.

The next morning Jean-Claude accompanied me to the 5.20. I rode on the bar of his bicycle and reached the station covered with mud and bruises. From that day we were friends again. It became a pleasure to go to our Pyrenees sector because he took me with him on small expeditions, and because we had the same education and background and could discuss for hours subjects which did not interest other people. From that day a deep and sincere friendship grew between us, cemented by common risks and common small successes.

CHAPTER VIII

The Resistance in the Toulouse region was already in an advanced state of organisation. For two years the AS, or Secret Army, under the direction of French officers, had been collaborating with the Patron: London provided arms, while they provided men and teams for sabotage expeditions. Jean-Claude trained groups of them in the new ways of guerrilla warfare and demolition technique. In the Pyrenees district, the various organisations of the Resistance were united together under the name of MUR or United Resistance Movements: representatives of the workers, of the railwaymen and of various political parties of the Left composed it.

Our aim was to arm them and ensure liaison between them and the Allied High Command, in order to coordinate offensive action on D-Day and after. Every night during the moon period, British aircraft dropped supplies somewhere in our circuit. It depended on the weather and on the location of the field. Colomiers' district was, as a rule, the best served. The Dordogne area was important; it controlled communications by road and railway between Toulouse, Bordeaux and Paris. They were to be cut, thus impeding seriously enemy troop movements towards the north of France.

I saw Colomiers regularly. As time went by he became more and more restless; he got into political trouble with certain groups of the Resistance in his neighbourhood and thought he was in danger of being shot by them. However, he remained poised and went on working.

"I shall do whatever the Patron wants. But I'm convinced I shan't last much longer," he would say, shaking his head. This he repeated every time we met, but he nevertheless lasted until the Liberation.

"I've got a surprise for you," he said one day. "Bernard, bring it along, will you?"

He remained mysterious but a mischievous gleam lit his eye. I usually met Colomiers at the Lantrets' house, in Eymet. Bernard Lantret, working as his private courier, ran about for him tirelessly. Jean Lantret, who had escaped compulsory labour in Germany by joining the *maquis* early in 1943, organised sabotage expeditions on enemy communications and dumps. The Lantret parents lived in constant expectation of arrest.

Bernard returned triumphantly, followed by a tall, fair-haired youth gazing nonchalantly round him. For the first time, Colomiers spoke English.

"This is Lee Davis," he said. "He's an American pilot and his plane was shot down on the return trip from Germany. Where did you say you jumped, Lee?"

"Vitry-le-François."

"Why, that's at least eight hundred kilometres from here!" I said.

"Yes," Colomiers replied with a smile and a nod. "He walked for two days heading south, in full uniform, fur-lined jacked and all… People fed him and hid him in farms and lonely barns during the night. Then someone gave him some civilian clothes and he went on walking: all the way down here, till he came upon some of my men."

It was a terrific adventure, and amazing that he should have travelled all this distance without being caught. He sat quietly and seemed quite unconcerned. He did not speak a word of French.

"They feed you well here," he said.

"Well, Lee, what do you want to do? I can fix your passage over the Pyrenees and get you on your way home. What do you think of it?"

It was the first time I spoke English since I had landed in France: my grammar had deteriorated dangerously. I felt a little silly under Colomiers' quiet gaze as I accumulated Gallicism over Gallicism. Lee looked up.

"Before we left, our Commanding Officer told the crew: 'Now if anything happens to you, do what you can to come back. But don't go and take any unnecessary risks'."

"Yes, well, it is a little risky. Maybe you'd like to stay here and learn French and learn about different ways to yours. What do you think?"

"Before we left, my Commanding Officer said to us: 'Now if anything happens to you kids, do what you can to come back, but don't take any unnecessary risks'."

"Yes, Lee, okay. So I suppose you want to go off. I'll get things ready and come and collect you later. How's that?"

"My Commanding Officer told us before we left: 'Now if anything happens to you, try to come back. But don't take any unnecessary risks'."

I have never had any patience, and this was more than I could endure. Colomiers was innocently looking out of the window and smiling to the sun, with an I-wanted-to-see-what-you-would-say face. As I turned my back to walk out, Lee mumbled:

"Yeah, they sure feed you well here."

I decided to leave him until he grew old enough to have a mind of his own. Later, the Lantrets told me how he had acquired it. He began to show the village kids how to play American football: they all played in the main street. Within a week the whole village had learned American slang and knew that he lived with the Lantret family. So they had to ask Colomiers to take him away and he was sent to a farm further north. He worked ten hours a day in the fields there, shirtless and happy, and refused point blank to go away.

"I think this place is swell. I'll join the boys when they get down here."

In fact he fought bravely in the *maquis* after D-Day. And that is how Lee Davis went to France and found his own mind.

"I've just received a message from London for Jean-Claude," the Patron said one day. It read:

"For Néron – Find out possibilities demolition of Empalot factory in Toulouse Stop Successful action by you would avoid bombing by RAF Stop Reply immediately giving details of targets and delay involved Stop Good luck."

"It's a nasty business," said the Patron. "Empalot is an enormous factory on an island in the Garonne on the outskirts of Toulouse. It's the third biggest powder factory in France and heavily guarded. The only way he can do it is to take fifty men and make a rapid fighting attack."[1]

I went to Montréjeau the next day. Jean-Claude took the news with his usual calm.

"Of course I can't answer right away. They don't suppose I can obtain the information they want overnight? I'll go to Toulouse tomorrow and see what I can do. I have no contacts there, except for a cousin of mine who will put me up for the night. But she won't be able to indicate anybody useful."

"I know someone who can help you," said Roger. "He is the father of a friend of my nephew and very much in favour of the Resistance; he's a retired engineer of Empalot."

Jean-Claude and Roger went to see him and returned with a letter for a Communist engineer in the factory. Later Miette, who had been shopping in Montréjeau, arrived home flustered.

"The Gestapo has been four times to Montréjeau this afternoon and I hear they're coming back tonight. I haven't been able to find out why or what is up. But I smell trouble."

"You always smell trouble and you live on gossip," barked Roger. "But nevertheless, better too much precaution than not enough: I won't sleep in Montréjeau tonight."

Miette shrugged her shoulders. For years now she had stopped paying any attention to her husband's imprecations. Jean-Claude went to the *cachette* he had built in the garden; it was packed with material he used for instructing the Resistance. He had dug a deep hole, lined it with wood, and fitted a wooden lid which he covered with gravel and branches. He brought back a small .32.

"I never go to sleep without one of those, and you're going to do the same tonight, Minou."

"What happens to me in all this is another question," Miette said. "Do I explain that I knew nothing about having terrorists in my house, do I jump from the first floor and run away, regardless of my thirty-eight years, or do I just sleep through the whole thing?"

"Don't worry," Jean-Claude said. "You know that I'll leave you enough time to get away."

Miette looked unhappy; she was perpetually haunted by the threat of impending danger. Yet somehow she managed to bear the nervous strain without losing her simplicity of heart or her spirit of enterprise.

"Minou, come with me."

"Why?"

"You'll see," Jean-Claude replied.

He led me to the window of my room on the first floor. It looked on the back garden.

"Now jump…"

"No. I'm not going to break my neck to give you a laugh."

"I tell you to jump. If you do it once, you'll see it's nothing at all and you won't hesitate if the need arises. You remember your parachute training? Feet together and parallel to the ground; then roll, knees, hips, shoulders, etc. Come on… I'll go first. I do it once a day."

I couldn't back out. The ground was freshly dug and the jump turned out to be quite easy. Jean-Claude was pleased, but I reflected that all physical courage is promoted by vanity. Vanity and ignorance.

"Do you think that people who have been unhappy all their lives can have courage, Jean-Claude?"

"It's not a question of being happy or unhappy: just of doing what people expect you to do; in fact often of doing it because they hope you will refuse and give them a chance to come out best."

"Yes, well, that's vanity. But people who have known only unhappiness are asked to give up the *hope* of achieving an improvement when they risk their lives."

"But they still keep the hope of coming out all right. And anyway, you never know happiness until you've lost it."

"But that isn't true of *un*happiness – you don't have to wait to know that. And

I should imagine that the risk of never knowing happiness would break the unreasoned impulse to go towards death. You don't mind dying so much if you've had some of the things you want."

"Listen, Minou, don't try to make out a thing like courage. It's only a question of impulse and I'll tell you what brings this impulse. Why do you think we're on this earth? To make people happy. But you can't make everybody happy. So you decide to make one person happy: just one. That's why you've been created through an intricate cellular procedure, given an intelligence and a set of emotions. Someone is trying to stop you, trying to prevent you from accomplishing your whole reason of existence. So you kill if you get there first. That's all. Some people call it courage."

Jean-Claude had put both his hands on my shoulders while he talked.

"Minou, you're my friend; so I'll tell you something," he went on gently, a soft shine playing in his eyes. "I know who I will spend my life making happy – I have a reason to stop at nothing against those who get in my way. Oh, she is very young," he went on, sitting on the edge of the window. "She's only eighteen. She's so beautiful, you know. I never have to tell her anything; she knows before I start to speak. I always do everything she wants, and she does the same for me. She's just part of me," he added simply.[2]

"Where is she, Jean-Claude? I'd like to know her."

"You will. She lives in Paris. Poor little thing, she's so thin now; she hasn't enough to eat. I don't know if you'll like her, you know. She's very quiet and shy; and very unsociable. She's so intelligent though: I taught her bridge in twenty-four hours…"

Jean-Claude was silent for a while and it seemed very quiet in the old house with its wooden panels, its tall, antique feather beds, and its porcelain statuettes on the mantelpiece. Outside, the wind rocked the pine trees in the garden; occasionally the iron gate rattled, recalling the possibilities of a silent encircling approach by the Gestapo.

"I've known her five years and I've always felt the same way," he went on, more to himself than to me.

"Well, you know, Jean-Claude, that means you've been happy. You've already lived something of the reason for your existence. That's why you're not afraid. Some people call that courage…"

He jumped up and hugged me. "I'm so pleased we're friends again. My goodness, how nasty you were in London and during our first days here… Do you know what?" he added, stepping back. "I've wanted to spank you for more than two months now, and I think I'm about to do it…"

Miette came rushing up, followed by all her cats, miauling and delighted.

"Jean-Claude, JEAN-CLAUDE..." she yelled. "Stop – I tell you to stop... You're going to kill her... What a demon you are! My goodness, what did I do to get such a brute in my house?"

Poor Miette was genuinely upset at the sight: I was flat on the floor, kicking and screaming, while Jean-Claude knelt on my back spanking to his heart's content. In a vain attempt to escape I had run round the table, caught at the tablecloth and upset books, hairbrushes, writing-pads and empty inkpots onto the floor, not to mention a couple of chairs. Fouffi, the white cat, was delighted with the noise; she jumped on Jean-Claude's shoulders and miauled at every hit. She was his favourite and had recently given birth to four white kittens in the middle of his bed.

Miette's dismay brought my correction to an end. She didn't realise it was a joke and stood over us with her head on one side and her hands clasped together while tears came to her eyes. She was quite irresistible, so we stopped and put the room in order.

"Do you know that tomorrow is the 16th of March and Paulette's birthday?" she whispered to Jean-Claude, later on.

"No. Why didn't you tell me before?" he whispered back.

"She's only just told me. I'm making her a cake. But don't tell her..."

I was hearing all this, although they did not know it, and enjoying the odours emanating from the oven at the same time. Jean-Claude vanished into his room.

"Do you know that François de Tranches is still here, Paulette?" Miette asked.

"No. Why hasn't he gone, and where is he staying?"

"He's living with the Picolets next door. One of the guides has caught pneumonia and the other one won't go alone in case anything happens to him on the way back. So he'll be here another week. I'll get him over to dinner tonight."

Dinner was animated. The Bear of Montréjeau, as we called Roger, was in a gay mood. He and his wife had spent some years in Indochina and he told us fascinating stories of life over there. He even brought out some armagnac in my honour, a rare gift, for he couldn't afford to buy it very often. At dessert, Jean-Claude went out and returned two minutes later with the cake: twenty-one multi-coloured candles burnt merrily around it, sending up twenty-one little puffs of black smoke. It was a wild success, but Miette knew better.

"Where did you get the candles, may I ask? They are impossible things to find."

"It's detonating fuse... I painted them with my water-colours. Miette, come..." he yelled.

But she was gone. She knew all the detonating properties of Jean-Claude's candles. Everyone laughed.

"I can never make her understand that it burns without blowing up," said Jean-

Claude. "You should see her when I put plastic explosive in the fire; she runs to the other end of the village. But sometimes I'm so cold that I have to do it to replace coal. It burns beautifully…"

Our hostess returned when the candles were out, and ate her share of the cake.

"That boy'll give me a heart attack some day," she concluded.

After dinner Roger went off; he cycled to St-Bertrand-de-Comminges, a village seven kilometres away, where he stayed with his friend Jules.

"I'll take François with me. The Picolets run the same risks as we do and it isn't wise to leave him there."

Miette unlocked the heavy gate to see them out. The night was very black: Jean-Claude took his flashlight and helped her to adjust a chain and padlock on the side door of the garden.

"Like this, they can't get us by surprise," she said.

"It's a good thing I don't believe a word of all the rumours going about, or at least don't let them influence me," Jean-Claude grumbled. "I'd be crazy by now… All these emotions and padlocks and looming dangers occur three times a week."

Nevertheless, he woke me up after I'd gone to sleep to say that he was leaving the cocked .32 on my bedside table. I was so sleepy that I hardly heard him: somehow I felt sure nothing would happen. Miette did not sleep a wink.

Jean-Claude and I left by the 5.20. It was a frightful business catching this train: at 4am he came and shook me like a plum tree. "Come on, wake up, WAKE UP!… What do you think this is? A vacation?"

It was cold and black, terribly black. The fields were muddy and wet, and my feet were soaked when we reached the station. Guards stopped us when we came onto the line. They were *gardes-voie*, or men ordered to watch the railway tracks for saboteurs. The whole organisation had been turned into a farce: half the guards belonged to the Resistance and sabotaged the lines themselves. The others would ask to be gagged and tied when they came on to a demolition party and next day would tell the Germans they had been assaulted and made powerless. They were only armed with a whistle.

When told we wanted to catch the train, they let us pass. At Toulouse, Jean-Claude said:

"I'll go and contact the engineer I want to see, before he goes to work, and ask him what he thinks about the Empalot demolition. I don't like the Patron's idea of making a large-scale attack. I think I'll do it with a couple of men and do it without being seen; it depends on what he says. I'll meet you at twelve o'clock on the place Wilson and we'll have lunch together. Then you can take my answer to the Patron this afternoon."

I was rather pleased to have an opportunity of wandering about Toulouse. I decided to start with the hairdresser. What a change from London: no question here of waiting days for an appointment. It was part of the German technique to leave France to live on her luxuries. Perfumes and make-up were plentiful, but soap and toothpaste non-existent. Ear-rings and hats could be found in any shop at fantastic prices, but woollen clothes and children's shoes had disappeared four years ago. The shops had an air of plentifulness, but all they sold was unpractical and part of the useless charms of existence.

I emerged from the hairdresser looking like a Toulousaine: my hair was piled at vertiginous heights on top of my head and swept into two heavy rolls at the back; it was a masterpiece of execution. Jean-Claude laughed and laughed when he saw me.

"Minou, this is absolutely terrific. I've never seen you looking so ridiculous. Now we're going to be a perfect pair of '*zazous*'."

The '*zazous*' were the French zoot-suiters. The fashion had started in Paris in 1940, in order to ridicule the Germans. University students wore their hair long in the neck and high in front to make fun of the Germans' close-cropped hair and fleshy necks, and long jackets and narrow pants to make fun of their short tunics and long, wide trousers. A favourite trick of the Parisian '*zazous*' was to hang a bicycle pump on a string round their waist, walk noisily into restaurants one behind the other and hang them on pegs next to the Germans' belts and holsters. The stiff Wehrmacht officers, furious, had some of them arrested. But the next day the '*zazous*' had some other tricks up their sleeves. The women wore bright-coloured shirts and very short, fully-gathered skirts; they had thick-soled wooden shoes, long dangling ear-rings and high hairstyles. '*Zazouism*' had degenerated since 1940 and become a fashion for artists and swing-fans, but the '*zazous*' were known, as a rule, as the dare-devils of the Resistance.

Jean-Claude grabbed my arm and dragged me to the market-place on the boulevard de Strasbourg, a wide avenue edged with plane trees.

"That's for me," he said, and bought a pair of bright-blue sun-glasses with wide, yellow rims.

"And that's for you." It was a pair of brass ear-rings about three inches long, representing a spider's web, with a pearl spider in the middle.

"You don't expect me to wear these horrors, I suppose?"

"I certainly do… We'll be a pair of '*zazous*'."

We looked like a perfect pair of fools, holding hands on the boulevard. I had a shock every time we passed a shop window. Jean-Claude was delighted. He distributed smiles to the '*zazous*' we passed, who kept stopping with the evident intention of talking to us; however, I refused point-blank to have anything to do with them. The ear-rings pulled my ears and hit my face every time I turned my head. Jean-Claude talked as we walked.

"That engineer is okay. He's a Communist; they're full of guts, so I don't think he'll let me down. He's all against the Patron's idea. He says no one would succeed in passing the gate without rousing all the Boches inside and giving the show away. I'll bring the charges to Toulouse and he'll smuggle them one at a time into his office. Engineers are the only people who are not searched at the entrance gate, but he can't walk in with a large bundle. I shall also have to inspect the machines."

"How will you get in?"

Four Germans walked by with their rifles slung on their back; their boots resounded on the pavement.

"He will give me an engineer's armband. With a soft felt hat on the back of my head, a blue pencil behind my ear, a yellow ruler sticking out of my pocket and a roll of plans under my arm, I can bluff my way anywhere."

"Do you know yet what machinery you have to attack?"

"Yes," he said, looking as though he was talking of the flowers of spring and smiling to a couple of 'zazous' strolling past. "I'll have to blow up the presses and the drying machines; that will interrupt the fabrication of the powder in the middle of the process. You ask the Patron to find out if London is satisfied."

"When do you think you can do it?"

"Not before three weeks from now. I have to prepare the charges, bring them here, and wait until the engineer has smuggled them inside. Until that is done I can't do anything."

We had lunch in a black-market restaurant.[3] It was against the rules of security, but some slackening inevitably followed the first days of tense attention. Also we looked like such a pair of local good-for-nothings that the solid customers shrugged their shoulders contemptuously at us.

"I'll be back soon with London's answer for you," I told Jean-Claude as he accompanied me to the station. "Don't come any further: stations are risky places and I can manage by myself. Be careful, won't you?"

Jean-Claude breathed an atmosphere of steadiness and self-confidence: I knew nothing would happen to him. At Auch I took the bus to Condom and cycled up to Nasoulens. I arrived in time for supper, as usual.

"Your hair is a mess... What *have* you done to it?" Cérensac said as I entered the kitchen greeted by general laughter. "But never mind – a happy birthday to you."

CHAPTER IX

Odilla Cérensac prepared a pantragruelian meal in honour of my twenty-first birthday. The whole family, after due consultations, bought me a small, travelling alarm clock. It was a very serious expense for them.

"It's for somebody who needs it very much," Cérensac said to the jeweller.[1] Then he winked. "The right sort of person, that's all I shall tell you…" And the jeweller had understood and fetched the clock from the hidden depths of his back shop. He was an outspoken enemy of the Germans and had been warned to keep quiet about it several times; he was a cripple. Nevertheless, after D-Day he took to the *maquis* and fought in the front line until he was killed.

The Patron lived in a small village called Castelnau-sur-l'Auvignon.[2] It stands on the edge of a plateau, a little fourteenth-century village, with thick walls, an old church and an ancient fortified tower. At the foot of the hill runs the Auvignon, a clear stream, the only source of water of the villagers; they carry it uphill in pails or cow-drawn barrels. At night, they eat under the bright flame of acetylene-lights, for electricity is unknown there. Castelnau is, or rather was, a delightful little place; it emerged honey-coloured and red-tiled from the green fields and dark pine trees around. Every night, the heavy bell on the church tower rang the angelus announcing the end of the day's labour; it resounded over the hills for miles.

The Germans came once, but left the next day, disgusted at the discomfort. It was a safe place for the Patron. His radio operator also lived there:[3] when an emission took place, the roads leading to the village could be watched from the top of the hill and DF cars would be seen long before they had a chance of being harmful.[4] The radio set worked on batteries brought each week from Agen by VanderBock. The Patron lived with a couple who had five children and a grandson.[5] In a disused cellar below the kitchen, two tons of arms were stored for guerrilla warfare. In spite of the presence of the Patron and his radio operator, both No. 1 targets of the Gestapo, and of an arms depot, neither of them ever winced or hesitated at the thought of what would happen if the Germans found out; they risked their homes, their lives and those of their children, and also the whole village.

The Sunday following my birthday, I was invited by the Patron to a feast in his village. I went up in an old pleated skirt, a shirt with rolled sleeves, socks and muddy shoes. I was horrified to find everyone dressed up in their best clothes.

"You should have known better," the Patron said. "They are going to be hurt when they see that you didn't make yourself smart for the occasion."

I felt ashamed. I borrowed a blouse from one of the girls, cleaned my shoes, took off my socks and painted my legs with a brown liquid to look like stockings. It looked a little better, but I felt uncomfortable all day. The meal lasted from noon until five-thirty: after it was over we danced in the village street to the sound of a gramophone. My head swam with all the wine and armagnac I had drunk and I had to spend two days without eating, following my birthday indigestion. It had all been a touching performance: I was given bottles of perfume and boxes of make-up.

"I'm sorry you can't stay at home and rest a few days, Paulette," the Patron said after it was over. "But you must go and see Cyprien tomorrow with messages for parachuting fields; I shall also give you a set of messages for D-Day which he will have to learn by heart. So will you: you can't risk carrying them."

The messages were divided into two lots, A and B. The A ones would warn us that Allied action was imminent, and that the Resistance must make its final preparations. The B ones would show that the invasion was to take place in a matter of hours: 48 hours after they had been received over the BBC, the Resistance was to begin guerrilla warfare, attack railways and telephone communications, and hold the chosen fields for airborne landings.

The Patron went on: "Don't fail to tell Cyprien that I order him not to set foot in Agen again. He's finished there; he's known by sight to many of the most dangerous Gestapo agents. Also tell him to stop, once and for all, eating in restaurants. He knows enough people who can feed him, without living in public places."

Cyprien was not in Agen. VanderBock gave me an address where I could contact him.

"I think he must be in Tonneins. He stays with wood merchants there, but I don't know them."[6]

Tonneins is a small and picturesque town on the Garonne, about an hour from Agen. I took the train after lunch and arrived in the early afternoon. The wood merchant's secretary received me.

"I would like to see your boss, please."

"I'm afraid he's busy. Can I do anything for you?"

"No, thank you. I'm here to arrange a purchase for a friend of his: he asked me to see him personally."

The secretary looked annoyed but fetched his boss; the boss looked even more annoyed.

"I would like to fix a deal for Cyprien," I told him.

"I'm afraid I don't know who you are talking about."

It was going to be difficult. "I've just arrived from Agen. I'm sure you've heard of Monsieur VanderBock; he asked me to say he was a friend of Cyprien and hopes you will be able to favour him with an easy arrangement. If I could see Cyprien, he would vouch for him."

"I tell you I don't know Cyprien. What is your name?"

"Paulette…"

He was quiet a second, then went out, saying he was going to ask his wife if she knew anything about all this. Two minutes later he returned, followed by Cyprien.

"I am under constant observation here," he told me. "I can take no risks with people I don't know. I apologise for the cold reception I gave you."

"Of course, I understand perfectly well."

"Now look here," Cyprien interrupted, "come with me. We mustn't stay here; it's dangerous. I'll take you to another place."

We left by a back door and went to a small radio-repair shop in the middle of Tonneins. The whole thing was like a medieval intrigue. We sat by a table in a darkened back room. The owner of the shop locked us in, locked his shop, pulled the blinds down, and stayed watching the street through a hole in the shutters. A cat sat majestically on the table. I wrote out the D-Day messages for Cyprien. He picked up the paper and slipped it in his wallet.

"Say… You're supposed to learn these by heart. You can't go round carrying them on you. The same messages hold for the whole circuit; it would be an appalling business to change them all, if they fell into the hands of the Boches."

"I'll learn them soon, don't worry."

"Now, come and have an *apéritif*," he went on, after we had finished.

"No, Cyprien. I don't want to. You and your precautions and theatrical security set-ups… You haven't an inch of common sense. And just after the Patron's message…"

Cyprien laughed good-humouredly. Instead, we drank an armagnac at the round table in the back room in the company of the radio repairer. He was very uneasy.

"I have a nasty feeling that something will happen… To be frank," he blurted out suddenly, "I'd like you to go away."

We left him to his terrors. In the square, I shook hands with Cyprien. "There's no point in coming any further: I'm catching a train in half an hour. I'll be seeing you."

I sat in the waiting-room reading my paper. A quarter of an hour later someone came and sat next to me, unfolding an evening paper. It was the radio repairer; he gazed steadfastly at his paper and spoke quietly from the corner of his mouth.

"I was right to smell trouble. When Cyprien reached the wood merchant's house, he saw him coming out with handcuffs and German soldiers guarding him. His wife followed behind; her face was bleeding; they must've struck her. There were two Gestapo cars in front of the gate and five of those swine stood around barking orders in their lousy jargon."

"What happened to Cyprien?" I whispered, reading my newspaper more intently than ever.

"He had time to turn into a side street and get away. I'm sure it was him they wanted to get: if you hadn't come today he would have been caught in the trap. He came straight to the shop and sent me here to see you. You mustn't come back to Tonneins; he'll let VenderBock know how you can contact him."

"What are you going to do?"

"I'll leave my shop to my assistant and go to the country for a while. If those two talk, the Resistance in the whole neighbourhood will collapse."

"Thanks for coming along. I think you'd better go back now, and don't forget to tell Cyprien to destroy the paper I gave him. Be careful, and good luck."

This had been a narrow escape: less than an hour after my painful introduction, the wood merchant and his wife had been surrounded by the Gestapo, reinforced by German soldiers. It was an unusual thing for them to come in full daylight: as a rule they came silently, at the crack of dawn, and caught people before they had time to wake up properly or gather their wits to attempt an escape. Later I learnt that the wood merchant and his wife had behaved like heroes; their children of four and two years were horribly beaten before their eyes, but neither of them spoke.

I went back to Montréjeau with London's answer to Jean-Claude:

"The RAF will give you three weeks only. After that they may come any day; they say they have to follow their bombing programme as it's been set out."

"All right, let them do what they want. I can't possibly get this demolition done before three weeks, and I'll probably need more. It's their own business if they want to make a bombing operation which they could avoid by waiting a few days."

Miette came in and kissed me.

"Mazères is becoming like a camp. There are so many people staying with me that I don't even know all their names."

"Who else has arrived?"

"Another police inspector from Agen. He came with a poor boy who escaped from Eysse and was forgotten among all the people you brought three weeks ago. He will cross over with François de Tranches; they are leaving in two days."

"Aren't you worried, Miette, with all those 'terrorists'?"

"My poor little Paulette, I'm getting past worrying. I'm continually ready to see the last of my hens, my cats and my house… I've packed my trunk with the sheets and embroidered materials we brought back from Indochina and I've parked them, with everything else I care about, in a good neighbour's house." She waved her hands in a helpless gesture: "I don't care. And deep down, I'd miss them if they went…"

François walked in followed by two men, the inspector, Lépine,[7] and the Last-Escapee. They all talked at once; the noise was deafening. Jean-Claude declared:

"Tomorrow I'm taking my explosive charges to Toulouse. I shall make them tonight. Paulette, you're going to help me."

"I'll help too, if there's anything I can do," François said.

"Are you going to take them by train?" asked Lépine. Jean-Claude nodded. "I'll go with you if you want: I may be able to help with my police inspector's card."

It was an excellent idea. After dinner I had a long talk with Roger; he wasn't happy about the D-Day orders. He learnt the A and B messages immediately and then went off to St-Bertrand-de-Comminges to spend the night. Jean-Claude was quietly preparing his charges in an inferno of parachuted stuff all over the floor, the bed and the chairs. Fouffi and her four kittens purred from the depths of the yellow eiderdown. François, sitting on the floor, had been given the stooging work: cutting the rubberised fabric into neat squares, making knots in the detonating fuse to prevent the primers slipping, sorting the two-hours time-pencils out of the heap of material lying around. We stayed up till well after two in the morning preparing ½lb. standard charges and 'tar baby' incendiaries.

"My camouflage as an engineer worked perfectly," Jean-Claude told us. "I went right through the gate and visited the whole factory without being stopped once. It was extremely interesting: sometimes I took a sheet of paper out of the carton under my arm and drew little sketches of the machines. The workmen thought I was taking notes and paid no attention."

"How are you going to do the demolition? Alone?" asked François.

"I'll go with one other person, probably Raymond Mautrens. We'll place the charges simultaneously in the two buildings I want to destroy. We'll also put incendiaries on the beams under the roofs: the whole place will burn and, as soon as it rains, the smashed machines will rust and be doubly wrecked."

The Last-of-the-Escapees was glum and sullen; he had been frightfully upset at being forgotten. Lépine was determined to make him laugh; he was a Basque, full of wit, and told crazy stories while we worked.

Lépine, Jean-Claude and I caught the 5.20 to Toulouse with four suitcases crammed with explosive and incendiary charges. The train was very full; people streamed past the barrier at the Toulouse station in a solid mass. Lépine went first, carrying two cases, while Jean-Claude and I followed at a distance with one each. Just after the barrier I noticed a man in civilian clothes making a sign with his head to a French policeman standing by. The policeman tapped Lépine on the shoulder and motioned him to follow: a Gestapo check. My heart was beating fast; it was amazing that amongst the hundreds of people who had passed in front of him, the Gestapo agent should pick on the right one. His flair impressed me. It was a sinking sensation to see a friend caught under your very nose.

The man had not moved and nobody noticed his game: Jean-Claude passed by unflinching. My heart beat faster as I came up to him. Once well away from the station I heaved a sigh of relief. I found Jean-Claude waiting at the top of a street some distance away.

"I hope nothing happened to him," he said. Then, looking at me: "You're pale, you goon."

"Goon yourself. You're pale too."

We waited in silence. Five minutes later, Lépine appeared.

"I'm all wobbly in the legs," he told us. "For God's sake let's go and have a drink. I need a hot grog."

"Quick, tell us what happened?" I asked, after we had sat down in a small café in front of a steaming grog.

"I just followed him without making a fuss: there was no point in appearing rushed. He took me to a room with two German and two French police officers who wanted to see my papers and search me. I put my case down, said 'French police', and produced my card – you know, the one with the red and blue lines across. They only glanced at it and apologised. I said it was perfectly all right and sailed out. But I can tell you I was glad to get out."

"Now, listen to me, you two," I told them. "I am not going to walk another inch in this town with either of you. Look at you; no wonder you were picked up. You look like a pair of *maquisards* on leave..."

Neither of them had shaved for four days; their hair was long and untidy; their pants and shoes were filthy and they walked about with the collars of their *canadiennes* turned up and their hands in their pockets.

"Please, Minou, we're happy like this. Don't make me clean up," Jean-Claude pleaded.

"Well then, you can go along all by yourselves. I'll have lunch at the Restaurant de la Reine Pédauque.[8] If you want to eat with me, you'll have to get a shave and a haircut and clean your shoes."

I left them to carry the four cases to the engineer's house and went on a shopping tour. At lunchtime they joined me, clean and a pleasure to the eye. The Reine Pédauque was a black-market restaurant: at the table next to ours eight Gestapo agents were enjoying a rich meal. Lépine said he knew one of them. They had close-cropped, mousy-coloured hair. All Germans like green: most of them wore green tweed jackets and all had grey-green felt hats hanging on the pegs near their table.

"They have a trick of going into cloakrooms and looking in people's pockets," said Lépine softly. Jean-Claude sprang up and disappeared.

"I'd left my toy in my pocket," he said when he had sat down again. "Silly of me…"

"I should think so… Why the heck do you have to travel with it?" I said.

"Because I like it," barked Jean-Claude.

After lunch, all three of us went for a walk round Toulouse. On the place Wilson, a pretty square with a flower garden and a fountain in the middle, people were laughing at a gathering of excited schoolboys who had just played a trick on the Germans. The Wehrmacht had a café reserved for their use in a corner of the square;[9] for some inexplicable reason, they had erected a barrier of wire-netting all round it and sat at tables on the pavement behind this defence. They looked utterly ridiculous: the Toulouse women made it a practice to pass by and glance at them with supreme contempt. The schoolboys had just put up a notice saying: "Beware – Wild Beasts". Every day some new form of mockery met the eye of the German soldiers at their Soldatenheim.

"Look," said Jean-Claude as we walked along. "This is the sort of thing that makes me sick."

With his chin he pointed to a German sentry standing in front of the Crédit Lyonnais armed with a Stengun.

"*Our parachutages*," he grumbled between his teeth. "They must have got hold of one of our depots or received some of our stuff. It's maddening." Lépine and I agreed: there was something grimly infuriating in the heavy calmness of the Boche sentry holding the Resistance's wearily earned, and often dearly paid for, material.

We went on walking round the town till it was time to catch my train. I was heading for Agen, on my way to Dordogne to give Colomiers the D-Day messages. Toulouse is an attractive city: cities with a river flowing through them always are. Wide avenues edged with plane trees border the Garonne and cross right through the town, knotted together here and there by gay squares with flower gardens and groups of trees. Unfortunately, it is riddled with smells varying from WCs to stale cooking. In the summer it is hot and dusty, but all the same rather lovable, with its southern charm and its population of gay and excitable people.

CHAPTER X

The days slipped by, sometimes slowly, sometimes too fast to follow. London had warned us to stand by for radio messages on the first and second, and on the fifteenth and sixteenth of each month. Nothing had come yet. People around us began to be discouraged. It was a dangerous state of mind to slip into because it immediately caused a relaxation in security measures.

Indeed, in the middle of April a succession of bust-ups occurred in the circuit. First, I received a note from Colomiers through VanderBock: the Lantrets had been arrested and I was not to return to Eymet. A few days later, I met him in a lonely farm near Bergerac, and he told me how it had happened. Bernard had jumped from the window and escaped through the garden, but Madame Lantret and her husband were marched to the main square of Eymet. There, they were handcuffed with a number of people and all were brutally beaten with a horsewhip before being taken to prison in Limoges.

It was a nasty shock. But not the last. One morning as I cycled down the hill to Condom, I met the Patron racing up in his small Simca. I was on my way to see Cyprien.

"You can't go to Agen today," the Patron said. The dust behind him settled gently back on the road. "Cyprien is dead. He was killed last night."

No... I couldn't imagine Cyprien dead... Only a few days before he was telling me how he couldn't do without women and adventure. Now he had had his last adventure. I wanted to cry; I had grown fond of the provincial beau, in spite of his ways.

"Unfortunately, that is not all: Lépine, the police inspector, was with him and he has been caught."

"My God... And he knows all about Roger and Miette; if he talks he blows up the whole Pyrenees sector. He knows about Jean-Claude and the Empalot demolition... He knows the engineer who is helping him... He knows VanderBock. What a mess!"

"Yes. VanderBock had already left Agen. It was Thévenin, the *gendarme* who accompanied you with the Eysse prisoners, who warned him to get away last night. He and Marie are hiding near Nérac. Now you must tell me one thing, Paulette: have you talked to Lépine? Does he know where you live and does he know anything about me?"

"No, I haven't said a word. Nobody knows where you live. Nobody knows where I live either, not even Jean-Claude. But how did it happen?"

"Cyprien had disobeyed my orders; he was dining in the private room of a restaurant in Agen and holding a war conference at the same time – the half-witted idiot! I suppose he had been followed or something. Anyway, the Gestapo suddenly walked into the room. Cyprien jumped up, grabbed his gun and fired; he killed one of the Gestapo men and wounded another, but he received fifteen bullets in the chest and died immediately. Lépine was taken away manacled."

"But, Patron," I cried suddenly. "The A and B messages… He always carried them on him. And Lépine had a photo of Jean-Claude for a driving licence…"

"Yes, I know. VanderBock also told me that. I'm afraid all the messages will have to be changed; London has already been warned. You will have to take them round again."

Lépine was tortured, but he didn't talk; he was deported to Germany and assassinated a year later. These arrests had a few repercussions in the northern part of the circuit, but they soon died down. Another person replaced Cyprien and the work went on without one day's interruption.

On my way to Montréjeau, one day, I had a queer adventure. The scheduled date for the Empalot demolitions was just past, and I had to get the results from Jean-Claude. It was nearly freezing that morning: we were having a cold spell which worried the Cérensacs on account of their fruit crop. In the bus for Tarbes, the only seat I managed to fight my way to was next to a broken window. I tied a woollen scarf round my head and pulled my collar up: somehow I had forgotten my gloves. I tried to keep my hands warm by tucking them up my sleeves.

A stranger sitting next to me suddenly handed me his scarf and his fur-lined gloves. I refused.

"You'd be silly not to take them," he said. "I'm not cold and I don't need them."

So I thanked him and accepted them. He was about twenty-four; he had a thin, intent face illuminated by shining black eyes and topped by a mass of black, curly hair. He wore a brown felt hat on the back of his head, riding breeches and a *canadienne*. His manner was self-confident, combining brusqueness and gentleness. He soon began to talk: after a few generalities, he asked me where I lived.

"Oh, you wouldn't know the place. It's a small village in the neighbourhood of

Condom." I couldn't invent a name in case he proved to belong to the police and asked for my papers.

"What do you do there? It doesn't sound the sort of place where a girl like you would live."

"Why not? I study there and work in the fields too… But not very often," I added, remembering that my hands might betray me. I told him the old yarn of how life in Paris had become too much for my income. He went on asking casual questions: I couldn't escape answering and invented lie after lie. I counter-attacked by asking him similar questions.

"I live in the country near Auch," he said. "I was also in Paris, studying journalism, but I had to leave…" Then he suddenly attacked:

"I know enough about you to be able to come and see you. I know you live near Condom and I can understand that you don't want to say just where." I began to feel uneasy. "I know the attorney there[1]. If you haven't the local accent everyone notices you, and he will surely know of a Parisian girl who has fair hair and lives in the region. I'll come and look you up some time…"

Damn that man. I was getting more and more uneasy. Who was he and what did he want?

"Why, do… I don't mind. It's quite possible that the attorney should know me, I go to Condom pretty often. But it is the first time anyone has suggested coming to visit me after talking to me on a bus…"

He felt that he had made a wrong approach and kept silent for a while. Then: "You intrigue me, you know…"

"Well, that's interesting. It's not very often that I intrigue people. Please don't stop being intrigued, but I'm sleepy and if you don't mind, I'll doze off."

I turned my back on him and closed my eyes. I felt annoyed and somehow worried. I wondered over and over again if I could have directed the conversation otherwise, if I had talked too much, and if he was going to go on bothering me. But I couldn't be openly disagreeable. And I couldn't refuse to answer; it would arouse suspicion. I couldn't tell lies that my papers could deny. When we arrived in Tarbes, he helped me out.

"I hope you didn't find me rude," he said politely. "Only I'm a little lonely and I like speaking to people."

I felt a bit relieved. I had two hours to waste before catching my train to Montréjeau and I meant to have lunch with the Mautrens as I usually did. But I couldn't risk being followed and possibly giving them away. Instead, I walked about Tarbes making sure he wasn't trailing me and finally went to the Restaurant Bleu where you could get a moderate meal. I sat at a table alone and read my book.

"Now, isn't this a coincidence?" a voice behind me said suddenly. "You won't mind if I sit with you, will you? It's so dull being alone."

My heart sank. The stranger from the bus again. Was it really a coincidence? I'd been so careful not to be followed… He sat down. The waiter knew him.

"You'll have an *omelette flambée* with me, won't you?" before I had time to reply.

"You still intrigue me," he began again. "You should not do your hair like that, you know. You look German."

No remark could irk me more. My hair was parted at the back in two plaits pinned on top of my head. The sides and front were swept up in a high smooth roll. It was convenient for travelling because it resisted the wind and stayed neat.

"I don't care. I do my hair in a practical way."

"What's your name?"

"Marie-Françoise."

"Marie-Françoise what?"

"Marie-Françoise Nothing. I don't give my name to strangers."

"Where are you going after lunch?"

"Now look here; it's none of your business. Nowadays you don't go about telling your life story to everyone you meet."

"Sh… Don't speak so loud," he said. "See those two men eating with that painted woman over there? They belong to the Gestapo."

"So what? I don't care. Why should I mind the Gestapo? Do you?"

"No, but I know them. I know people who belong to both sides: this restaurant is full of them."

"Well, I'm glad to hear you have so many acquaintances. Why don't you go and sit with them? Or don't you want to compromise yourself one way or the other?"

"I only know them by sight. And I don't know if I'm not compromising myself this very minute, one way or another."

This was getting more involved. This odd man with his penetrating black eyes had something of the human sincerity and adventurousness of an anarchist. He was attractively dangerous. I was divided between curiosity and caution. Had I been the only one involved, I would have attempted to reach the bottom of the mystery he so carefully wound around himself – and tried to wind around me.

"No, you couldn't know," I replied.

"Well, I suggest you tell me what you're doing here. If you don't want to, I'll conclude one of two things: either you belong to the Resistance or to the Gestapo."

He was clever and his trap was a dead end. I made a movement.

"No, no, don't interrupt me now," he cut in quickly. "Now, if you belong to the Resistance, you are either a liaison officer or a local organiser: I can't quite make out which it would be. If you belong to the Gestapo, you are a very efficient *agent provocateur*, because I should think that you can use your feminine charm to its full effect." I was getting furious; also he was deliberately blurring my mind. "Quite sincerely, I have no idea which you might belong to. You have an old and ugly handbag, such as nobody working with the Gestapo would have; on the other hand, I observe that your suit is made of very good material such as is not found on the market now. Then, your hair and your colouring could be German, but your personality and appearance are entirely French. Now – will you tell me what you are doing in Tarbes?"

"After this avalanche of observations and deductions I'm afraid you are going to be rather disappointed," I replied dryly.

"Never mind, go ahead."

"I'm in Tarbes on my way to St-Gaudens. My sister-in-law lives there: her husband, who is my brother, is a prisoner in Germany. She is leaving for Paris in two days and I am taking charge of her children during her absence. I'm on my way to fetch them and bring them back with me… If you want *more* details, my small niece is five and my nephew is seven. If you want more details…"

"No, no… That's fine. You're right, I'm disappointed. I quite sincerely thought that you were something special. In fact, in spite of what you say, I'm still not sure that you're not."

I had averted most of the trap anyway.

"Well, between you and me, it is rather exciting to be thought 'something special' these days. At least as long as you don't have to start proving that you're not."

I wanted to get out of the restaurant, breathe fresh air, and be somewhere I could run if the need occurred. I couldn't make out my opponent. He was too Resistance- and Gestapo-conscious not to belong to one of them. He was too indiscreet and childish to be a leading personality in the Resistance, but he had an indefinable honesty and casualness that suggested that he belonged to it. Then he dressed like someone who lives out-of-doors and has to be ready for any change of weather. But that could be a trick. In fact, his whole act could be a trick.

My last remark finished disarming him; but that could be a trick too. I was surrounded with possibilities and I felt tense and angry with myself.

"I'll come with you to the station and carry your case."

I hated giving him my case: there was 75,000 francs in it, but he grabbed it before I had a chance to say anything. I took a ticket for St-Gaudens, the station after Montréjeau. He accompanied me onto the platform.

"I wish I could see you again some time," he said as I climbed in. "But I suppose you don't want me to. It's a pity; we could have had interesting arguments." Then, suddenly, "Please get down. I'd like to tell you something."

I had regained confidence, knowing that the train would leave five minutes later. I jumped off. He caught hold of my arm and pulled me to one side.

"I'll tell you something. I must tell you: I like your face. I've been in the *maquis* for more than a year now. That's the truth… My father was tortured by the Boches to make him reveal where I was, and deported to Germany when he said he didn't know. I hate the Germans; I hate them, do you hear? I've been in the Resistance more than two years: I gave all my money to it. And I had a lot. Now you know the truth… Yes, now you know the truth," he added more calmly. Then suddenly, cold and smiling: "Now, what's the truth about you?"

"The truth is that I'm a very ordinary person on her way to collect her niece and nephew. But you are a fool: I, nevertheless, *might* be something. I might belong to the Resistance and report that there is a crazy, black-haired guy who goes round telling everybody that he's fighting the Germans; I might tell the Resistance to get rid of him before he is caught and talks more… Or I might belong to the Gestapo; I might always be followed by a couple of Gestapo men, maybe the ones you saw in the Restaurant Bleu… And you might be arrested as you step out of the station. You might be in an awful trap this very minute… No, I'm sorry," I said – the train was about to move off. "You've behaved like a dope and if I can give you one piece of advice it's 'Shut up'…"

I jumped on the train as the first cars trembled in the effort to get moving. He looked rather stunned and I felt pleased with my little effect… I didn't lean out of the train and a moment later it pulled out of Tarbes into the green countryside.

My self-satisfaction turned into annoyance after a while: my final explosion had been unnecessary. I promised myself not to tell Jean-Claude, feeling I'd be in for a few sensible and crushing remarks. The pale and intelligent face, however, stayed clear in my memory: I thought I would never see it again.

Mazères was in a turmoil. It was getting to be a habit.

"What's happened now, Miette?" Miette had discovered a cupboard full of things she had brought back from Indochina; she had forgotten about it. Miette had a weak memory. She was packing furiously.

"The Communists…" she moaned. "They have no arms and they say we don't use the ones we have; they've threatened to raid our depot. I'm afraid they'll take my stuff too."

"Of course not, Miette. For goodness' sake relax. Which depot are you talking about?"

"Jaunac." Jaunac is a tiny village on the way to St-Bertand-de-Comminges.

"Where's Jean-Claude? How did his demolition operation go?"

"He's out, trying to find more details about this fuss." Then suddenly affectionately: "He's got so much courage, Jean-Claude. He will tell you himself how he did his demolition; he was all alone and he was lucky to get out. He wouldn't tell me much about it though."

He arrived an hour later.

"Minou, you've come at the right moment. I need someone who will help me to prepare the depot to be moved tonight. Everything's got to be counted and packed ready for transport."

"I won't. I've got a new skirt on and I'm not going to mess it up just to save you an hour's work..."

"You and your skirt, you make me tired. You're damned well going to come. I can't do it all alone this afternoon and the truck is coming to take the stuff away tonight."

I determined to have the last word. We cycled off to Jaunac.

"How long is this disagreement with the Communists going to last? Why can't everyone cooperate?"

"It will last as long as they lack any arms. They are the most daring people here, but they haven't anything to fight with. And we have so little ourselves that we can't even give them a bullet."

"But didn't you have a *parachutage* the other night? I heard a message for you."

"*Parachutage...*" shouted Jean-Claude. "Yes, let's talk about it. Do you know what they did? They dropped it at *five thousand feet*. Yes, five thousand feet, instead of five hundred. They're scared of the mountains, that's the only thing I can think of. You should've been here; up there in the sky, parachutes, tiny little specks... They took a quarter of an hour to come down. And not only that, but the pilot dropped them *with* the wind; they went miles and miles off the field. The *parachutage* was done at midnight and I searched for the confounded containers till two the following afternoon. Eight of them were lost..."

It was a disaster because the Pyrenees was a poorly armed sector. For many reasons. First it was very far from England; then the weather was often bad near the mountains; finally, as Jean-Claude had said, the pilots hated diving low because of the proximity of the mountains.

"Never mind all that, tell me about Empalot."

"A mess. It wasn't as successful as I wanted it to be, but I couldn't do any better. I was alone..."

"I thought Raymond Mautrens was going to do it with you?"

"Yes, but he caught bronchitis a couple of days before. There was no one else I could trust, so I went by myself. One piece of bad luck was that three days earlier a rule was made that the buildings should be lit up all night: it was a blow. I dragged along two sacks with fifteen explosive and fifteen incendiary charges in each: one sack for each building. I left one in a corner outside and crawled into the presses shop. Five men were patrolling up and down and I had to crouch every time they approached. It took a long time to place all the charges: nearly an hour, when I had counted on less than fifteen minutes."

"Were you able to place the incendiaries too?"

"Yes, the machines were high enough to hide the beams from the patrol. Anyway, I did that, and I got out and slipped into the next building. I hadn't placed two charges on the drying machines when my very first charge, placed on the water system in the presses shop, went off…"

"Why? Did the pipe vibrate, or what?"

"No, because the other charges went on exploding at intervals of four or five minutes after the first. The temperature must've been too high and the two-hours time-pencils went off fifty minutes too soon. As you can imagine, the uproar in the factory was terrific: people shouted and ran about all over the place. They thought there were *many* saboteurs."

"Did you run away?"

"Run away? Why should I? I knew they would never expect the saboteurs to carry on, so I did…" That was Jean-Claude all over. "I had time to place fourteen charges, but then it got too hot: people had begun to search the other end of the drying machines' building. So I left."

"How did you get away?"

"Quite simple. I cut my way through the barbed-wire fence – I had a pair of cutters with me – crawled along the bank of the Garonne and climbed up to the railway bridge. The fools were only guarding the road bridge, next to the railway one; so I crawled along the tracks and got away. From the opposite bank of the river I watched the last charges going up: it was so beautiful, Minou. I wished you were with me."

"I wish I had been: it must've been wonderful. But did the buildings burn?"

"No, that's where my plan failed. It is due to a curious phenomenon. The blast from every explosion of a standard charge put out the incendiary next to it. I was awfully disappointed."

I was proud of Jean-Claude; the only emotion he felt about the whole thing was the disappointment of not having entirely succeeded.

"We'll leave our bicycles here…" he said. We were on top of a small hill, and parked them behind a bush. Everything was strikingly green around us: the sun was hot and the light, pure and soft, edged every leaf and blade of grass with a golden halo. At the foot of the hill, the Garonne sang a crystal-clear melody as it rolled over its stones. The air was heavy with the smell of trees and flowers. A renewed sense of incongruity struck me: how could there be any danger or misunderstanding in such peaceful surroundings?

But Jean-Claude was practical. He cocked his gun.

"You do the same. We'll have to approach through the fields by the back. Don't talk, and be careful: if they should happen to be there now, it would be a nasty business. Let me go first."

He caught hold of my hand and we approached through the high grass, taking cover behind trees. The depot was under an old water-mill: a little stream gurgled by. We crept cautiously along. All of a sudden I slipped and fell on my behind while stones bounced about and made a terrible noise.

"Shh...you goon."

"Shh...yourself! I'm sitting right in a bed of nettles. Get me out of here," I fumed. My seat and legs burnt all the rest of the day.

The mill was quiet and the depot untouched. Jean-Claude led me through holes and secret doors, over rotten, shaky boards until we crawled through an opening in the wall.

"How do you ever suppose the Communists would find this place?" I asked. I was covered with dust and earth and spiders' webs.

"The man to whom it belongs is a Communist. But he hasn't said anything yet. He may, though."

We spent the whole afternoon making detailed accounts of the quantity of plastic explosive, incendiaries, Sten guns, rifles, Bren guns, hand grenades, magazines of all descriptions and bags of ammunition the depot contained. As things were counted, we put them into sacks, labelled them and piled them ready for easy transport. There was a hole in the roof above, from which the material could be removed rapidly. At one moment, Jean-Claude threw his arms around my neck and slapped two noisy kisses on each of my cheeks.

"Well... Does that happen to you often, Jean-Claude?"

"It's just that you ought to see yourself," he replied, putting on his cherubic expression. "The tip of your nose is all black, your face is red and puffed and your hair is white with spiders' webs... And you're dirty; but dirty, you have no idea! I simply felt I wanted to kiss you..."

My skirt was ruined; it was covered with the heavy grease used to keep the arms from rusting, and dust stuck to the stains. What would Suzanne Laroche[2] say if she saw it? She had cycled four times to accompany me to a dressmaker she had recommended, and she and her sisters were so neat and tidy. But there was nothing I could say to Jean-Claude when he played the cherub: I could just imagine him cherubbing to Miette until her kind heart melted – she worked and slaved for him.

"I want to bring a Bren gun back with me for instruction," he said. "Will you take it on your luggage rack? Mine's broken."

Together we camouflaged the Bren by covering it with long oak branches and added bunches of hastily-gathered flowers. I waved heartily to people as we cycled by.

"This looks more like a return from a romantic week-end than anything I've ever seen," Jean-Claude grumbled. "It makes me mad. Stop grinning like that… You look stupid."

"Thanks, you ill-mannered chump. Thanks for the romantic return, too…"

"All right, all right, don't get angry. Only there's nothing I hate like puffing and merry people returning from a merry week-end by a merry river in the merry sunshine. Their flowers are faded, their clothes are crumpled and they smell. It's depressing."

CHAPTER XI

"Oh, heavens, but you are going to catch your death of sunstroke if you don't put a hat on. Goodness, goodness, what have you girls of today come to? In the freezing winter you sleep with your window wide open and in the torrid sun you go about without a hat... I've never seen anything like it."

It was the last day of April and the sun was bright and hot: the cherries were pink, the flowers in bloom, and the approaching summer seemed to burst out of every living thing. Odilla's mother, with black woollen stockings, and a wide and decrepit old straw hat pulled over her ears, flew daily into shocked indignation at the sight of me lying on the grass in shorts and offering my face to the rays of the sun.

Every colour had acquired a new richness. Odilla in flowered aprons chased the poultry in and out of the henhouses; chicks and ducklings and squeaky little turkeys ran under your feet and filled the air with perpetual noise. Henri and André came back from the fields browner every day: I watched their bright-checked shirts from a distance as they bumped and swayed on top of the hay-cutter. Now, the cows were taken out in the evenings. I used to be terrified of cows; now I didn't mind them any more: I led them to the fields at sunset. La Brunette was the only milk cow; the others worked. She was temperamental; she seemed to think that she was better than the others because she lived a leisurely life. She would glance sideways at me, then throw her head up and walk straight into a flower-bed, or run suddenly away and make a mess right in front of the house; she gave me more work than all the others put together.

Reports had come in from Agen that the French police were looking for me: no one was quite sure whether the Gestapo was in on the search or not, but it was probable. The leakage had come after the Tonneins arrests, no one quite knew how. The Patron limited my visits there to a minimum.

I'd acquired four identity cards now, one for each of the departments I travelled to. They all had different names and details and it was no small enterprise learning each of them well enough to become a reflex. Roger had obtained the most perfect one for me; it was a real identity, but the original human being to whom it belonged was finishing her days in the Lannemezan asylum. When I went to the Pyrenees sector, I was Alice Davoust, born in Rennes (Brittany), and living at 25 route de Bordères, Tarbes. The papers were registered at the Hautes-Pyrénées Préfecture.

For a long time now, I had lost the sensation of being an outlaw. I felt just like any other French girl. I had had to buy some summer clothes and had ceased to wear French fashions as if they were fancy dress. Again I thought, dreamed and reacted in French. But I was still Gestapo-conscious: I carried my messages in toilet paper. Once at a bus stop, I found myself in a snap-control. One of the Germans searched my handbag while another examined my papers; he pulled out a crumpled little bunch of toilet paper and looked at me. I blushed modestly. He put it back tactfully. There were thirty BBC messages inside... I had blushed from sheer fright.

It was on a return trip from Montréjeau that I had my most disagreeable encounter with the Gestapo. I had found Mazères in a turmoil again.

"Now what, Miette?"

"This time it's the *miliciens*. Somebody killed a *légionnaire* last night, in Mazères... I ask you. They were in the village this morning and may come back any minute. I wouldn't mind if it wasn't for all those arms hidden in the garden."

"But nobody will find them..."

"I'm not so sure. That's providing nobody gets picked up and talks. Anyway, Jean-Claude has guns all over the place. He's out with Auguste,[1] finding out more about the movements of the Milice."

"Who is Auguste?"

"He's a law student who lives outside Montréjeau and helps Jean-Claude. He escaped compulsory labour in Germany last year and has been 'camouflaged' ever since."

I suggested cleaning up Jean-Claude's room. It looked like a dormitory for active anarchists. The accumulation of books had overflowed from the mantelpiece to the floor; filthy pants on the back of chairs, socks under the bed, suitcases opened on the floor. But no guns: Miette's imagination was in such a flutter that she had forgotten Jean-Claude's common sense. Not an incriminating thing could be found.

"Paulette..." Miette shouted suddenly. I went to the kitchen. Her face was close to the radio and she put a finger on her lips.

"Listen," she whispered.

Messages. I recognized nearly twenty warning Colomiers that *parachutages* would take place in Dordogne the same night. Then a number for the Lot-et-Garonne and the Gers, then four for the region of Tarbes. "The cigarettes are green" – that was the Montréjeau district...

Miette was as excited as a child; so was I. A few minutes later the Picolets from next door rushed in. Had we heard? Yes, we had. We all went out: it had been a fine day, but low clouds were rolling towards the mountains. Picolet predicted rain.

"What about the *miliciens*? They're sure to set up road blocks all over the place," said Madame Picolet.

"Can't help that," said her husband. "We'll have to crash them. We can't miss this *parachutage*; we need the stuff too badly."

Jean-Claude came in followed by Auguste, a tall young man with long, straight black hair. He had a Slavonic face – high cheek-bones and a flat nose. He was twenty-one – later I was to see a lot of him.

"The Milice are all over the place," they informed us.

At six o'clock Roger arrived. He had heard the messages in Tarbes and rushed back by the first train. Raymond Mautrens and his men had spent the afternoon in frantic organisation of transport and preparations for their *parachutages*. Everywhere the excitement was terrific: the planes had been hoped and prayed for during so many months. *Parachutages* were the life-blood of the Resistance.

"Minou, you'd better not come. There might be a clash with the *miliciens*," Jean-Claude declared.

"If you don't let me come, I'll never speak to you again."

"All right. Do what you want. I hoped you'd say that."

Every five minutes somebody rushed out to look at the weather. The wind got up, the clouds rushed ever thicker and gloomier across the sky: at eight o'clock they broke into torrential rain. Our hands were moist with emotion: everybody clung to small hopes.

"The wind usually drops after nine," said Picolet.

"If it rains now, it might be over by the time the plane comes," said Roger.

"They must know the weather ahead, in England," said Auguste.

"We can't possibly have that much bad luck," said Miette.

But it went on raining endlessly: the elements seemed to have settled for the night.

"That might keep the Milice in," said Jean-Claude.

At 9.30 we got ready to leave. The emotion was so general that we had forgotten to have dinner. Miette distributed bread and sausages to everyone. Jean-Claude lent me his *canadienne* and produced a .32 Colt.

"I cleaned it this morning, Minou. It's on safety."

We climbed into Picolet's small, open truck and started out. The rain hammered monotonously on the tarpaulin overhead, the night was as dark as sin. The truck bounced up the rocky country lanes to the main road: the Nationale 117 or Toulouse–Bayonne road, by day, full of German traffic, and by night, full of looming perils. As soon as we speeded on the tarred and smooth road the truck began to zigzag painfully.

"Stop this, Picolet," Roger growled.

"I can't. Seven people is too much for this car and the road is slippery. We just have to hope for the best."

We zigzagged along in silence. The rain moderated its downpour and fell, soft as silk.

"Watch out…" A light shone in the distance. We drew our revolvers and waited tensely: inside I was cold and calm. But I knew I would feel bad after it was over. I hoped the truck wouldn't overturn: it seemed the worst danger.

We whizzed past unchallenged: it was only some man lighting his cigarette. He will never know the emotions he caused with this common gesture. Reactions were different: Picolet, and a few men I didn't know, giggled nervously. I did too. Roger fumed and cursed at the rain, at the truck, at the people who light cigarettes on the roadside and at the Milice. Jean-Claude and Auguste said nothing and put their guns back on 'safety', but Jean-Claude caught hold of my hand and kept it all the rest of the way.

We stopped near a small wood and parked the car. It was nearing eleven. A group of silent men joined us in the dark: I shall never know their faces, but I saw their wet Stens shining. After Roger had given brief and precise orders, they went off to their positions without a word. Jean-Claude, Auguste and I started out to the middle of the field; we seemed to walk for hours. The earth was soft and wet. We crossed a wheat field: the wheat came up to my knees and water ran down to my shoes. They gurgled at every step. At a clearing we stopped.

"Minou, you take charge of the 'Rebecca', if you want to. I'll take the light signal, and you, Auguste, you can take a red flashlight," said Jean-Claude.

The 'Rebecca' was a DF instrument which captured and re-transmitted a signal from an aircraft, thus indicating our exact position. Jean-Claude helped me to set up the aerial and test the batteries. Auguste vanished in the darkness with his red flashlight.

At that time, parachuting fields were indicated to the pilots by a number of lights. Three red ones at intervals of 100 metres, placed in a line parallel to the wind. The direction opposite to the wind was shown by a white light signalling the Morse code-letter, placed 50 metres from the top red light: the effect was an "L", the vertical bar being the three red lights and the tip of the horizontal one, the white light. At the noise of the approaching aircraft, the lights would be put on and made to follow the sound. The aircraft had to fly low, dead over the red lights, and start dropping the containers over the white. According to the speed of the wind, the fifteen containers would fall in given places.

Jean-Claude and I sat on the ground and huddled close. The rain had stopped but the wind blew more fiercely, piercing right through my *canadienne*. I kept the ear-phones on and occasionally tested the battery: di-di-dah-di, di-di-dah-di – the code-letter was 'F'. Eleven-thirty, twelve, twelve-thirty struck from a distant church: the wind carried the sound. At a quarter to one Roger joined us.

"I don't suppose it will come: the weather is too bad." His voice was full of disappointment. "Everybody is asleep on the ground…"

I tested my batteries and listened out once more. Nothing but the usual low whistle. Then it conked out.

"Jean-Claude, the battery is flat."

"That's the end of everything. I was afraid this would happen… I can't tell when it's charged, I have no ammeter."

Roger went back: discouragement sounded in his step. We sat, silent while the rain began to drop softly again.

"Listen…"

My head beat through the effort: miles and miles away I could hear a vague drone. I wanted to yell "Shut up" to the wind. The drone became a steady rumble. Black figures sprang up at the other end of the field; they had heard too. The expectation had reached such a pitch that if blood could have revived the 'Rebecca', I would have cut a vein there and then.

"They'll never find us…" moaned Jean-Claude.

"They are flying above cloud and trying to catch our signal. Oh, why, why did the cock-eyed thing have to go flat now?"

He ran to his position. I joined him there; he was tensely pointing a two-watt beam of light to a distant sound in a tormented sky. It seemed naive. Further along, red specks followed the sound too: I could nearly hear the prayer rising from these men's hearts to the pilot, up there. The sound got closer.

"Jean-Claude, your light is out," I cried. He shook it until it came on again, a dying, blinking orange glow. Would our troubles ever cease? "I'll get you another one."

I ran to Roger as fast as I could: mud stuck to my shoes, making them heavy. I twisted my ankle and fell flat on my face on the soppy earth, but nothing seemed to matter outside the battery. The drone had receded again. I ran back with Roger's last one.

"If they don't drop us some this time I don't know how we'll manage next time," he had muttered.

The sound approached again. "They're circling above cloud," Jean-Claude groaned. "If we had the 'Rebecca' it would be done by now. Dive, for goodness' sake, dive… The mountains are miles away, you won't hit them."

Above, the heavy Halifax circled for twenty minutes. I could imagine the despatcher, next to his open hole, his packages ready by his side, peering down at a dirty mass of grey clouds, his face stiff with cold. Below, we're *below*!

Finally, the low drone went off further and further until it mingled with the wind once more. We waited another hour, jumping up at any sound, cold, wet and miserable. Our ears were full of wind. But nothing came.

"He's gone back. *Our* plane," Jean-Claude said.

They had waited so long. It meant so much. How many others went through the same thing that night? And all the other nights? Even Roger was too empty to grumble. No one spoke as we climbed into the truck: no one even thought of the *miliciens*, although the danger was the same. Picolet did not zigzag; he drove slowly. The last time they had had a *parachutage*, half of it had been lost. This time it didn't come at all.

Miette had prepared some *café-au-lait*; she had heard the aircraft. Madame Picolet had waited with her. Both of them had tears in their eyes when they heard that no arms had arrived. The women of France – all they wanted was grenades and Bren guns.

"I'm going to Tarbes tomorrow with stuff for instructions; will you come with me, Minou?" Jean-Claude said.

It was more complicated returning to Condom via Tarbes, but I was so unhappy that I agreed to go. It was nearly a quarter to four. I was so wet and cold that I thought I never would find enough warmth in me to warm up a bed, so I stayed by the fire of the kitchen cooker and put my shoes to dry in the oven. Jean-Claude stayed with me; we fell asleep against one another. Miette came in at half-past six.

"Wake up, you two pigeons, your train leaves in an hour and a half. I'll get you some breakfast."

I was cramped and stiff, cold and hungry. It was a bad start for the day. Jean-Claude had two cases full of material, from small arms to demolition stuff, for his instruction. We reached the station twenty minutes before the train left, and walked about trying to warm up. Three or four Germans stood on the platform opposite; they seemed to be talking about us. I began to feel uncomfortable.

"Jean-Claude, I'd like you to go away until the train comes in. I don't like those four, over there."

"Nonsense, I won't go."

But I insisted so much that he finally did. Two minutes before the train arrived, two of the Germans guarded the door of the station while two others, revolver in hand, arrested every man on the platform. It was a *rafle*, a regular German trick. The men would be bundled into trucks and taken to the nearest police station, where they would be searched and their papers examined. From there they would be deported to Germany, unless they had papers issued by the German authorities certifying that they were unfit or doing vital work. Their families or relatives would never know what had become of them and very few would escape.

Jean-Claude reappeared and he and I jumped into a first-class carriage just as the train moved off. It was packed but I managed to find a seat in a crowded compartment. A young woman sat next to the window, trying to hold on to two small children who were laughing and shouting and trying to climb on everybody's lap. I had to ask her to move some of the numerous parcels she had with her to be able to place one of our suitcases on the rack. Jean-Claude kept the other one with him.

He stood in the corridor looking out of the window. I tried to read a book, but my feeling of discomfort still persisted. Jean-Claude had chosen my book; it was called *From the Infinitely Big to the Infinitely Small*, all about the splitting of the atom, and the particles of light, right to the galaxies. I couldn't possibly concentrate on neutrons and protons in my compartment.

"Minou, come here a second, will you?" Jean-Claude said politely. I went to the corridor. He went on looking straight out of the window and said, smiling vaguely:

"Don't be upset, but the Gestapo is on the train. I just saw them at the other end of the car. They're searching cases and asking questions. Don't worry, Minou. It'll be all right."

Which was just like Jean-Claude. There was no question of moving away; the corridor was full of people and the Gestapo might have some agents ahead. I sat in horrible suspense, singing little tunes to myself. Maybe they wouldn't search my case. If they did I would deny that it belonged to me. But they would arrest the whole compartment, including the young woman and the two babies. They would make a close check on papers and addresses and would soon find out that I was 'irregular'. Jean-Claude and I had one ticket for the two, so he would probably get arrested too. My brain wouldn't work clearly. I have nothing of Jean-Claude's calm and collected attitude before impending peril. Only when faced with a sudden and unexpected crisis can I deal with it coolly.

I tried to read my book: protons, neutrons, photons… It was all a blur. My heart beat until I thought it would jump out, my knees wobbled and I felt thousands of ants running up and down my back. Now – when a proton is projected in a vacuum against a phosphorescent plate…

"Papers…"

I had known he was there for a few seconds… Now he was talking to Jean-Claude: my heart made such a noise that I couldn't hear what they were saying. They talked for hours. The man was frowning. He didn't notice the case behind Jean-Claude's legs. He came in.

"Monsieur…" he said, putting his hand out to a man sitting in the corner next to me.

"In what capacity do you want to see my papers?" the man said, looking up quietly from his newspaper. The other one pulled a bronze badge from his pocket; it bore a wide German eagle and swastika.

"Gestapo."

Politely but unhurried, my neighbour gave his papers and resumed his newspaper. It was a good method; he was left alone.

To me: "Your name?"

"Alice Thérèse Davoust."

"Born?"

"Rennes, Ille-et-Vilaine."

"Occupation?"

"Student."

"Where?"

"Paris. I left three months ago."

"What are you doing now?"

"Nothing. I help in the house."

"Where are you going?"

"Back home, in Tarbes."

"You live…?"

"25 route de Bordères."

He returned my papers abruptly. Jean-Claude was looking at me; he closed his eyes in affectionate reassurance. The smallest hesitation in my answer to this cross-examination would have meant a closer examination. I felt empty of all substance, my emotions tied in a knot on the seat beside me. The Gestapo agent went on with his careful examination: outside in the corridor, another one had slipped by and looked on.

"Now, open all cases…" he said suddenly. That was the end. Paulette? Caught… they'd say back in England. I got ready my case, adopting an air of utter boredom, a why-can't-I-go-on-reading-in-peace air. But it was the end. I looked outside the window; the trees were flying by, at top speed. If ever you have to jump from a moving train, they'd said in England, remember your parachute practice. But how would I get to the window? Feet together and parallel to the ground… I could see Jean-Claude from the corner of my eye; he was rubbing his hip, feeling for his gun. A little bit of shooting, what a perfect frame for an end… And not a hope. My mind was a blur again, my legs cotton-wool and I felt slightly sick. But, something was happening… The woman in the corner, the woman with the babies, was talking.

"You can't make me open all that..?" she was saying. "I'll take hours to do these parcels up again. They contain butter and fat; this one contains some wool. And how would I hold the babies while I untied them?" Then more gently and full of charm: "Please? It would mean so much work and nothing in them would interest you..?"

"All right," said the man, gruff and surly. It was probably the nearest thing to a good action he had done in all his criminal existence. "Just open your big case – also, I want to see this one and this one," he went on, pointing to two others, one of which was my neighbour's.

Not mine... My heart sang. Two seconds later he went out. I remembered François de Tranche's admonition and went on reading until Jean-Claude walked into the compartment. He was as white as a sheet: I was sure to be the same. My neighbour had gone into the corridor for a while; Jean-Claude took his place and leaned against my shoulder.

"It was awful, wasn't it?" he said softly.

But, in the corner, the woman with the babies looked on with a smile. Had she understood? Had she done it on purpose? I smiled back, but I couldn't help wondering what was in her parcels... You became like that, suspicious of everything. She was young and she was pretty.

Maybe she will recognize herself here. In that case, all I can say is: Thank you.

CHAPTER XII

"I tell you they won't come…" Robert Laroche was saying. "They've been making fun of us, all this time."

"Don't be silly, Robert. You know very well that the whole point of our being here is because they will invade."

"I bet that's just a pose to make the Boche jumpy. For nearly three months now, we have been expecting them daily. You'll see they won't come; they'll let the Russians kill all the Germans first. They played us the same trick last year, in October, when they warned us to stand by and never came. The Americans want to make money out of the war while the British try and pose as the saviours of the world. Meanwhile here, every day that goes by, people get caught, arrested and deported… I tell you I'm sick of waiting and I'm going to quit."

"Well, you are nothing better than a coward," I replied, furious. "You've worked for years with nothing but hope, and just before the end you make a big noise and let everybody down. And I'll tell you something more: you are a defeatist and what you say is as bad as fifth-column work… Let me talk… You undermine the organisation around us just because you're discouraged, and you do a lot of harm. Deep down, you know as well as I do that the Allies will invade, and you ought to be upholding the morale of people around you."

Robert Laroche didn't quit. No one did. But everyone felt the way he did. Even the peaceful and optimistic Colomiers in his summer-specked Dordogne began to think that the invasion would not take place. They all thought that the Allies were going to smash Germany from the air only, and that it would take months. The Patron was discouraged; his radio operator stayed up night after night in the hope of receiving the preliminary A messages. The four marked days of the months passed each time in tense listening to the radio, but nothing came.

I was getting discouraged too. I wondered what had become of my family, whether they had any news of me. I had received two or three messages: "Whole family well and safe – send their love." Or, "Father says: Quote – Thinking about you every day. All well. Mother back in Oxford – Unquote." Why was she back in Oxford? Had they been bombed in London? I had read hair-raising reports in the French press on the bombing of London in the early part of 1944; they were exaggerated, of course, but I knew that raids had started again. Nevertheless, I did all I could to encourage people: sometimes I invented vague messages of warning from London, but the most effective thing was to look mysterious – "Ah, Paulette knows something, but she can't tell us…" they thought. And hope would spring again, a little weaker every time.

The Patron arrived at Nasoulens one warm afternoon.

"You wanted to go on a longer trip, Paulette; well, here it is. You must leave for Paris tomorrow morning."

"My God!… But I washed all my clothes this afternoon. I won't have anything to wear. Can't it wait another day?"

"I'm afraid not. You have to go there to contact Galles.[1] I told you about him; he used to work with me, then went to England, and was dropped back in Brittany a few months ago. His radio operator has been caught and he sent a courier to me while you were in Montréjeau, with a number of messages to transmit to London for him. Now they've sent a long answer which you will have to take. It concerns dropping-fields in Brittany, a new system of signals to the planes, coded pin-points, and the key to code messages he will receive by regular broadcasts. You will have to travel by night, I'm afraid. I expect you to be in Paris the day after tomorrow. After that you must go to Tours and contact T— who is a radio operator: here is a message which he'll have to transmit to London."

He handed me five slips of paper with orders which I learnt by heart and then burned. I was filled with the same excited expectancy as before my first missions at the beginning of the year. I dried my clothes in front of an open fire and pressed my black suit which I'd never worn yet.

I had a rendezvous with Colomiers a few days later. Marie would have to go in my place, so I went to Agen the next morning and gave her all the necessary details. In the afternoon I took the train for Montauban, where I caught the night express from Toulouse to Paris.

The middle of May 1944 was an ill-chosen moment to travel in France. The BBC warned French people several times a day not to travel by night, because all trains were attacked indiscriminately under cover of darkness. Besides the little disadvantage of being bombed on the way, the Resistance sabotaged the lines at frequent intervals. Derailments caused large numbers of casualties, because the Germans removed most of the modern carriages, and those left were made of wood.

I climbed into one of the last carriages, those being the least destroyed in accidents, and walked into a compartment, empty except for one man slouched in a corner, his hat pulled over his eyes. As I placed my case in the rack:

"Hello," he said. "Now, isn't this a coincidence?"

I nearly fell into my seat with astonishment and horror. The stranger of the Tarbes bus... For a second I thought of running away, but the car was nearly empty and he could easily follow me. Also, I would have appeared guilty of something.

"Hello," I said. "I didn't expect to see you here..." Which was an unintelligent sort of remark.

"Ah," he said, pushing his hat to the back of his head, "that is what fate does to people. It was written that we would meet again. Do you know, I like you much better with your hair in curls: you should never wear it otherwise... And my, but you are smart, all dressed up like this. Altogether a great improvement on the last time I saw you."

"Well, Paris and Tarbes aren't the same..." I replied weakly.

"No, certainly not. And what are you going to do this time? Fetch more little nieces and nephews? Or am I being indiscreet?"

"Yes, you are. I'm just going on a little pleasure trip. I miss Paris terribly and I'm going to see my friends for a change."

"Now isn't that true. So do I... Only I wouldn't risk bombs and sabotaged rails for it..."

"Well, why *are* you risking them, then?"

"I'm going on business; it's not the same thing. Do you know, I've often thought of you. And the more I think of it, the more I wonder what you do. Now I'm intrigued all over again: there you were, with plaits around your head, with an old skirt and handbag – your coat was crumpled and your shoes dirty, but one was of excellent cloth, the other of excellent leather. And now, you've completely changed personality; you look younger and yet more sophisticated. That suit of yours is of still better cloth than the crumpled coat, and you have a decent handbag... You must be pretty rich to buy all that stuff on the black market, because you can't get it anywhere else. *Who* are you, anyway?"

"Now look, once and for all. I told you who I was; I can't be bothered to repeat it. What is more, you annoy me. What is more you are rude and indiscreet. What is more, if it is your wish to make me a mysterious heroine of your imagination, go ahead – I don't mind. Only leave me in peace. I want to read my book..."

I buried my face in another book picked out by Jean-Claude. It was a mystic satire of life: something between Voltaire's *Candide* and *Alice in Wonderland*. But I couldn't concentrate properly. This man had a fiendish memory. In England I had been told to vary my appearance according to my surroundings. In Tarbes I looked like a Tarbaise; in Paris I would look like a Parisienne. But I never thought someone might bump into me at both ends. Or rather, I had not counted on meeting anyone so observant and intelligent as this man. He had put on a childish expression and sat looking at me steadily. After a time, he couldn't bear it any longer.

"That's an awful book you're reading. Talk to me. I've just concluded that you belong to the Gestapo…"

"Well, aren't you scared?" I said from my book.

"Possibly. But then maybe I do too… In that case wouldn't you be scared?"

"No, why should I? There we are, two people belonging to the same organisation. Perfectly comfortable…"

"Hem, I'm not so sure…"

Neither was I. If he *did* belong to the Gestapo, I would never get off the train. If he belonged to the Resistance and thought I belonged to the Gestapo, I wouldn't get off the train either. I was slightly frightened and very restless. Yet I had an instinct that nothing would happen to me. At Cahors, two people entered the compartment: I wanted to hug them. The dark young stranger leaned back in his seat and said no more, but he did not take his eyes off me for a moment. Further on, at Brive, the compartment filled up completely. He offered me some bread and cheese and a drop of armagnac. In the night I was cold; he insisted on taking off his *canadienne* and wrapping it round my legs. He shivered all the rest of the day, but nothing would induce him to take it back.

As we pulled out of Brive the sirens went and I wondered at the irony of being bombed by the RAF. However, I was lucky: Châteauroux and Brive were both bombed after the train had passed. In the morning we passed the railway yards of Juvisy, outside Paris, which had been smashed a few days earlier: the sight brought a heavy lump to my throat. Of several kilometres' width of tracks, one single one remained open: the train drove by slowly. Everywhere rubble and ruins, pylons twisting their steel arms in frantic agony, electric engines standing with their tails to the sky and their nose in the ground; others, upside down like dead animals, had several rings of rail twisted right round them. Everyone looked out of the window in dead silence: how can such a sight be forgotten?

In spite of everything, we arrived in Paris less than an hour late. At the station, the stranger-from-the-bus insisted on carrying my suitcase to the cloakroom. I could see I would never get rid of him without resorting to tricks. Fortunately he ran into a friend as we walked out of the station.

"Please come and have dinner with me tomorrow night," he pleaded.

"I'm sorry. I've already got an engagement. I told you I was going to see friends: I shall be very busy."

"Never mind your friends… Come anyway. I'll be at eight o'clock at the buffet at the Gare St-Lazare, whatever happens. I'll look out for you."

I wonder if he did. And I wonder who he was.

The address the Patron had given me was in Vanves, a rather poor suburb in the southwest of Paris. I found the flat just before lunchtime and was shown to a narrow drawing-room by a small, dark-haired woman who eyed me suspiciously. She rushed back to the front door and locked it, then disappeared for five minutes. It was a typical French petit-bourgeois room: a wallpaper covered with violently-coloured shapeless designs over every inch, heavily-framed pictures representing the sunset over a cornfield, the sunset over the sea, and the sunset over a mountain, a buffet taking up half the room with flowered plates leaning against it, and mass-produced chairs with red, plush coverings. I sat on one of them, feeling rather depressed. The woman returned with her husband.

"I hear you want to see Galles?"

"Yes, as soon as possible. I have some messages for him."

"He's away…" looking at his wife uncomfortably.

"Well, I'm afraid I'll have to chase him wherever he is."

"He's in Morlaix," he admitted reluctantly. In Brittany. And what's more, in the forbidden zone of Brittany: I had no hope of getting to Morlaix without a special coastal permit. And I had no contacts to smuggle myself through the lines… These people evidently were not going to be helpful; they were frightened.

"Well, can you let him know that someone is here to see him, and get him to come to Paris urgently?"

"Yes, I can do that. I'll write and say his mother wants to see him; he'll understand, because she's been dead four years. He'll probably be here within five or six days. Why don't you come back on Saturday?"

Obviously they didn't want me to stay. In a way I was glad; their flat offered no possible way of escape; it was on the sixth floor. Moreover, I distrusted them. I found myself in the street. Where should I go? I didn't know what had become of people I knew who lived in Paris before the war, but a friend of my parents, the only other person beside my father who knew before I left England that I was going to France, had told me to go to his daughter Janet,[2] if I needed any help in Paris. I had not seen her for ten years, but she was my only hope. At least she might indicate some hotel where the number of my Lot-et-Garonne papers would not be taken down. I had lunch in a little restaurant in a park just outside Vanves, then proceeded to find her flat.

"Mademoiselle Périer? I don't know who that is," I heard her say as the maid announced me. "But show her in."

"I don't suppose you will ever recognise me, Janet…" I told her.

"You're quite right. I have no idea who you are."

"Anne-Marie Walters…"

It was the first time I had spoken my name in five months. It sounded strange, as though I were talking about someone else.

"Anne-Marie," she cried. "But what are you doing here? Weren't you in England?"

"Yes. And I saw your father four months ago, too."

Janet sat down, speechless.

"Yes, indeed, I recognise you now... Or rather, I recognise your mother's mannerisms. But how on earth did you get here?"

I told her how I had come and what I was doing.

"I'll think all this over while I get some tea ready," she said. "I found some in the black market a few days ago."

While she was away, I filled my eyes with the sight of soft carpets, ruffled lampshades, cushions and flowers. A sense of well-being began to creep slowly over me, beginning from the contact with the deep and cosy armchair I had sunk into. As Jenny set out the tea on a low Chinese table, the front door opened and the flat was filled with voices.

"Here are my daughters. They've been out on their afternoon walk."

Babet, three years old, came running in and flung her arms around her mother's neck.

"Babet, this is Anne-Marie."

"Sainte-Marie," Babet repeated docilely. "*Bonjou'*, Sainte-Marie." Which was my name from then on...

"Now, here comes the problem child," said Janet, as Caroline, eighteen months and screaming, was brought in. "These are the worst moments of the day..." Caroline, red-faced and furious, was placed on her pot, right in the middle of the room: there she kicked and jerked herself along until she reached the edge of the tea-table. Before anyone had time to interfere, she caught hold of a cup and threw it on the floor, spilt the sugar-bowl and covered herself with jam. She howled with delight as her mother cleared up the mess.

"Imagine, it appears that the gas supply is going to be completely cut and that we shall have to eat in Communal Restaurants. Can you see me queuing for my food with this fury under my arm?"

"But why Communal Restaurants?"

"Of course, I forget that you don't know what life is like in Paris today. We have electricity from 8pm until 7am, and none during the day. The gas is so low that half a dozen potatoes – that's when you can *find* half a dozen potatoes – take two and a half hours to cook... So you see that, without gas, there can be no question of eating cooked food. And you can't get tinned food, so that the Communal Restaurants will be unavoidable. I shrink from the thought. But, Anne-

Marie, don't bother about a bed for tonight anyway, we have so much to talk about that you can't leave tonight."

It turned out, Janet found that we had so much to talk about that I stayed with her all the time, to my intense relief.

Walking about Paris the next day, I had a most extraordinary encounter. As I walked down the crowded and busy Underground station of Marbeuf, I ran into Marie's brother, Georges VanderBock, coming out.[3]

"What on earth are you doing here?" I asked.

"I came to see you." It was already a shock to hear the Agen accent.

The coincidence was almost unbelievable. "Now look here, don't be funny, Georges…"

"I assure you, the Patron sent me urgently to see you. I arrived this morning."

We went up into the open air.

"I didn't find you at Vanves: I was going to wait until Saturday and meet you there then."

"But why? Has something happened?"

"Yes. The radio operator in Tours has been caught. The Patron received a message from London yesterday, warning him that you must not go there… Apparently, the Gestapo has laid a trap and is waiting for whoever is to contact T—; two people have been caught already like that."

"And what were you going to do if you had missed me on Saturday?"

"Go to Tours and meet all the Paris trains until I found you… I couldn't do anything else. I didn't want to tell those people in Vanves about all this: I didn't know what they knew and I didn't like them. They nearly threw me out of their house."

Two amazing coincidences in three days, one mysterious, the other warning me of danger…

I stayed in Paris a fortnight. Galles never came; instead he sent a messenger to explain that his circuit was in the process of breaking up, and asking me to leave my messages at Vanves. I left a long, coded letter to him, which he found when he came to Paris a few days later.

There was an anaesthetising feeling of security in the big city. It seemed so easy to be lost in a crowd, so easy to be going about with the simple excuse of shopping or sightseeing. Yet, a persistent discomfort trailed behind me: it was also so easy to be followed a whole day without being able to detect it, and so easy to forget all rules of security amongst many people and temptations. But, had I not been worried for Janet's safety, the discomfort and self-consciousness would have quickly receded. That was how so many agents were caught in Paris and other big cities.

One afternoon I went to the rue des Saussaies, one of the Gestapo's headquarters,[4] drawn by a sense of morbid curiosity. How many of my own friends, the men and women I had trained with in England, had spent endless and terrifying hours of cross-examination behind those black walls? How many were there now? Being tortured perhaps? After a while I turned my back and fled.

The trees on the banks of the Seine were in bloom. The quays were tinted with mauve, and a sweet-scented cloud shadowed Paris. The streets, wide and bare, were silent. Few cars drove along them, and then, they were German army cars or the suspicious, petrol-driven tractions. The swastika flapped arrogantly on the Madeleine. The perspective of the big cross-roads was wrecked by enormous and hideous black-and-white indicators, showing everything, from the nearest lavatories to the Opera. Paris stood big and cold under the occupation.

But the women's hats, like the 'zazous' in 1940, were a defiance to the unimaginative Prussian stiffness, tall, coloured, gay, flowered, ribboned and overwhelming. At first, with my eyes still full of the memory of the flat, small London hats, I was shocked, then soon delighted: I bought one. It took me two days to make up my mind. A hat with two tall feathers emerging from a cheeky bunch of red, blue and yellow marabou feathers.

Babet exclaimed: "Sainte-Marie has bought a hat..." and tried it on. Her whole face disappeared beneath it. Caroline howled with rapturous joy; she wanted to try it on too. But I had got wise to Caroline, and laid my treasure on a high shelf.

On May 24th, I went back to my warm south, but not without creeping cautiously into my compartment. I was through with coincidences... At the farm, I was greeted with the usual open arms and gay welcome.

"Hello, Petite. How was Paris?"

Fany and Sirrou licked my hands, the white cat rubbed herself against my legs, Brunette opened an uninterested eye between two mouthfuls of the front lawn: I was Paulette again. It was easy. In Paris, I had stepped right out of my assumed personalities in the home-like atmosphere of Janet's family. Back in the familiar surroundings, all that appeared distant and nearly artificial. With sincere pleasure I resumed my blue apron, my *sabots* and my wide straw hat – for, with the summer sun, the grandmother had won the last round of the battle. She stood gazing at my Paris hat, rubbing her hands on her apron: then she picked it up gently, between two fingers, and, without a word, looked at it all over. She had never been any further than Condom, and listened to my stories of the capital, at dinner-time, like wondrous fairy-tales.

While I was in Paris, Jean-Claude had been ordered by London to undertake another demolition: the Lorraine-Dietrich factory in Bagnères, which repaired railway material damaged by bombing. He did it with Auguste, Raymond Mautrens and another boy.[5]

"You could roller-skate in the power-room," was his sententious conclusion after he had told me about it. "The only trouble was that we didn't get away quickly enough and received a shower of broken glass on our heads. But we had only a few cuts…"

The Patron decided that Jean-Claude was to be transferred to the Dordogne. Colomiers had reported the presence of suspicious people who claimed to have come from England; he couldn't enquire into it himself in case it turned out to be a Gestapo trap and because his capture would endanger the success of D-Day action in his whole district. Jean-Claude enquired into it and the matter was soon cleared: the men were genuine London-sent agents.[6] But I was not to see Jean-Claude again for many weeks.

Moondrop to Gascony

Part II

Chapter XIII

June 1st, 1944 – The A messages, the first warnings of impending action, were broadcast over the BBC at lunchtime.

The few people who knew what they meant could hardly believe their ears. The work they had done for so many months was to be suddenly crowned: but crowned with success or failure? No one knew. The issue was looked upon with vague disbelief and mistrust: it was better that way. But hopes rose to a peak where security had no reach: the following days were certainly the most dangerous for the Resistance. In the southwest of France an airborne landing was expected, and all plans of action were centred around it.[1]

The Patron sent me urgently to Montréjeau to make sure that Roger had heard the news and was ready. In Tarbes, I went to Raymond Mautrens' shop, to make sure his teams were ready too. In his back shop I found Miette, morose and dejected.

"What are you doing here, Miette? Who is looking after your cats?"

"My poor Paulette, I don't know… The Picolets were arrested two days ago. It was sheer luck that I wasn't caught too."

"My God, what awful news… How did it happen?"

"We don't quite know yet. But we believe that it was through double-agents of the Gestapo. Some men saying they belonged to the Resistance came about a week ago, to ask for a contact with Pyrenees guides: they said they were closely trailed by the Gestapo. Then they left, saying they'd be back in a few days…"

"And then?"

"Well, it was the Luchon Gestapo who came. We think that those men belonged to it, and that the Picolets fell into a trap." Miette could hardly talk, she was so upset.

"Come on, Miette. What happened next?"

"They just walked into her kitchen, and before she knew what was happening a gun was pointed at her stomach and she heard her husband telling her not to move because there was nothing to be done. They have been taken to the prison of St-Michel in Toulouse."[2]

"Did they go to your house? How did you escape?"

"I was having my hair washed in Montréjeau when someone rushed into the shop saying that the Picolets had just been arrested, and that the Gestapo was waiting for me in my house. Fortunately Roger was in Tarbes. I came out of the hairdresser's and took the next train for Tarbes, without going back home, of course. I haven't been there since... God knows what's happening to the cats."

It was terrible ill-luck, so near the end. I thought of Jacqueline Picolet's baby face; of her constant good-humour, of the pancakes she had cooked, way into the night, while Jean-Claude and I warmed ourselves near the big open fire in her kitchen.

Also, their arrest endangered the Pyrenees sector: they did not know the A and B messages, but they knew the positions of various arms depots and of the landing fields. These would all have to be changed and it meant heavy work for the Patron's radio operator. Miette assured me that the Picolets would never talk: but no one could tell with the methods of the Gestapo.

Roger came in a little later on, and fumed and cursed.

"Of course I've heard the messages, of course... What does the Patron think I am? Of course I'm ready. As soon as I get the B messages, my teams will cut the railway and telephone lines, but I can't do any more; we haven't enough arms. If I started making ambushes on the Nationale 117, there would soon be no ammunition left. And then, how would I hold the grounds for an airborne landing?"

Back at Nasoulens I found a message from the Patron. It appeared that the Feldgendarmarie had spent the afternoon in Condom, asking about a "fair-haired girl who lived in the neighbourhood." The Patron thought they were looking for me, and ordered me not to leave the farm. Did the mysterious stranger from the Tarbes bus have anything to do with this?

The next few days were spent in feverish expectancy: how, when and where would the Allies land? They would soon reduce the Germans in the southwest to a nasty memory. There were only three or four divisions in the Toulouse area.

The Patron told me how he was going to start up a *maquis*. To carry out London's triple orders – attacks on railway lines, attacks on telephone and telegraph lines, and general guerrilla warfare[3] – a starting point and headquarters were necessary. He would make them at Castelnau. The village seemed well situated, being on high ground and safe from surprise attacks.

At eight o'clock on the morning of June 6th, the Patron arrived in his small Simca car. The sun was shining in a cloudless blue sky. "Well, have you heard?" he shouted, as I poked a sleepy head through my window. "They've landed in Normandy..."

"No…? Wait a minute, I'll be downstairs in a second." I didn't *go* downstairs, I *flew* downstairs.

"Quick, tell me more…" I tuned the radio onto the BBC wavelength. "*La Marseillaise,*" "*The Star-spangled Banner*" and "*God Save the King*" filled the kitchen.

"Yes, they landed at 6.30 this morning. We were warned in the middle of the night. Eisenhower has made a broadcast to the French; de Gaulle will speak at lunchtime; and I'm going to start the *maquis* tomorrow…" The Patron was so excited that his already poor French was getting completely incomprehensible.

"We must tell the Cérensacs," I cried. Henri had been cautious and doubtful of the enthusiasm brought by the messages of June 1st. I couldn't wait to cry to him: "See? The Allies keep their promises after all… Finished the doubts and mistrust of four years of lies. You can hope openly now… And no one will stop you…"

I ran all the way to the vines where the whole family was at work, jumped over the wire supports and waved my hands over my head.

"They've landed!…" I yelled.

They dropped their instruments and ran to meet me. Everybody kissed everybody else and wiped away furtive tears of emotion. We all returned to the farm for a quick celebration, shouted the news to the neighbours, who'd already heard it from other neighbours, crowded into the kitchen and sipped a small glass of deep golden armagnac, while the radio trembled under the thundering national anthems of the Allies. All day it played them.

The Patron went back to Castelnau, after suggesting that I should stay at Nasoulens until things got started: there was nothing much I could do anyway. No one worked that day, all the neighbours dropped in to discuss the Allied strategy: some said the Germans would collapse right away, others that it would be a long fight because of the Siegfried Line, but no one expressed defeatism – in two days Paris would be taken, in two weeks Berlin…

The young men of Condom rolled their fathers' old army kit and a few warm clothes in a blanket and started up to the *maquis*. Within two days Castelnau was so overcrowded that there wasn't room for a cat. The enthusiasm had to be quenched and the young farmers sent back to their homes to cut the corn and help feed the *maquis*. For a few days the muddle was frightful: people were disappointed to see that the Allies were not going to land in the southwest right away and that the fighting and rounding up of collaborators shouldn't start immediately.

After things began to get organised, the Patron came back. He had pulled back the roof of his small car and, as he approached, I caught sight of a pointed head sticking through in the most comic fashion.

"This is Mike," the Patron said in English.[4] "A New Zealand pilot who has just joined us. He was shot down a month or so ago and has been moving from *maquis* to *maquis*. Now he will stay with us for a while."

Mike was six foot or more high, with large blue eyes in a thin, bird-like face. He stuttered a little because he was shy. He stepped out of the car like an overgrown spider.

"I-I'm very glad t-to meet you," he said, nearly shaking my arm off. That's the only thing he said that day.

The Patron told me that the *maquis* was more or less organised, that the constant flow of people had at last been stopped, and that guerrilla action was going to start. An important store of arms had been made at Castelnau from the numerous *parachutages* made in the neighbourhood. He suggested I should go up and help with washing up and other fatigues "proper for women." He was tired and jumpy.

"I haven't had a single night's sleep since the *maquis* was started," he declared. That was four days ago. I began to see the change that would take place in my life: he had his 'staff' now, mostly young French officers who had been hiding for the past months and working with the Resistance. I would no longer be a confidante, he was too busy. And I was a woman, and not supposed to understand 'military strategy'. Also I was becoming part of a crowd, no longer an individual in the underground movement.

In the afternoon, I packed a few things in my old travelling bag, tied it on the back of my bicycle, put on my oldest farm skirt and got ready to go.

"You'll come back, won't you, Petite?" Cérensac said. "I don't like to see you go up there."

"Of course I will. First because I'll miss you. Then because I'll soon crave for a little rest…"

Castelnau was full of noise and movement: men dashing about, car engines running all over the place, women peeling piles of carrots and potatoes on their doorstep. Everybody talked at once, no one listened to what the other was saying: the *maquis* looked more like a busy market-place than fighting headquarters. The headquarters themselves, or PC as we called it (Command Post), were in the old schoolhouse on the village square. In front of it, Robert Laroche, Privat and other men were organising an expedition.

"We're going to re-take a depot which the Milice captured four weeks ago," they told me. "They're in an old castle near Agen; maybe we'll get a chance to shoot a few down…"[5]

They looked very business-like and important; their sleeves rolled up, scarves tied around their necks, and guns, Sten and magazines stuck out of every pocket.

They had mounted a Bren gun on the front of their car, and started out like heroes, followed by a storm of good wishes. The rest of the *maquis* looked on, hands in their pockets, longing to go too.

I went in search of a room. Most of the men slept in barns or disused houses or, as the nights were already warm, simply rolled up in blankets under the trees. After endless difficulties, I was allowed to sleep in the drawing-room of the smartest house in the village. Half of it was taken up with piles of crockery and glasses. I laid a thin, hay mattress in the furthest corner, and hid my little bag under the sofa. The sofa had two large, fancy cushions on top of it: on the cushions, two dolls, with wide, pink satin dresses and white silk hair, sat with dangling legs and a stupid expression. They looked absurdly incongruous in the dirty room and, after a while, irritated by their half-witted faces, I wrapped them up in an old cloth and pushed them under the sofa. They were indignantly retrieved the next day by the proprietor, who packed them up carefully in a trunk.

At seven, the heroes returned, but not so noisily: the expedition had brought no result, except the using up of precious petrol. The Milice had vanished to an unknown destination with the captured depot, and was nowhere to be found.

I had dinner with the Patron and his personal staff; I was made to understand that I was to consider myself lucky to be treated with such honour, which put me in a bad mood. Already I was not too pleased, because Robert Laroche and Privat had been telling everyone that I had been parachuted: people wanted to know "what it was like," and stopped considering me like any other French girl, to my great disappointment. The Auch bus driver, who had joined us, exclaimed:

"Do you know that I once reported you as a Gestapo agent to the Resistance in Condom? No wonder they said they thought you were not…"

At ten, I retired. That night, and the following ones, went something like this. First the room stank of acetylene gas; it caught at my throat and choked me. I put the lamp outside, but even then the fumes found their way through the open window. Then, the room had no shutters, so I had to undress in the dark. I crept to my hay mattress, stumbling over my bag and crashed head-first on it. Utterly bad-tempered by then, I rolled myself up in my blanket, mumbling and swearing under my breath. I could feel the floor right through the hay, tossed and turned and finally fell asleep at about 3am. At five, two men walked into the room, chatting and joking gaily. I woke up with a start. They each picked up a pile of plates and went out. I turned over and tried to fall asleep again. But two minutes later they walked in again, shouting at someone in the corridor – they hadn't seen me in my corner. I shouted furiously:

"Don't make so much noise!…"

They looked at each other, startled. "Say, someone is asleep here," and, little concerned, walked out laughing. They kept coming back until they had removed all the plates; they were getting breakfast ready. The mess was right opposite my room. When the last dish had gone, I heaved a sigh of relief and thought I would snatch a little more sleep. But, too soon: breakfast began. Thirty or forty men shouted and laughed right outside my window. It was six o'clock. At seven, the two returned with their piles of plates neatly washed: pile after pile… I gave up. They took hours before it was all back and I had to wait until they had finished, to start dressing.

Finally it was over. I got up and dressed hurriedly: there was no key to the door and anyone could walk in at any moment. I went to the kitchen for a wash: five people were queuing for the only pail of water. Despair drove me all the way down the hill to the Auvignon. But there I found all the rest of the *maquis* indulging in a thorough morning toilet… I tried not to see them, washed my face hurriedly and ran all the way up again.

And so it went on. After four days of this, I went to Nasoulens, scrubbed myself in the duck-pond and slept fifteen hours at a stretch. André Cérensac came back to Castelnau with me; he couldn't bear to stay out of the *maquis* any more. Odilla burst into tears.

"I-I had a son and a daughter," she sobbed in her apron. "Now I have no one left…"

The life of the *maquis* was desperately dull. After the first two or three days of enthusiasm were over, the men became terribly bored. They had nothing to do all day: the Germans were scattered at great distances from Castelnau and expeditions were rare. The telephone lines had been cut in hundreds of places and a number of *miliciens* and collaborators were caught. We had fifteen in all; they had to be shut up in the church, as no other house was available as a prison, and were marched to one of the barns for their meals, twice a day and under heavy escort. The men booed and scorned them on the way. Then nine Germans were added to them; they refused point-blank to be kept in the church in the company of 'traitors', as they asserted, spitting on the ground. So they were kept in another place and made to do the dirtiest fatigues in the *maquis*, at their own request.

The padre of the *maquis* was an old priest, the *curé de* B—.[6] He had become famous in the region for his patriotic sermons. Already in 1942 he would curse and condemn the Germans from the height of his pulpit, in the simple and outspoken language of the district. He would get so excited that he'd forget the time and talk on and on for hours. One day the Bishop had called him and warned him to be careful, but he declared "I'm darned if I will…" and had turned his back and walked away, leaving the Bishop speechless. Everyone had thought that he would be removed, but the incident was not pursued and he had carried on. He tore about the countryside on a bicycle, his *soutane* flying in the wind and his bare feet in the dirtiest pair of worn-out old *sabots*.

On Sunday mornings now the *miliciens* and collaborators were all parked in one corner of the church during Mass. The altar was brilliant with flowers and flags and the door had to be left open, as the church was too small to hold all the *maquisards*.

"Nazism and the Vichy Fascist institutions are anti-Christian," the *curé de* B— declaimed, walking up and down in front of the altar. "We have taken up arms because it is our duty to contribute to the defeat of evil. We shall carry on until the Germans are beaten. *Vive la France!…*"

And with a wide, sweeping gesture of his arms he spurred the whole congregation to a stirring "*Marseillaise*", bursting out of the men's hearts to the roof of the little village church and out into the serene, Sunday blue sky. All the *maquisards* turned to the *miliciens* in patriotic defiance, and their message was so strong that the traitors turned to the wall in shame and humility and stood gazing at their feet. The *curé de* B— followed us during all the following weeks, saying Mass wherever he could to the *maquis*, then rushing off to his parish church, always on his bicycle, always dirty and unshaven, doing a bit of fighting here and a lot of sermoning there.

The instruction of the men was a difficult subject. There were about one hundred and fifty of them, mostly ignorant of the use of firearms. They were organised in small companies under a regular army officer and trained as well as possible; practice firing was an impossibility: ammunition was too short and it would have raised chaos in the neighbourhood. They learnt how to strip and clean their arms, how to take firing positions. It was all rather incomplete and theoretical, but the best that could be done. A few accidents occurred: Dr Driziers, who had joined us, fixed a small infirmary in the schoolhouse and looked after them.

The worst problem of the *maquis*, at all times, was the feeding. The farms around provided us with vegetables, fruit and wine. Also with live cattle: Privat, the butcher, killed them and cut them up in the main square. I used to hide when these disgusting operations took place. I couldn't bear watching the dead calves being blown up with bicycle pumps. The Condom cooperative sold us sugar, coffee, bread and cigarettes and the trucks went daily on the rounds for food. VanderBock was in charge of the quartermaster's stores. At first I helped him with his work, but soon refused to go on; he would not keep any accounts or follow any given plan, and I could not stand the lack of organisation.

One morning I ran into a young Parisian journalist. We agreed to try and edit a *maquis* paper, to inform the men of the war news and keep them interested. They were students, workmen, farmers or shopkeepers, all thrown together with nothing to do but wait for their meals, or argue over who would go on the rare expeditions; they were utterly bored and fast losing their initial spirit. I got hold of a typewriter and reams of paper from the cooperative, and together we started a daily news-sheet. We worked way into the night, issuing eighteen copies of detailed news of the Normandy fighting, which we listened to on small radios parachuted from London, and working on batteries. Also news of the Resistance in the southwest. They had to be typed three times over: we relayed our painful labour to the companies and the smaller groups. Our little paper was quickly popular, as the men had no other means of knowing the news.

A number of Republican Spaniards joined us at the end of the first week. They were hardened to guerrilla warfare and used to a tough life, being all veteran fighters of the Civil War. Their chief, Alcazio, was an amazing character.[7] He had lost a leg in the Civil War, but had nevertheless fought the 1940 campaign in France. He had been part of the Resistance since the defeat of France.

"My little Paulette," he used to tell me, "I don't know what will become of me on the day I stop fighting. I'm a warrior and nothing else. I think I shall go to Mexico or South America and make revolutions there. I can never hope for a normal life," he would add sadly. "No woman would marry me, with this leg…"

"Now, Alcazio, why not? All women don't look only at men's physique. I don't see why one should not fall in love with you?"

"Do you think so?" he would say, trying to convince himself and very ready to believe me. All he wanted was to be told that as often as possible.

Alcazio had thick, long black hair shining with icy-blue lights. He wore it long down to his neck and usually said he had no time to have it cut, to excuse his secret pleasure at his romantic appearance. He had a hard, sun-tanned face with large, pitch-black eyes. He walked on crutches, and refused to admit a physical inferiority because of his leg, driving cars at hectic speeds, and wrecking engines in a few days with the rough treatment he imposed on the gear-box.

"I used to race in Madrid," he would tell me as we whizzed around road bends. It looked more as though he had raced in tanks. Alcazio never bothered to get out and open gates; he went clean through them. The result was that the fronts of his cars were made to hold together with wire or, more often than not, were just not there.

I wasted hours with Alcazio in Castelnau. At two in the morning, he would call me to type reports for him.

"You must do what he wants," the Patron told me. "I want the Spaniards to stay with us. They are good fighters and very helpful."

So I would spend hours typing six lines of a report on Alcazio's activities of the day. He always began: "To the Colonel, from the Commander of the Spanish forces

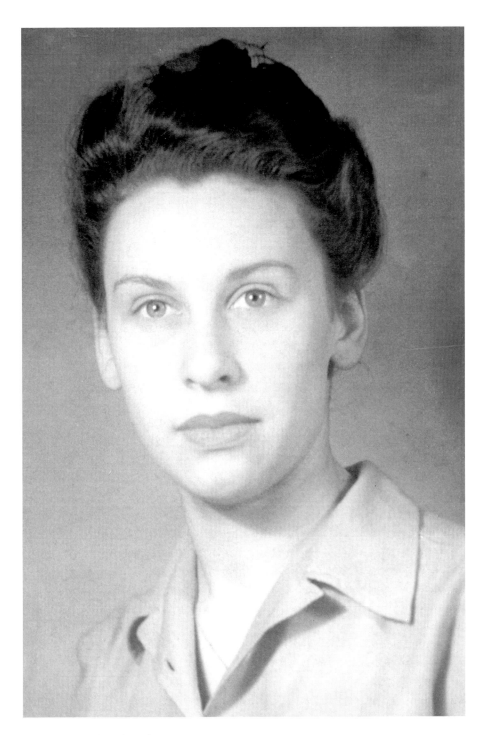

Anne-Marie in the early 1940s.

LEFT: Anne-Marie at Ecole Internationale, aged 13.

RIGHT: Anne-Marie in WAAF uniform, early 1940s.

LEFT: Claude Arnault (*Néron*), sabotage instructor for WHEELWRIGHT (known in the text as 'Jean-Claude').

RIGHT: Lt Col G R Starr (*Hilaire, Gaston*), DSO, MC, Légion d'Honneur, Croix de Guerre ('The *Patron*').

WHEELWRIGHT memorial, Lapeyrade, Landes.

ABOVE: Anne-Marie with the Castagnos family at Mamoulens. *Left to right:* Maria Dupourquet (mother of Odilla), André, Marcelle (André's wife), Odilla, Anne-Marie and Henri Castagnos.

LEFT: Roger Larribeau, Mayor of Castelnau-sur-l'Auvignon 1935–1971.

Above: Agents of the Wheelwright circuit at Gabarret. *Front row, left to right*: Didier Bengué, René Barbères, Robert Barrère, Omer Duprat. *Back row, left to right*: Albert Cantal, Gabriel Cantal, Georges Fleutiaux, Jean Duprat, Gervais Dumergue, Emilie Cantal, Justin Téchené.

Above: Joseph & Alice Darroux, owners of the café at Fourcès.

ABOVE: Juliette Mansencal ('Miette'), wife of Roland Mansencal ('Roger').

ABOVE LEFT: Flight Officer Yvonne Cormeau WAAF (*Annette*), MBE, Légion d'Honneur, Croix de Guerre. Radio Operator for WHEELWRIGHT.

LEFT: Railway timetable Southwest France, November 1943, used by Yvonne Cormeau.

Baron Philippe de Gunzbourg (*Philibert*), MBE ('Colomiers'). De Gunzbourg estimated he covered 20,000 km by bicycle whilst organising WHEELWRIGHT's Dordogne sector.

LEFT AND ABOVE: Paul Dufazza ('Picolet') and his wife Marie ('Jacqueline'), members of WHEELWRIGHT in Mazères.

BELOW LEFT: Jeanne Robert, schoolmistress at Castelnau-sur-l'Auvignon.

BELOW: Marius Sorbé ('Monsieur Chénier') and his wife Etiennette, owners of outfitters shops at Seissan and Boulogne-sur-Gesse.

ABOVE: Albert Bordes, painter and decorator at Condom ('Monsieur Laroche').

ABOVE: Olivier Prieur, butcher at Condom ('Privat')

RIGHT: Albert Cantal, son of Gabriel Cantal ('Morel'), both members of the WHEELWRIGHT circuit at Gabarret.

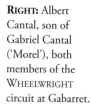

ABOVE: Maurice Rouneau ('Galles'), one of the founders of *réseau* VICTOIRE.

LEFT: Denis Parsons (*Pierrot*), second radio operator for WHEELWRIGHT.

Funeral of Comdt Parisot, Auch, 9 September 1944. *Front row: left*, Tomas Guerrero Ortega ('Alcazio'); *fourth from left*, George Starr. *Back row: from right*, Yvonne Cormeau, Guy de la Roche, Hod Fuller.

ABOVE: Lt Col H W Fuller ('Ross Halsall'), OC JEDBURGH BUGATTI team (*centre*). Capt Guy de la Roche ('Yves de Changins'), Second in Command (*right*). With unknown soldier, possibly Michel Guillemot ('Bouboule'). Taken by Anne-Marie, August 1944.

ABOVE: Tomas Guerrero Ortega ('Alcazio') talking to Mme Parisot at the funeral of Comdt Parisot, Auch, 9 September 1944.

LEFT: Commandant Maurice Parisot, leader of the Panjas *maquis*.

Château de Castelmore, Lupiac, Gers, the "beautiful seventeenth-century house" from which 'Alcazio' and Anne–Marie commandeered cars for the *maquis*.

ABOVE: Castelnau-sur-l'Auvignon after the German attack, 21 June 1944.

ABOVE: Communal grave at Meilhan, taken by Anne-Marie, July 1944.

Visit of JUDEX mission to Auch, December 1944: 1. Dr. Deyris; 2. R A Bourne-Patterson; 3. Roland Mansencal; 4. G R Starr; 5. Yvonne Cormeau; 6. Juliette Mansencal; 7. Lt Col M J Buckmaster; 8. André Coulom; 9. Juliette Coulom.

Anne-Marie on holiday in Mexico, 1954.

of Castelnau." And ended: "From my Headquarters, signed —, Commander of the Spanish Force." After dictating one line which I took ten minutes to understand, for he spoke an exotic and completely incomprehensible mixture of Castilian and Toulouse slang, he stopped.

"Paulette," he would say dreamily, "I know you'd love Spain…"

"I'm sure I would, Alcazio, but, about this report…"

"Yes…" he went on, "the sun there annihilates all the strength of the day: you are left smooth and soft, you have no energy to do all the boring things that life expects you to do. Just rest and sing, think of trees and women. Everything is so colourful: the stones are very white, the earth is very red and the sky is of a blue you never know here."

I didn't know how to interrupt Alcazio's reminiscences without hurting his feelings. He was so dreadfully home-sick.

"Eight years I've been gone now. My father and mother have been shot by Franco. I never think of it; what's the use? All I would like is to go back to my home for a few hours, hear people speak my language all around, smell the women's strong perfume and look at their brown legs. You can hear music in the streets way into the night, in Spain, you know?"

At three or four in the morning, I usually succeeded in extracting myself from Alcazio's confidences and take the crumpled piece of paper with his six-line report to the Patron. The Patron would smile and throw it in the fire without even bothering to read it. I looked on with growing anger.

"He only wants to talk to me because he's lonely. I can't go on spending half my nights typing bits of paper that don't interest you!"

"You must do it, because it pleases him and I want him to be happy. We need those people badly…"

All the time we were at Castelnau I went on "pleasing" Alcazio and doing this futile work. After a while I was so exhausted that I had to go and sleep at Nasoulens for a break.

The *maquis* had now been going on for nine days. A few reports came in, showing that the Germans were getting disturbed about our presence in Castelnau. A column, reinforced with *miliciens*, was reported at Fleurance, a small town between Condom and Auch. A column of the *maquis* was sent to attack them. They started out at lunchtime on June 15th. In the afternoon I ran into André Cérensac.

"Nothing has been heard of our column," he told me. "I'm going with a small reconnaissance party. I'll drive the traction…"

"But André, you can't go! You can't even handle a gun."

"Oh, well, I've been shown how…" André replied. "That's the barrel, that's the trigger and that's the magazine. I put it in, I cock it and I shoot. It's easy enough: I've just been shown…"

Just been shown… That was a poor recommendation for a young man who started out to attack Germans.

"Can't anyone else go in your place?" I asked, very unhappy at seeing him go. If something happened to him, I would never forgive myself.

"Nobody wants to go, so I said I would," he replied as though it was a natural thing to do. I saw him go off with an unpleasant apprehension. That night he wasn't back. I cycled to Nasoulens again.

"How is André?" the family asked after they had kissed me.

"Oh, fine. I saw him this afternoon." I did not tell them that he had gone off to attack the Milice and had been away eight hours already. I rushed back to Castelnau in the early morning, and went in to the Patron's PC.

"What's happened to the party which went to Fleurance? Are they back yet?"

"No. And all I know is that there has been a fight; I have no other news." He wiped his brow, his face dark with worry. I went out, unable to think of anything else, after he had promised to let me know the first news he received.

At lunchtime, Mike came to say that I was to go up to the PC.

"I've just heard," the Patron said. "The first party who went out had a regular fight. But the second, the one with André, unfortunately fell into an ambush: I believe that the ten of them were killed. André has disappeared though, and I haven't found out yet what happened to him."

I went off overwhelmed with misery. I should never have allowed André to go off; I should have made a fuss, called the Patron or something. If he was dead, how could I go and face the Cérensacs who lived only for their son? After all they had done for me…

But André was not dead. He and his party had fallen into an ambush of one hundred and fifty *miliciens* at the foot of a hill. Meanwhile, at the top of the same hill, the first party was approaching in full fighting order. The *miliciens* ordered André and his nine friends to stand in a line, shoulder to shoulder, while they took cover behind them. The first party saw that the *miliciens* were hiding behind a line of their own friends and stopped for a while. Then they began firing over their heads in the hope of scattering the enemy. But the *miliciens*, panic-stricken, shot the ten men point-blank in the back. They all fell to the ground, some dead, some screaming. André was at one end of the line, his head hanging down a ditch, a 9mm bullet through the lung. He thought his only way of escape was to pretend to be dead.

"Shall we finish them off?" the *miliciens* said. And killed all those they thought still alive.

"They all died thinking that they had been killed by their own people…" André told me later, with tears of powerless rage in his eyes. "I'm the only one who knows that the bullets came from the back: mine went through my right lung and out near my collar-bone."

André stayed eight hours on the road while the fighting went on. He bled continuously. He was finally rescued and taken to the Lectoure hospital. The doctors, who were terrified that the Germans might come and take reprisals on them, declared that he was lost, but a little Spanish Sister tiptoed to André's bed and whispered in his ear:

"I heard the whole story of the fight: I know that you are a brave boy and I promise you that I am going to save you."

She had remained by his side all night, giving him an injection every half-hour. He had lost a great deal of blood, but next day he was still alive, when we heard of him. I had rushed to Nasoulens, but the Cérensacs already knew. Odilla packed a small bag, with tears streaming down her face; Henri was pale and trembling all over. Dr Driziers drove them to Lectoure in his car. The next day he had André transferred to the Condom hospital, where he and the local surgeon fought death, and then a purulent pleurisy, for nearly a fortnight. At last he was saved, the only survivor of a massacre organised by Frenchmen against Frenchmen.

I shall always consider André's miraculous escape the most fortunate thing that happened to me during all my months with the Resistance.

The same day, a few hours after I had seen André off to his expedition, a group of six Spaniards ran into a German column as they patrolled the Agen neighbourhood. They took cover behind a small, fortified tower and fought sixty-five Germans for more than an hour and a half. Eventually, the six of them were killed. Someone cycled to Castelnau at top speed to warn us of the fight, and Alcazio jumped in his car and went off, followed by a couple of fast trucks, filled with his compatriots. By the time he reached the scene of the fight, the Germans had left. He picked up his comrades and brought them back to the *maquis*.

We had a parade in front of their bodies. Alcazio had a tremendous sense of drama. On one side of the square he placed his Spaniards in two rows; on the other side, the Patron placed the French companies. The six bodies were drawn in a wooden cart and placed in the middle of the square; the men presented arms. Alcazio walked before the cart and made a short speech in Spanish: we understood nothing, but we knew that he spoke of hate, revenge and honour. His face, gestures and his tone were more eloquent than words. I couldn't help tears rolling down my cheeks: the six Spaniard's naked bodies were thrown in heart-rending positions on the cart; one foot had been torn off and the bloody stump hung over the side; the others were blue, and red with dried blood. Their lifeless faces showed signs of having died in fearful agony! I recognised one to whom I had spoken the same morning.

It was a painful parade: for the first time in our safe and secure *maquis*, death had been brought right before our eyes. We felt that the incalculable backwash of war was at our door.

CHAPTER XIV

The following day, the Patron's hostess came into the kitchen as I was cutting bread for the men's breakfast.

"I've been hearing shots at the edge of the plateau, towards La Romieu, for some time," she said. "I wonder if the Patron ought to be awoken: this is the first time he has slept for so many days… I've prevented people from waking him up."

Many of the men had been handling arms for such a short time that misfires occurred more than once a day: this might be another instance. But we could take no chances, so the Patron was awoken.

I went outside: people had begun to be worried. Various reports were coming in from the direction of La Romieu. Some said it was practice firing; others, a group of *miliciens*; others, a German attack. The Patron rushed out, zipping his cycling jacket, and vanished into the PC. Mike came perambulating calmly down the only street with his shirt wide open. Mike had a habit of wearing his shirt unbuttoned.

"What's all the fuss about?" he asked. "When all these Frenchmen start running about and talking at once, I can't understand what they say. It's already bad enough trying to understand a simple conversation with my school French…"

Someone ran up to us.

"Please tell him," he said to me, "that the Patron wants him at the PC with the Bren gun which he will find hidden under his bed."

After Mike had gone: "Do you know what is going on?" I asked.

"I think the Germans are attacking us, but, we don't know how many yet."

Alcazio came striding down on his crutches. The sun was hot and dry; it was about 9am.

"Paulette, come *here*…" he shouted before entering his quarters.

I followed him into the dark, damp room where he lived. Five or six Spaniards were gathered around, sitting on upturned pails.

"Paulette, I've just had a report from the advanced post of La Romieu: my men are holding it. This is a real German attack. We don't know how many more will arrive, but there are already more than four hundred of them."

"What about the Condom and Agen roads? They won't surprise us that side, will they?"

"No, they won't surprise us because we have sent reconnaissance patrols there, but if they come this side, it will get rather hot. If we are encircled, we have little chance of getting out. Now, you must go and warn all the village women to be ready in a quarter of an hour. They will be evacuated with their children. Will you and Marie go with them too?"

"I'll tell Marie about the evacuation; she can do what she wants, but I don't think she will want to go any more than I do."

I heard Alcazio laughing as I walked out. "I thought you wouldn't want to go…" he shouted through the window. I had no idea of the way things would develop, but nothing in the world would have made me go off. I might miss something interesting.

The Patron came running out of the PC. He looked thin and tired.

"Evacuation going on all right?" he asked. I nodded. I was terrified that he would order me away.

"Shall I go and work in the armoury and release one of the men there to fight?"

"Yes, do what you want." He rushed off again, wiping his forehead; the sun was already hotter.

Shots became more distinct as they got closer. I cleaned hand grenades, still thick with their preserving grease, while people ran in and out excitedly. No one quite knew what they were supposed to do. One of the staff officers of the PC walked in with a bundle of papers under his arm.

"I've been looking for you for quite a while, Paulette," he said. "Will you please take charge of these papers? They are all our security records and the details on the next-of-kin of the men: if the Germans should get them, there would be terrible reprisals in the region. They are your responsibility: if the enemy comes close, you'll have to burn them. Otherwise hide them; they've cost us many hours of work."

He had left before I had time to answer. Mike poked his head through the window, his Bren gun slung across his back.

"Why do Frenchmen get so excited?" he said desperately. "I don't understand anything that's happening. I'm going to the advanced post anyway: as far as I can gather, they've started retreating."

I went on cleaning grenades. People were becoming nervous. Nervousness is catching: I cleaned and armed my grenades more and more feverishly. Now and again someone would rush in and fill his pockets with them. Alcazio went by; there was something fiery about him. He loved fighting. His long hair was held back by driving glasses, his open shirt flapped in the wind. He waved and shouted that the Boches would be sorry they attacked… I hoped he was telling the truth. I began to feel the strain of being shut up in a room, while outside people ran about, apparently knowing what was going on. A young boy rushed in.

"Come on… We're evacuating!" he yelled, and flew out again.

The armoury was empty in a second. I picked up a Sten gun and put three magazines in my overall pockets, and ran to my room. Identity card, identity card…was the only thought I had in mind: the same evening I was supposed to go and see Roger to report on his activities. Slung on a chair, Jean-Claude's *canadienne* which he had left me, all my clothes brought back from Nasoulens the day before, my alarm clock. I looked for room in my pockets, but I thought I would break it against the magazines and decided to collect it later. Not for a second did I think that I might not be coming back…

Outside, the sun was hotter yet. The air had a dusty dryness and smell of sweat. It was past ten-thirty: shots rang close now. The village was already half empty. VanderBock went by; under his right arm cartons of Gauloises cigarettes, under his left arm a box of rifle ammunition. He walked like a man who doesn't want people to know that he has the devil at his heels.

"We are retreating in good order, Paulette," he said. "Follow me…" And he walked faster.

"OK, Monsieur VanderBock, I'm following…" and marched behind him. We passed the edge of the village and turned down a narrow path, hidden by the bushes.

"Monsieur VanderBock, I must hide these papers. I'll catch you up."

"All right," he replied. "I won't wait…" And he walked yet faster down the lane.

I climbed to the old arms depot, hidden by brambles and rocks. It was an ancient cave dug in the rock below the village church. I removed stones and old container tops, scratched a hole with my hands in the earth and laid the large bundle of papers in it, after wrapping them up in a stray sack. Before leaving, I covered it all up with stones and dry branches and jumped about on it with both feet, until it looked natural again.

Outside, the shooting was becoming closer and closer. I walked along the side of the hill towards the PC, under cover of the bushes.

"You'd better go slow here…" someone said at my feet. Three men were lying on the ground, hidden by the high grass. I lay flat next to them.

"Why? Are the Germans anywhere near?"

"They are on the crest of the opposite hill; they might see you. We are trying to reach the PC."

Stens in hand, we crawled through the grass until we got to a lane climbing up to the village square. We stood up, ran across and flattened ourselves again, by the side of the bushes. Before we had time to catch our breath, bullets began to whistle by in an uninterrupted stream; they cut the branches a few inches above our heads and rang shrilly in our ears.

"Hey, stop it! STOP IT, will you?" cried one of the men. "We're with you. STOP IT, you half-witted idiots!"

The firing ceased. "Well, that was a hot one…" said another. "Being killed by your own people, wouldn't that be fine? Thank God they shot too high. Wasting precious ammunition…"

"Unless they were trying out their Bren on us!" said the third icily.

"Don't be stupid. Everybody is in such a muddle up there… They don't seem to know exactly what to do. I've lost my company. Others are like me… But I suppose they must've thought the Germans had succeeded in crossing the Auvignon and were climbing up the hill."

We crawled up to the PC. The square was shadowed with dust: nearer and nearer I could hear heavy bangs. The dust receded, falling slowly over the edge of the dry village well. On the side of the square, turning his back to the PC, I caught sight of Alcazio. He was like an epic hero: straight and tall, his hair white with dust, he stood in the front line of the fight. He was an easy target for the enemy, hidden in the vines on the opposite hill, but it left him unconcerned. He shouted orders right and left, punctuating them by hitting his right crutch on the ground, his hot blood bubbling with the hysterical joy of a fight, and his passions overruling the thought of danger.

I took cover behind a five-ton truck and strained my eyes in the hope of seeing something. Far in the distance, small black figures sprang out of the green vines and disappeared a few yards further. Alcazio turned round.

"Paulette, what the hell do you think you're doing? Come out of there and follow me!" he yelled.

He caught me up behind the PC and dug his nails in my arm.

"Why are you still here? Nearly everyone has gone."

"Well, I came up from the Auvignon side…" I said, feeling like a scolded schoolgirl.

"They're shelling us with mortar fire," he went on. "One fell right in front of the PC. Can you see the crater there?"

So those were the loud bangs and the cause of the dust!

"You follow me everywhere I go. We're leaving now; we're encircled on three sides, but the Condom road is still free, we—"

Bang!… Thirty yards behind us, a mortar shell had fallen. Right on top of the truck behind which I had sheltered…

"Look where you'd be now, if I hadn't called you out?" Alcazio said quietly. Our ears and eyes were full of dust and noise. The truck was nothing but a pile of smoking wood and twisted wheels: the engine was on fire.

"Look, here's the Patron running up. He'll be furious to find me here."

"Don't worry," Alcazio said. "I'll tell him I told you to stay."

But the Patron paid no attention to me; he had other things to think about. His rifle, slung on his back, flapped against his short legs.

"Alcazio, it's time we left. The reinforcements are not here yet; they will be too late."

"Yes, that's what we're doing," he replied. Another shell fell ahead of us, making a hole in the wall of the Patron's house. Alcazio's car was ready to leave, behind the church.

"I'll be back!" he yelled, hopping away on his crutches. "I must warn one of my liaison men that we are leaving: I don't want the Condom advanced post to be abandoned."

I ran into the Patron's house. I don't know what prompted me to do it. Just behind the door, thousands of bank notes lay on the floor – three or four million francs. Someone had dropped them in a frantically hurried exit. I filled my pockets, my blouse and a large tin with them and gave them to the Patron.

"I must get the papers," I cried to the Patron, suddenly remembering them. But he stopped me as Alcazio returned.

"No, we haven't got time…"

Later, however, they were safely recovered.

We climbed into the car and jerked off, Alcazio's only foot passing rapidly from the clutch to the accelerator. Hardly anyone could be seen in Castelnau: the enemy was at the other end of the village. It was 1pm.

"They're there in the valley," Alcazio shouted, his hair flying in the wind. "Take that rifle and try to get a few…"

Alcazio was impractical. He was running the open Renault down the steep hill without touching the brake: at every one of the abrupt turns we skidded right into the bushes. But only he was sure that we would not overturn: the Patron and I gripped the edges of the car, trying not to be thrown out and praying all the saints in Heaven to preserve us from an accident. I picked up the rifle and tried to aim at the black specks still hopping in and out of the vines and firing at us. As the car bounced and jumped over stones and small ditches, the heavy rifle nearly flew out of my hands, and my bullets made harmless trips to the pure blue sky.

A little later, we arrived at one of the companies' PC.

"Commandant Parisot[1] has sent a liaison officer to say that his *maquis* had an alert just before leaving to come and counter-attack," a young officer told the Patron. "He will be here in an hour…"

"It's too late…" the Patron mumbled, shaking his head.

A tremendous explosion concluded his words. From Castelnau, high on the top of the hill, a heavy black cloud curled slowly up to the sky, a sinister finality. The rearguards of the *maquis* had blown up one of the ancient towers of the village where 400lb. of high explosive had been stored. All the material left behind was thus safe from falling into the hands of the enemy. The rearguards fought several hours longer in a slow retreat, saving us from pursuit. The men silently watched the black smoke curling up into the blue sky; they all felt that it meant the beginning of a wandering life – the end of the delusive feeling of security brought about by the company of other men and the possession of firearms.

Alcazio passed his fingers through his thick hair and turned to me, smiling. His smile brought an extraordinary softness into his hard, sun-tanned face.

"They haven't got us, they haven't got our material. We couldn't hope for more. Paulette, do you know how many Germans there were?"

"No, I have no idea."

"Approximately seven hundred… Seven hundred trained Germans against one hundred and fifty *maquisards*, half of whom don't even know the difference between the butt and the barrel of a gun. We're lucky to have come out of it, do you know, Paulette?"

"Do you know anything yet, Alcazio?"

"No. All I know is that my men destroyed eight of their trucks with hand grenades at the advanced post of La Romieu. Also they must've had a good number of losses, otherwise they would've encircled us completely."

In the distance, the sound of rifle fire and explosions could still be heard. A group of men arrived, helping some of their wounded comrades.

"Paulette, you'd better go and see if you can help there," the Patron said, between two arguments.

I walked to a nearby farm, supporting a young boy wounded in the arm. His eyes were full of tears, but he clenched his teeth in a childish attempt to hide the pain. Having no knowledge of first aid, I expected to pass clean out at the sight of ugly wounds: however, I forgot to do so. In the small kitchen, one of the Spaniards lay on the floor; one side of his face, abominably swollen, had taken a blue-green colour. At first I thought he was dead, until he groaned softly. His mouth twitched.

"He's had a piece of shrapnel in the eye," said the farmer with consternation. "I don't know what to do with him."

Water was boiling in the big fireplace. I removed the Spaniard's soiled handkerchief. He uttered an agonised cry as I uncovered his eye: nothing but a mass of coagulated blood and torn flesh. My head swayed. I cleaned it as best I could with boiled water, bandaged it again, and called Dr Driziers, just as he was passing by. The wounded man shook with pain while tears ran out of his only eye. Dr Driziers gave him a morphine injection.

"I've got a truck filled with the most seriously wounded men. It's going to the Condom hospital, where the Sisters are already looking after a number that I sent a little while ago. He'll go too..."

The black cloud now hung motionless in mid-air over Castelnau. Explosions occurred at regular intervals: the Germans were blowing up the remains of the village. Were they going to take reprisals on the neighbouring population? Panic struck me at the thought that Nasoulens might be destroyed. But there was nothing I could do, nothing I could offer...

"Where's the Englishman?" one of the men asked me. I had forgotten Mike in the general emotion.

"I don't know. I saw him sometime ago... I hope he's all right."

"Yes, that I know he is. You should've seen him fighting," he went on excitedly. "Ah, these phlegmatic Englishmen... There he was, right in the front line, firing single shots with his Bren gun... Single shots! I ask you! One, then another, bang, bang! And every time you'd see one of the Boches in the vines drop to the ground, or little puffs of dust rising just next to him... Ah, what a man!" he said, shaking his head.

Mike, l'Anglais (the *maquisards* never remembered his patient explanation of how he was not an Englishman, but a New Zealander), became the legendary figure of the Castelnau fight. Everybody spoke of his calmness and his accurate shooting, while a lot of the boys had wasted ammunition, excitedly firing long bursts of their automatic firearms. Later on, the men would go and ask Mike's advice on all sorts of things.

"First, I can't understand what they say," he would tell me, throwing his arms to the sky. "Then, I don't know a damned thing about guns and grenades. I try to tell them I'm a pilot, not an army instructor. But they don't understand me either – what a picnic! Ah, what wouldn't I give for a glass of beer in a quiet pub."

But he loved it. In his filthy shirt and torn pants, he spent hours learning French and discussing things with the men. He refused to stay at the *maquis* headquarters, and was attached to one of the companies. L'Anglais was the most popular man of the Castelnau *maquis*.

At 4pm I went to Condom in Alcazio's car. Most of the men were already there; the population fed us and shouted gaily: it was all a great adventure. We joined Commandant Parisot's troops who had arrived a little earlier.

"Just as my *maquis* was ready to move off to your help," he told Alcazio, "a

German column passed on the road a few kilometres away. We had to race to our battle positions, as we expected to be attacked. It didn't happen but we wasted a couple of hours starting out again."

Parisot was a major in the regular army and an Armée Secrète man. He had worked with the Patron for a long time. Tall and dark, with a moustache like Charlie Chaplin, he had a frank and honest face. His eyes gleamed with perpetual mischief. He was surrounded by young officers in uniform; they seemed better organised, or at least more professional, than we were.

Towards evening, a long convoy started out. Alcazio had asserted himself as a commander, and he and the Patron requisitioned trucks and buses with the help of the Condom police authorities.

"We're going to Panjas," Alcazio informed me. "It's about a hundred kilometres from here. I hope we won't meet a German column; the men are too tired to fight well."

There were approximately forty-five trucks and cars, slowly advancing along the wide, straight road. The men were piled high in the trucks, legs hanging over the edge, Stens and rifles in hand. On top of each truck, a Bren gun was mounted. Next to it, the French flag, with the Cross of Lorraine, flapped in the wind. Some of the trucks carried the lightly wounded with bandages round their heads, or their arms in slings; they waved their firearms and sang. We passed through towns and villages like the liberation armies: people stood on their doorsteps, shouting, waving and singing "*La Marseillaise*", reinforced by the voices of the *maquisards*. The women brought us wine and food: some of their men rushed home, put on their heavy boots and grabbed a coat, jumped on the trucks and came along with us. Marie was in a car with her father and Dr Driziers; she had got out of Castelnau about the same time as me, but I had lost sight of her. The Patron drove with Parisot, while I went with Alcazio, busily giving orders as he went along.

We arrived at Panjas at ten: night had fallen and there was little chance of organising sleeping quarters, so the men slept on the ground or in their trucks. Parisot's cooks had prepared some food; it was the first meal we had had all day, but excitement had kept me completely unaware of it. Alcazio, who possessed the valuable quality of being able to go for days without sleeping or eating, found a room in an evacuated château for me.[2] I slept on an antique bed, in a wide room with cretonne curtains and old furniture, while six Spaniards slept, rolled in blankets, on the floor. My white blouse and pleated skirt were filthy, covered with black grease, dust and earth. I kept them on. As a matter of fact, it was nearly a week before I could take them off.

I fell asleep, wrapped up in the cretonne cover of the bed, unaware of Alcazio in the next room, walking up and down, dictating reports and taking account of the day's loses. We heard later that out of 380 German casualties, they had lost 248 killed. We had 40 casualties, of which 19 were fatal. Castelnau was pillaged by the Germans, then set on fire and blown to bits: only a few walls are standing today.[3]

CHAPTER XV

When I awoke the next morning, the Spaniards had crept out of the room: I could hear them arguing, in their rapid musical language, below my window. I sat up and tried to make out the balance-sheet of my own losses. My heart twisted in misery at the thought of my alarm clock, the Cérensacs' own souvenir. How would I ever have the courage to tell them that the Boches had it? All my clothes were lost, except for a few winter ones I'd left at the farm. Jean-Claude's *canadienne*. My books, including my precious *From the Infinitely Big to the Infinitely Small*... And the last remains of the soap and toothpaste I had brought from England. Tooth-brushes were impossible to find; French soap was so rough and hard that it scratched your face and hands.

One of the Spaniards came in with a pail of water.

"Mademoiselle Paulette, I thought you might like to wash and freshen up a little," he said with a brilliant smile. The Spaniards had kept sentimental memories of their women fighting in the Civil War. They treated me kindly all through the following weeks.

My hands were still black with grease and I had left uncouth marks on the cretonne cover of the bed. I washed as best I could. Alcazio came in when I'd finished, and sat on the edge of the bed.

"Listen, Alcazio," I told him, "I *must* go to Eauze today and get some decent clothes. I can't go off on a mission like this: I look like a *maquis* side-kick. Also I need all sorts of things like soap and tooth-brush and other clothes."

"I know. All the men need them too. You can come with me if you want: I intend to go and see what I can get for them."

Alcazio bought half the town. He filled the back of his white Renault with everything he could get hold of. I found a minimum of underwear, a cheap skirt and a rayon blouse. It shrank so much at the first wash that I had to give it to Marie, who was smaller than I.

"Mademoiselle, I've got something in my back-shop which I think you might like," the owner of one of the shops told me. "I'd put it aside for my sister, but I saw you in the convoy yesterday and I guess you must need it more than she does…"

She came back with a small, woman's *canadienne*, lined with brown rabbit's fur.

"Three thousand francs—"

"But I can't afford that…" All I had in the wallet rescued from Castelnau was 700 francs.

"Well, I give it to you," Alcazio said. He had walked in unheard.

So I went back to Panjas, clutching my swazzy *canadienne*. The Patron called me into his office.

"Paulette, did you manage to save your identity card from Castelnau?"

"Yes, I have the Hautes-Pyrénées one with me."

"Good. Because you have to leave straight after lunch for the Pyrenees sector. I have a car ready for you: you'll go with Plucci, an Italian from Condom.[1] It's his own car."

"Has it any papers?"

"No. You must avoid all the big roads; the Germans are very tight on road control now, so you must avoid them like the plague."

"That I do anyway. But what is there to do in the Pyrenees?"

"I told you a short while ago that I had received a message from London warning me of the arrival of three Allied parachutists, in full uniform, who will organise guerrilla warfare from a military angle – we're not specialised in that.[2] Anyway, their message came over the BBC a few minutes ago: 'Cream cheese is rare…' Now I want you to be at their reception. They ought to have some money for me; you'll bring it back. Also, I want you to come back with the senior officer of the party. I want to tell him how things stand in the region."

"What ground are they arriving on?"

"The Tanet ground.[3] I gave Choulac's name to London as a safe house for the parachutists, in case they happened to be dropped off the field."

The Tanet ground: the one where Jean-Claude and I had spent a long night under the rain, six weeks before, in vain expectation of a *parachutage*. Tanet was a tiny village, some two kilometres away: five or six houses dotted on the hillside, between bushes and small woods. I had seen Choulac only once; he was the mayor of the village and had struck me as being rather characterless and watery.[4]

I left after lunch with Plucci. He was a sturdy, blue-eyed Italian with a dry wit and a gay temperament. He had two passions: his wife and his car, the latter being a fast, petrol-driven Renault.

We took the big road for the first part of the journey, Commandant Parisot having assured us that, according to reports from his patrols, no Germans were about. We made a detour to Seissan, where the Patron had asked me to take a message to Chénier. I had not seen him since my first visit, in January.

"You must be careful," he told us. "I've just heard that that the Boches seem to be in a panic about an Allied landing at Bordeaux. They have blocked all the side roads turning off the Nationale 117, because they want to have it clear for their traffic between Toulouse and Bayonne. Also they have controls and patrols all over the place."

We studied the map and decided to go through Boulogne,[5] a fat village on a secondary road leading straight to the parachuting field. Chénier had a clothes shop there.

"I'll come with you as far as Boulogne," he said. "I have to attend a burial there."

In Boulogne I bought a few more things in his shop. At four we started out again. We soon left tarred high-roads behind, and started driving along small, dusty country lanes. As we came round a bend, we suddenly found ourselves faced with tommy-guns and rifles in the hands of dishevelled and unshaven men. We stopped. One of them approached; he had a dark face and a sombre look. Black eyes shone uncannily in a thin, hard face, overshadowed by a green hat pulled low over one eye.

"Who are you?" he asked, poking his nose through the window of the car and pointing his tommy-gun at Plucci. I noticed with discomfort his finger on the trigger. They were very obviously men from a neighbouring *maquis*. The only thing to do was to tell the truth.

"We are on a liaison mission for the Resistance."

"Who is the liaison agent?"

"I am."

"And what are you?" he asked Plucci.

"Her driver."

"What group of the Resistance do you belong to?"

"I don't know. Just the Resistance."

"You must belong to a political group of it. We are the FTP. What are you?"

"I don't know. We don't do the Resistance for the sake of politics, but to fight the Germans. We think that's enough…"

He eyed me sourly for a few minutes. The FTP (or Francs-Tireurs et Partisans) were Communist *maquisards*. They had a reputation in the region for bravery and daring, but acts of terrorism were also attributed to them, and this gave them a bad name. They had little or no contact with London and were unarmed for the most part, and so carried out raids on depots of the other Resistance groups. They had no money, so they carried out raids on banks. They had no food, so they raided the *mairies* for ration cards. As a matter of fact, their reputation was also suffering as a result of German and Vichy propaganda, all acts of brigandage and ordinary robberies being attributed to them.

"This is very curious," the Green-Hat said. "Have you any papers to prove that you are on a mission?"

"No, of course not. How can I risk being stopped by the Germans carrying papers of the Resistance?"

"Don't talk so much," he snapped. "If you have no papers, how can I know that you are speaking the truth? Stay here…"

He returned to the group of men, waiting menacingly with their sub-machine guns pointing at us. He came back with another one, tall and fat, and trying to look like the wrath of the gods.

"What is your mission?"

"I'm afraid it is none of your business. But I would be grateful if you could let us go on. I'm expected shortly and I shall be late."

"Where are you going and who is expecting you?"

"That is none of your business either."

"Yes, it *is* our business," the Wrath-of-the-Gods put in furiously. "Don't you know that a German column is expected at any moment along this road? They're going to inspect the St-Loup petrol wells, and nobody belonging to the Resistance in the region is ignorant of this fact."

"I belong to the Resistance of the Gers. I've come from the region of Mont-de-Marsan, two hundred kilometres away. Now, will you let us go?"

"No. We have no proof that you are speaking the truth and we shall have to keep you until we can check your assertions."

"But you *can't* do that," I cried. "I have to accomplish my mission by tonight…"

The two men went back to their group; they talked with the others for a while, then returned.

"Do you know anybody near here who can prove your identity?"

"No…" Then I suddenly remembered Chénier, attending his funeral in Boulogne.

"Yes," I cried. "A man called Chénier, in Boulogne." They looked startled, then softened up.

"Chénier? Which Chénier?"

"I don't know *which* Chénier. I only know one. All I know is that he owns a clothing shop in Boulogne."

They were silent for a while. Then the Wrath-of-the-Gods broke in:

"There are two Chéniers in Boulogne. One is our chief, an FTP leader. The other is a collaborator. You have to come back with us and make sure that you are speaking the truth…"

"But we can't do that," I said desperately. "Boulogne is fifteen miles away, and

I am already late. Of course I wouldn't give you the name of a collaborator as a reference: it wouldn't make sense."

"Well, if you know Chénier, why hasn't he given you a password to go across this region? He knows no one can get through without it."

"I don't know why he didn't give me a password. I saw him less than an hour ago. You must believe me, and you must let me go, please."

"No. I'm afraid there's nothing doing," said the Wrath. "Your driver will stay here with his car and four of my men. You will come with us and we shall see whether Chénier knows you."

There was nothing more to say. I climbed into a large Hotchkiss: two men, finger on the trigger of their guns, sat next to me. They kept their hands on the handles of the doors: another, sitting in front, kept his door open and a foot on the running-board "in case anything happens," the Green-Hat informed me graciously. Outside Boulogne, the Hotchkiss stopped.

"We'll have to go in on foot. We can't appear like this in the town…"

The townsfolk of Boulogne eyed me with suspicion and surprise as I walked in with my escort. We made a sensational group: one woman with four tough, bearded *maquisards*, arms in hand and finger on the trigger. Everyone thought I was a captured Gestapo agent. I was furious. As we approached the church, the funeral march was slowly winding its way to the cemetery, just behind it. I caught sight of Chénier and waved. He stopped dead with astonishment, while two people walking mournfully behind collided with him. He left the procession and ran towards us, his hat in his hand.

"What the hell do you think you're doing?" he asked my escort, panting with fury.

The Wrath-of-the-Gods looked modest and humble. "She said she knew you, but she had nothing to prove that she belonged to the Resistance."

"Put those tommy-guns away immediately. It's all my fault," he said, turning to me. "I forgot to give you the password. I'm terribly sorry all this happened. And you will be late, if you don't rush off, too." Turning back to the Wrath and Green-Hat: "Now, you are going to accompany her all the way, do you hear? And see that she gets there safely. And from now on, will you please be careful with this mania you have for stopping every citizen on the road. You are going to get me into endless trouble if you go on."

I was revenged, so I held no rancour against my escort. We went back to the Hotchkiss great friends, to the bewilderment of the population of Boulogne who had gathered on their doorsteps to watch the event. We caught Plucci up; he was sitting forlornly on the edge of the road, under the unswerving glance of two *maquisards* pointing their Stens at him.

The Wrath went in front in his Hotchkiss, a Citroën followed with Green-Hat, then our Renault with *maquisards* on the running-board, and finally another Citroën with five men inside.

"What a death-trap…" Plucci muttered under his breath. "If we run into a column of Germans, not one of us will get out of it. What a bore, this idea of being escorted!"

"I know," I muttered back. "But there was nothing I could do: Chénier felt he had to make up for the scandal of my entry into Boulogne and for having made us so late."

We horned the small convoy to a stop as we approached Tanet. I didn't want them to know our destination. It was 7pm. We all shook hands; more apologies and more forgiveness ended the episode.

Plucci hid the car behind bushes on the edge of a cornfield, while I watched the road. No one saw us. We cut branches and covered the car up, to make it invisible from the air. To avoid sun rays catching the shining chromium headlamps, we wrapped them up in sacks and dirty cloths. Then we went down narrow lanes and wooded drives towards Tanet. In Tanet, we entered Choulac's farm by the back. He was in the kitchen.

"What are you doing here?" he said, frowning and closing the door behind us.

"There's going to be a *parachutage* tonight, and we would like to stay here until Roger and his reception party arrive on the field," I replied, all bright and breezy.

"No, you can't. No, you can't," he cried. "There's a *milicien* next door. I'm sure he's spying on me; I'm sure he'll know that you're here. He'll report me. No, you can't stay here."

"My goodness, what a fuss. What will you do about the *parachutage?*"

"I don't know; I won't go, anyway. I'm sure he'll follow me. Besides, I've heard nothing about a *parachutage*. Usually Roger comes here to warn me beforehand. Or at least sends someone…"

"What do you mean?" I cried. "Do you think Roger doesn't know there's a *parachutage* tonight?"

"No. I'm sure he would've let me know if there was one."

"Maybe the message didn't come over again after lunch," Plucci suggested. "It might mean that the weather has deteriorated."

"Can't we listen to your radio, Monsieur Choulac?" I asked.

"All right, but you will have to go afterwards. The *milicien* might already know that you are here."

I was getting annoyed with the man. If he were terrified it was his right to be, but he had no right to refuse assistance after having promised it. We listened to the messages: "Cream cheeses are rarely sold…" What did this mean? The message was distorted. The Patron had given me the list of messages straight from decoding, and I had brought "Cream cheese is rare" to Roger, some weeks previously. How could London make a mistake, or choose two sentences so nearly alike, considering the multitude of opportunities they had for making phrases in the French language? This last argument convinced me that the message was really for us. But would Roger think differently and not come?

"Now look, Monsieur Choulac. There seems to be a probability that Roger and his men won't come. In that case you must help us, and get the men of Tanet, whom you can trust, to make the *parachutage*."

"I know only five…" he whimpered.

"Well, we'll have to do it with only five, since you don't want to come," I replied impatiently. "One of the men will have to come up with a cart to carry the containers off the field. We have no depot, so we'll have to dump them in the woods where the Germans won't find them. Your men will have to bring some straw and small firewood, also a flashlight. There's a new signalling system."

"I'll tell them," Choulac replied weakly.

"I'll have to count on them, Monsieur Choulac. I'll go out of your house now, since you don't want me: I shall be on the field at ten-thirty, waiting for them."

As Plucci and I stepped out, we ran into Choulac *père*.

"What are these two doing here?" he yelled at his son. "I told you I don't want any of your compromising people in my house."

We went without bothering to reply. It was infuriating to be received like this before an important operation. Choulac was cleaning up to go to a christening the next day, and nothing seemed more important to him than brushing his best hat. On the success of the *parachutage* depended the pay of many *maquisards* who had to support their families, as well as the proper training and arming of the Pyrenees region.

We were to use the new signalling system I had taken to Galles in Paris. Three fires, best lit by small incendiaries, in a triangle, with a white flashlight signalling the code letter at the top: the aerial picture was that of a 'Y', the tail showing the direction of the wind. It was more risky as it could be seen some distance away, but the importance of each *parachutage* after D-Day was greater than the danger involved. The most exposed fields would be used only once.

Plucci and I sat next to the car, killing time as best we could – eating bread and sausage, generously given by Madame Chénier, talking and arguing. After a while, he went to sleep in the high corn. The sun went down and the air became colder: I wrapped myself up in my *canadienne* waiting for the moment to go onto the field. I had thought of going to Montréjeau, but it was impossible. Montréjeau was over twenty kilometres away; I couldn't go by car because of the road blocks and German patrols, and there was no time to go by foot. Seven of us could do the *parachutage*; with the three parachutists we would be ten.

At ten-thirty, Plucci and I were on the field. We waited at the top of the lane leading to Tanet, to make sure we wouldn't miss Choulac's men in the dark. At eleven we became anxious: no sign of them. Roger was definitely not coming. At eleven-thirty, they had still not arrived: we were desperate. On the stroke of midnight, alone in the wide field, under a brilliant moonlight, we heard the distant drone of the aircraft. A few minutes later it was overhead: the Halifax flew dead over the field, silhouetted clearly on the sky. I wanted to shout and stamp my feet. Plucci and I were powerless; we had no lights, no fires, no way of signalling our presence. It was an unusual thing to find a navigator who directed the plane dead over a dropping point at the first attempt. The Halifax circled and circled over us for half an hour. I sat on the ground and wept with unmitigated fury. What could we do? Up there the men were on the edge of the hole; they had gone through a long and strenuous journey, reached their goal, and were waiting for the signal… But there would be no signal. Below, two people were helpless to put an end to their nerve-racking wait.

Plucci, walking up and down with clenched fists, and I, weeping with rage, saw the bomber go off on its long return journey home. After it had disappeared on the black horizon, we ran all the way down to Tanet and burst into Choulac's kitchen. Choulac's son was nowhere to be seen.

"What happened?" I shouted to the old father, sitting next to the fireplace, as solid as the walls of Jerusalem. "Why did he let us down? Do you realize what you've done?"

Choulac walked in, meek as a mouse; his father frowned, ready to blow up.

"The men started out," Choulac's son said, "but when they were beginning to climb the hill they heard a noise behind them, and thought they were being followed…"

"You double-crossers," I said, out of myself with rage. "Why the hell should they all start out together? It's an elementary principle of security to go to a rendezvous one by one. I told you there were some paratroopers up there. They are on an urgent mission, they had a lot of important stuff with them – we've been waiting for them for days. You are slowing up the Resistance in the whole region, all by yourself. You may be responsible for a lot of misfortunes…"

"We're scared, see?" the old father cut in, his voice shaking with anger, "scared… You don't have *miliciens* living next to you. You don't risk a whole family and house. I don't care what happens to your damned parachutists. I don't want my household to be broken up by the Germans or the Milice…"

"I know, I know. If you're scared, I don't care. But you said that you belonged to the Resistance, and offered your house as a safe place. What would've happened if these men had jumped tonight..? Where would I have taken them? You agreed to let your name be sent to London. Now you're backing out. If you're scared, *don't* belong to the Resistance... If you belong to it, *don't* let people down..."

"Get out, GET OUT..." the father yelled. "I don't want these rude good-for-nothings, or the likes of them, in this house. Get out, before I *chase* you out..."

"Of course we'll get out. If you think we want to stay with you, you're making a big mistake... We have miles and miles of fields to sleep in..."

We went out, hot and puffing with anger. Choulac's son caught us up in the front yard.

"I'm sorry about this row," he said. "Where are you going to sleep?"

"Just where I said. In the fields. Or we have a big large Renault to sleep in, too: I'd forgotten that..."

"No. You can't do that. Now look, why don't you stay here? You can sleep in the cow-shed: if you go out before dawn breaks and make sure no one sees you..."

I was so furious that I refused, but Plucci, calmer and more reasonable, urged me to accept. We would be frightfully cold, and there was no point in catching bronchitis. Choulac's son generously threw a pile of straw into a corner of his cow-shed and left us there: the cows looked astonished at first, but soon resumed their ruminating. I put the light out, lay down and tried to sleep: continuous noises crowded my mind – cows chewing, cows sighing, cows moaning and cows' tails hitting the wooden partitions. Pats falling near me made me jump up with disgust. I fell asleep for a few minutes, but awoke with a start as slimy feet skipped over my legs: I put the light on and saw two enormous rats staring at me with perfect unconcern.

"Plucci, look!..."

"Yes... I've been pushing them off for some time already. I was afraid you'd jump up and scream."

"Do you think they'll bite?"

"I don't suppose so. I wouldn't pay any attention to them..."

I tried not to, but tossed and turned until dawn. Bits of straw scratched and dug into me, so I hid my face in my rabbit's fur. When streaks of white light came through the barred windows, Plucci and I got up, removed the straw from each other's hair and clothes, and departed.

"I'm not sorry to see the last of those people," Plucci said.

I thought of the three parachutists; they must be back at their aerodrome now, and have reported that no one had waited for them... It was 5am. Plucci and I sat in the car and ate the last of our bread and sausage: the bread was stale and we were terribly thirsty, and cold.

"We'll have to go and find a warm drink," Plucci said.

"Yes, and also a bicycle. I must go to Montréjeau and see Roger, and warn him that the message might be distorted again."

We waited three hours before being able to go to one of the local farms without appearing suspicious. The farmers worked according to the sun, or two hours behind the German time. We approached a farm and I poked my head through the window.

"I wonder if you could help me?" I said to three sleepy-looking figures drinking coffee by the fireplace.

"It depends, come in…" said one of them.

Plucci and I went in and explained that we had arrived by car the night before and had run out of petrol, so had to spend the night in the car.

"But you must be frozen," said the farmer's wife. "Come and have some coffee and warm yourselves."

We accepted gratefully. I told them I wanted a bicycle to go and collect a can of petrol, and that Plucci would stay as a guarantee of my honesty.

"I'm sorry I can't help," the farmer said. "I have no bicycle. I suggest you go to the doctor, a little way up the road. He has all sorts of means of transport and might be able to help you…"

I had a feeling he was lying. The nearest village was more than ten miles away; he had to have some form of wheeled transport to take him there. But we thanked him and went to the doctor's. He was only just getting up. We waited half an hour.

"Good morning," he said, putting his hand out. I shook it; it was hot and slimy, soft and sloppy. I felt immediate distrust.

"Could you tell me where the nearest chemist is, please?" Plucci looked at me with surprise, but said nothing. "I would like to get hold of some M & B. You wouldn't have any, would you?"

"No," he said, his full lips pursed. "The nearest chemist is at Lannemezan. Have you got a prescription?"

"Of course," I lied. To avoid further questions: "Thank you very much. I'll go to Lannemezan. I had thought I might save myself the trip."

"Whatever made you do that?" Plucci asked, when we were out.

"I don't know, to tell the truth. I just didn't like him. And he didn't like me… I wouldn't tell him about the car: I didn't want him to know we had one."

There was another farm in the vicinity. A short, wrinkled little woman was busy in front of the door: a torn, straw hat wobbled defiantly on her head. We repeated our request.

"Well, the only one who has a bicycle is my son, and I'm not sure he'll be ready to lend it."

The son came in. He had just returned from Germany, where he had been a prisoner. We expressed our sympathy for his sufferings and obtained the bicycle. Plucci stayed with the farmers. Their name was Bérard.[6]

"Don't forget the Patron expects us today," he shouted as I went off. I waved that I knew.

At the cross-roads onto the Nationale 117, the Germans had felled a tree right across the way. A group of soldiers was waiting to inspect papers, on the other side.

"Hey, you, could you help me?" I shouted.

The Germans picked up my bicycle and pulled it through the branches and greenery. I forced my way through without their help.

"What's the idea?" I asked, while they checked my papers.

"To stop hay-carts and other slow-moving vehicles from getting in the way of our traffic," one of them replied.

"Why? Has something happened?" I asked innocently.

"No. But it might… And we're ready all the time, you know."

"Of course, of course…" If only you knew, I thought, that just a few miles away some parachutists will drop right under your noses, maybe you wouldn't be so sure.

I found Roger in Montréjeau. As I supposed, he had thought that the message couldn't be for him. He promised to try and find another safe house.

"I had no idea Choulac was so scared… But then I never really saw him in action. The trouble is that all the other safe houses I can think of are very far from the field."

My Germans helped me amiably through the barricade again, and I arrived at the Bérards' farm in the early afternoon. Plucci and they had become great pals, as I had hoped, and were all talking together about the dirty Boches and what they did to prisoners. We thanked them profusely, and started back to Panjas, taking great precautions that no one should see where the car was hidden. The old grandmother, bent by her eighty-two years of age, but as hard and healthy as a rock, saw us to the gate.

"*Au revoir,*" she said. "God protect you."

CHAPTER XVI

We returned to the *maquis* without further encounters. At lunchtime the next morning, the Patron sent a motorcyclist to fetch me: my room was four miles from his headquarters.

"The message has come through again. It seems distorted again, but you will have to go back," he informed me.

Plucci was cross; he had found nowhere to sleep, and had crouched uncomfortably in his car all night. We filled our cans with petrol from the *maquis* dump. It was petrol stolen from local collaborators, who always seemed to have endless reserves of it, or presented by rich members of the Resistance who had bought it on the black market and stored it. Parisot gave me a chit for it, together with the latest news of German troop movements in the vicinity of the *maquis*. Alcazio produced a bicycle, which we dismantled and put in the back of the car.

We drove fast, on secondary roads all the way. We stopped at the Bérards' farm.

"What, back already?" said Monsieur Bérard. He was tall and lanky, with an exceedingly red face and a notable absence of collar.

"Yes, I have some people to see in Montréjeau, and I can't take the car all the way because of the road blocks..."

We were invited to a glass of *piquette* and sat around chatting for a while.[1] It was arranged that Plucci should stay with them, while I cycled to Montréjeau to make sure Roger's reception party was well on the way. This time there was no snap-control at the barrage. I called at Auguste's house and found him chopping wood.

"Yes, we know about the *parachutage* this time. You can be sure we wouldn't miss it twice."

Another young man straggled in; he had a squirrel's face, topped with black hair cut *en brosse*, according to the best tough fashion of the day. He observed me silently through small almond-shaped eyes.

"This is my friend Jean Monégas," Auguste said. "We have been working together in the Resistance for more than eight months now."

Jean and I shook hands, and the three of us started back for the parachuting field. Roger was scheduled to arrive at ten o'clock: Jean and Auguste would prepare everything. We carried Stens and guns, and an arsenal of small incendiaries to light the fires. The corn would have to be cut in the appropriate places, to prevent the whole field catching fire.

"I'm not very happy with all those Germans around," Auguste said. "We shall have to send the parachutists away from the vicinity of the field as soon as possible, because the Boches are sure to know that some operation has taken place. Yes, Roger has found a safe house," he replied in answer to my question, "but it is nearly ten miles away, and it is rather a nuisance using a car to take them there, when it could be carrying the containers away quickly."

Jean spoke little. He seemed to have deeply satisfying thoughts all of his own. A smile lurked on the edge of his lips all the way. Below his leather blouse his short shirt flapped in the wind, showing a bit of his brown back. I told Auguste about the Bérards and the possibility of asking them to feed the paratroopers on arrival. Jean and he decided to meet them and judge.

Plucci had done more good work; he and Bérard *père* were full of *piquette* and wise-cracks. Madame Bérard's mother tapped her cane on the floor and bid us enter, grinning with all her only tooth. She bullied her daughter and yelled at her grandson; she prepared the meals, fed the pigs and looked after the house, in spite of her eighty-two years. The farm had only two rooms and she lived in the kitchen. At night, she would remove her *sabots* and climb into her high bed without taking anything off, not even the black scarf she wore round her head all day. She would fall asleep, her rosary in her fingers and saying her prayers. She and Jean became great pals at once.

"I like people who know what they want," Jean informed me. "She is the only one in the family who knows her own mind."

We talked about the Germans and how much we all hated them. Then we spoke about the Resistance, and all agreed it was a wonderful thing.

"We belong to it, you know," Auguste said suddenly.

"Oh, I had an idea you did – yes, I had an idea you did," Madame Bérard said, her torn, straw hat shaking approvingly on her head.

Auguste made a sign, and Jean and I followed him out. We decided that they seemed all right. They were too simple to lie to us. But the sky was clouding over, and the wind had got up. We went in again.

"We would like to ask you to help us," I told them. The old grandmother jumped up before I had time to continue.

"You are good children. You have the right ideas. We will help you…"

"Wait a minute. You might find it too dangerous. In that case we would quite understand that you should refuse. We would like to point out that we are all independent and unattached, and we may risk our necks, but we don't risk our family, we don't risk our home and we don't risk our livelihood. You would."

There was silence for a while. I went on:

"You may risk it, but it depends on you. If you know how to keep quiet about all this, nothing will happen to you. We won't talk, none of us will ever talk about you at any time." Jean and Auguste approved with a nod. "If you don't either, no one will ever know that you had anything to do with the Resistance…"

"What do you want us to do?" asked Bérard.

"Shelter three parachutists who will arrive tonight in this region. They will need food: of course, we will pay you back. We only ask you to shelter them for a few hours. They will be in Allied uniforms, and that's the most dangerous thing about them."

"Of course, of course," the grandmother shouted before anyone had time to reply. "And they'll have my bed too…"

I saw Jean and Auguste turn away to hide their laughter, and had great trouble repressing my own, at the thought of our parachutists sleeping in the never-aired feather bed.

"Thank you very much, but—"

"Of course, of course they'll have it," she interrupted, tapping her cane impatiently on the floor. "These brave young men, these brave young men – I'd sleep out of doors to make sure they can rest in comfort."

The three of us finally convinced her that the brave young men would hardly want to rest on arrival and would be contented with a welcome and a cup of coffee. The Bérards were eager and excited with the adventure. Although they were very poor, Madame Bérard talked of killing a sheep to feed the ravenous bears she expected to see marching in. But the rain had started to fall and thunder rolled in the distance: the *parachutage* began to appear doubtful.

At ten-thirty we joined Roger and his men on the field. The rain had stopped, but the sky was full of electricity and thunder. At twelve nothing had come. We waited, cold and weary, in an extraordinary setting of elements. Above us, the sky was black and shining with stars, but in the distance a ring of purple clouds circled the horizon, lit the whole way round by a continuous stream of red and purple lightning. This mass of uncanny and overpowering beauty seemed to oppose a steady barrier to the approach of a lonely plane. We waited until three o'clock, but nothing came. We went back to the farm: the Bérards had waited in excited anticipation and kept a large fire burning in the chimney. We dried ourselves and drank hot milk before climbing up to the hayloft, where Auguste, Jean, Plucci and I slept, rolled in old army blankets.

The wind was blowing loud and brutal the next morning. The *parachutage* seemed improbable that night, so Plucci and I started back to Panjas. We drove slowly and cautiously because Jean had warned us that German columns were patrolling the whole region. We reached Panjas just after lunch, but found it deserted. After roaming disconcertedly around the district for a while, we ran unto a car-load of *maquisards*; they knew me by sight and escorted us to the new *maquis*.

"We heard that the Germans in Mont-de-Marsan knew all about Panjas, so the Patron and Commandant Parisot decided to leave before we were attacked. We are at Lannemaignan now."

At Lannemaignan I found the Patron's PC with great difficulty. He was becoming a little queer, the Patron; he went whole weeks without sleeping, and took his *maquis* more seriously than a general his army group. His PC had now become secret: I had to fuss and argue before being finally shown to it. I gave him an account of our trip, then asked what had become of the few things I possessed.

"Alcazio must have them, as you were staying at his headquarters," he said with a gesture of indifference. "I suppose he's also found sleeping quarters for you."

Alcazio was out on patrol, and I waited until he returned in the evening. Plucci fell asleep under a tree. I wandered about, visiting the new *maquis*. It was spread over several square miles, on the very edge of the Landes. The Landes forests were a good escape route: the enemy could not possibly carry out a search through miles and miles of pine woods.

Alcazio had thrown my things into the back of his car, but had no idea where I would sleep.

"I didn't think you'd be back tonight. But don't worry, we'll find something…"

Alcazio had the greatest confidence in Alcazio. But all he found was a straw mattress on the floor of one of the *maquis*-occupied farms. Nobody had thought of me during my absence, and while the staff officers slept in comfortable beds in the best houses, I had to be satisfied with my bug-ridden mattress. I was peeved, and tired. I couldn't sleep through the noise the men made, talking and singing all night.

I got up the next day stiff and bad-tempered. As I chewed a cold rabbit's leg, sitting on the doorstep of the house, and chatting with Mike, a messenger came in from the Patron. I was to report to him immediately. This was beginning to sound like real army life.

"The message has come over again," the Patron said. "You'll have to start out right away. I hope things will turn out better tonight: I have to pay the men some allowance for the upkeep of their families, and I've become terribly short of money."

Plucci was already informed and more bad-tempered than I.

"Nobody thought about me either," he fumed. "I had to sleep in the car again.

I'm sick of it. And what's more, I'm so tired I'll probably drive straight into something…"

It was the third night we had spent practically without sleep. We were both filthy, but we had nothing to change into and no time to wash what we had. Plucci peeled his socks off and chucked them away.

"I can't bear dirty socks," he said fastidiously. "I'd rather go without."

We started out just before lunch and took our usual road. To reach the parachuting field, we had to cross the Nationale 129, the long, straight road from Auch to Lannemezan. It was the most dangerous stage of the journey. We usually crossed it at Castelnau-Magnoac. As we approached a town or village, I would get out and enquire whether the Germans were around. Someone said that a column was somewhere in the region, and warned us to be careful. I had an indefinable feeling that we ought to avoid Castelnau-Magnoac, so we decided to cross the Nationale 129 further down. Later, I heard that eight hundred Germans had occupied the town for the day.

We drove along dusty country roads, winding up small hills and down narrow valleys. As we neared the Nationale 129, Plucci pointed at some obstruction at the cross-roads; it looked like a number of hay-carts, but he slowed down cautiously. A hundred and fifty yards from the obstruction, he jammed on the brakes fiercely.

"German cars," he said hoarsely. He backed the car round on the spot, avoiding the ditches on both sides with miraculous skill. I grabbed my precious *canadienne* and my bag, and opened the door, ready to jump out and run if necessary. To avoid any further delays through *maquisard* patrols, Commandant Parisot had given me Resistance papers, stating "The holder, Mademoiselle Paulette, belongs to the Armagnac Battalion of the Resistance. She is on an urgent mission, and it is requested that all facilities to accomplish her mission rapidly should be given her." It was written on thin paper, and in case of arrest I was to swallow it. We drove back at top speed on the road we had come by. Plucci stopped near a farm and I jumped out and ran to the gate. A sturdy old man was working in the front yard.

"Are they Germans over there, on the cross-roads?" I shouted to him.

"Yes, and they're all over the place," he shouted back, with a sweeping gesture. "I can't understand how you didn't run into them. They're searching all the farms and houses in the neighbourhood. They've blown up four farms outside Castelnau-Magnoac and shot four people in the main square…"[2]

"Look out, they're after us," Plucci called, starting the car. "I can see a traction racing up the road."

I jumped into the Renault as it moved off. Plucci, setting his teeth, drove fast; we had two minutes' advance on the German car.

"They must've seen us backing," I said. "We can't go straight back on the road we came from: it's full of them there too. It seems extraordinary that we didn't run into them. We must turn uphill somewhere soon."

We went on for another couple of miles, then Plucci swerved up a stony path, scraping the bushes and leaving a cloud of dust on the road behind us.

"Come on, I know you can make it," Plucci mumbled to his car. "Don't let me down now..."

The grey Renault bumped its way up the steep path, well hidden by hedges. At the top of the hill, he drove it right into a wood and parked it under bushes and undergrowth. We heard the Germans whiz past straight along the road: they had lost us.

"If they meet one of their patrols, they'll know we've turned off," Plucci said. "We must camouflage the car and hide for a few hours." We covered it up with branches and greenery; we'd become great adepts at the job. We hid in the woods some distance away and waited three hours. No more Germans were heard.

At six, we got my bicycle out of the car, and I cycled off on a fifteen-mile reconnaissance of the road. The Germans had left.

"They always go off in the evenings, the swine," a farmer told me. "They're scared of being attacked by the *maquis*. Under God's bright daylight, they're not afraid of shooting innocent people right and left, but long before night comes down, they run away like a lot of scared rabbits."

My enquiries were generally answered without surprise or inquisitive questions. We arrived at the Bérards' without further incidents.

"I was waiting for you," the old grandmother declared. Everyone else was out with the sheep and cows. "Monsieur Auguste came this afternoon to say that you would probably be coming. He told me to tell you that the message had come over only once and that the *parachutage* seemed to be off again."

Three times...

Plucci and looked at each other in dismay. We decided to stay and see whether the messages would come again the following day. I would go to Montréjeau while Plucci stayed behind. We camouflaged the car again, in one of the Bérards' fields, and I helped him to make a snug little corner for himself in the hayloft, in the hope of smoothing his discontent. I cycled to Mazères, where I found Miette, back and happy with her cats.

"Paulette, I've been so worried about you," she said, throwing her arms around my neck. "Jacqueline Picolet was freed from St-Michel yesterday. Come and see her, she'll tell you all about it."

Arm in arm, Miette and I went to Jacqueline's house. We found her pale and thin with large circles below her eyes.

"Oh, Paulette," she said, putting a hand on her cheek, "how glad I am to see you. I thought you'd been caught…"

"Will you please tell me what all this is about?"

"Well, about three weeks ago, a young girl was thrown into my cell. She was exactly like you: fair hair, blue eyes, your height and your profile. She even had mannerisms like you. She was crying and showed us blue marks where she had been beaten. 'They think I'm somebody called Paulette,' she said. 'They say I'm a liaison agent of an English circuit. I don't even know what it means…' I couldn't say anything," Jacqueline Picolet went on. "I had denied having anything to do with the Resistance and I couldn't let anyone guess that I knew you. She might even have been an *agent provocateur*."

"What happened to the girl, Jacqueline?" I asked, aghast.

"I don't know. That's the awful part about it. Apparently the Germans told her that they were looking for Paulette and Jean-Claude. She was picked up at the restaurant La Frégate, in Toulouse, on the 28th of May."

"La Frégate? On the 28th of May?" I cried. "But Jacqueline, on the 27th Jean-Claude and I had lunch there on our way to Dordogne. Why weren't we arrested then?"

"I don't know. Her boyfriend was arrested with her; he was deported to Germany immediately. The Germans seemed convinced that they had you two. They told her she had been denounced and obviously they have your description, since she answers to it so well. A few days ago she was told that her photo would be shown to the people who gave you away, and if they recognized it, she would be shot right away. They took her away two days later, and I've heard nothing since."

"Have you any idea who gave me away?"

"No. But the only people who were caught in May, apart from my husband and me, were people at Bagnères-de-Bigorre. You went there only once, but you are known there somehow."

I was the cause of the arrest and maybe the death of an innocent person. There was not a thing I could do. I didn't even know her name. Or where she came from…

Jacqueline Picolet told us how the Toulouse Gestapo, panic-stricken, had destroyed all their dossiers on D-Day. Later, when they saw they were not in immediate danger, they tried to rebuild them and asked her why she had been arrested. But Jacqueline was a quick-witted little person. She replied innocently that she had no idea and had been asking that for a long time herself. And the next day she was set free, after a month in captivity.

Her story haunted my night. How had all those denunciations happened? Who had known that Jean-Claude and I had had lunch at the Frégate? We must have been recognised there, but why weren't we arrested then? Why was someone *else* arrested the next day? By the end of the night, I had reached the conclusion that the girl could very well have been an *agent provocateur*: it was a good German trap anyhow, although not good enough to catch Jacqueline. The thought calmed my conscience a little. But I never found out what really happened.

At lunchtime the next day, the cream cheeses came over the radio once more. Auguste and Jean were with me, with Raymond Mautrens, who had left Tarbes, and a friend of his called Jacques.[3] Jacques had been made a prisoner during the Battle of France in 1940. He had been wounded, and, during his stay in Germany, the Boches had used him as a surgical guinea-pig: nine operations were performed on his stomach. When he was on the verge of dying, he was repatriated and looked after by French doctors, who saved him. He was still weak, and looked sick and unhealthy, but nothing could convince him that he had done his share and ought to rest at home.

The five of us cycled singly to the field, carrying the Stens and the Brens, camouflaged with branches and leaves. We were careful to watch that no one should follow us: the FTP were again after our depots, and we feared that they might try and intercept the *parachutage*.

At ten-thirty, we all met on the field. The night was calm and quiet. An orange moon hung heavily on the horizon, on the first part of its sweep across the brilliant, starry southern sky. The boys cut the corn and prepared small wood for the fires. Roger gave me the white code-signalling light. The corn was high and ripe, the night was warm and soft, the air smelt of trees and earth, giving back to the night their sun of the day. At eleven, a steady drone filled the sky: it couldn't be them, so early, surely..? I made a rapid calculation; they could not cross the coast before dark, and it was not dark before eleven – it was a two hours' flight from the Channel to the southwest. Roger caught me up.

"What do you think? So early? I can't tell them to light the fires: what if it is a German?"

"No, I agree with you. I think we must wait. I can't understand how they can be here before one…"

So we waited. The plane circled patiently some distance from the field. I grew more and more restless, and after a while ran to Roger, whom I found pacing nervously up and down.

"It must be them. We can't risk missing them again. We must just keep as far from the fires as possible, in case it *was* the Boche and he wanted to strafe us."

Two minutes later, the fires burst alight. I signalled the letter 'L' and suddenly realized that my piece of good advice was of little use for me: how could I keep away from a light I was holding in my hand? The plane approached and circled over us once. Then it went off in the night and came back suddenly, very fast and very low, straight at me.

"Look out!…" I heard Roger cry. The men scattered. My heart was beating like a drum. Just as the heavy bomber crossed the edge of the field, the engines slowed down and the plane shivered.

"It's them…" I shouted, as I caught sight of the lit-up aperture below the fuselage. The next second three parachutes slid into the night, the engines picked up again, and the Halifax climbed back and away in the darkness. The parachutes glided with the wind. I saw the first one make straight for the trees just beyond the field, and ran towards it, forgetting all about my flashlight and my signalling. The ripe corn cut my bare legs as I ran. In between two of the first trees, I found a tall, tough figure half hidden under an American steel helmet, and caught up with his parachute in the brambles and bushes.

"Are you hurt? Are you all right?" I asked in English.

An astonished gasp. Then a strong American voice assured me he was okay. I heard the drone of the engines in the distance, and suddenly remembered my code letter. I ran back through the corn to my marked place and flashed the 'L' to the fast-approaching and low-flying plane.

"Who are you?" someone said behind me. The voice spoke English with a strong French accent.

"My name's Paulette," I replied, in French and without looking back. The Halifax was just overhead and, one after the other, fifteen white parachutes cracked into the sky, under the wings.

"I must say we didn't expect to find a woman on the field," the voice went on. "We were expecting machine-gun bullets, and instead we find a woman asking us if we're okay…" The containers landed one after the other with a thump.

"Yeah," said the American, who had joined us.[4] "I guess that's about the only thing we hadn't thought of, hey, Yves?"[5]

I heard the one called Yves laugh, as I ran down to the place where the first container had landed.

"Paulette, can you see it? I can't find it," I heard Jean shout. This was the most noisy *parachutage* I had seen. Our British instructors would be wild if they saw the little heed we paid to the rules they had so patiently hammered into us. I had seen the container fall; its parachute lay white and shining in the moonlight, spread on the wind-rippled corn. The wind was stronger than we had thought, and some of the containers were swept beyond the field. Up in the sky, the engines still droned away. I went back to my signalling position.

"Our parcels," the American was saying excitedly, "our parcels… They haven't been dropped yet. All our equipment and our radio sets…"

"Don't worry, the plane's coming back on a third run," I said. "I can't understand why he didn't drop your parcels with you, and save himself a run and us from being pin-pointed by the Germans. When I was dropped not only parcels but also the containers came down with us."

"You were dropped?" the one called Yves said. Then he laughed and laughed until I wheeled around on him.

"Anything wrong with being dropped?" I said crossly.

"No, I just think it's funny, when I think of what we expected to find here." Tears were glistening on his cheeks. But I stopped paying any attention to him. The Halifax was approaching on its third run: low – fast – then slow – then, out of the aperture, six parachutes swinging gracefully. The American was standing three yards away from me: suddenly, with a whistle and a crack, a parcel crashed clean between us, then another, just half a yard on the other side of me. The American jumped high enough to make Serge Lifar jealous, but I was pinned to my place, shaking all over.[6]

"The bloody fools," he raged. "Why the hell do they use cardboard containers to drop things? They always break when they hit the slip-stream. We might've been killed. If any of those parcels had hit you or me, we would've been killed straight… Say, you, do you realize that?" he added, shaking my arm.

From the damp earth, a smell of coffee rose slowly: good coffee, real coffee, such as I hadn't tasted for weeks, and even months. Good coffee, like they had every day in England, like people stole for and dreamed of in France. Five pounds strewn right across the ground, wasted because of cardboard containers. The men around threw themselves on their knees and filled their dirty pockets with the smooth ground coffee.

"Excuse me, Mademoiselle," said a timid voice next to me. "The third man is here; he's a Frenchman, and wants to know if he can kiss the first French girl he meets in France. He's been away for four years…"[7]

I hadn't the heart to disappoint him about my nationality. A tall, thin boy planted a big, resounding kiss on my cheek; his face was cold.

"Say, I never would've dared do that," Yves exclaimed. "And I'm not shy…"

I hadn't seen any of their faces yet. Overhead, the Halifax zoomed by on its way home and flicked its wings in farewell, just as it had, six months earlier, after I had landed. It felt like years ago… The fires were out. The tenseness had gone. The *parachutage* was over. I suggested going to the Bérard farm, where the three men could get rid of their heavy clothes.

I walked ahead with Yves. "I'd like to introduce myself," he said. "My name's Yves de Changins." There were three captain's stripes on his shoulder. "The American is Colonel Ross Halsall, and the little French lieutenant who kissed you is a radio operator. We just call him Bouboule. So now you know everybody."

"Well, will you tell me why you arrived so early? Did you fly by daylight over France? You must've left England terribly early?"

"But we didn't come from England… We took off at Algiers. We flew over the Mediterranean by daylight and crossed the coast at night."[8]

We walked in silence for a while, then Yves caught hold of my arm; his voice choked a little:

"I'm sorry if I laughed a while ago. I was so happy that I had become a little hysterical. Do you know that I've been away from France for four years? I feel I want to lie with my face flat on the earth and smell it, and smell it, till it becomes part of me again. When I had tears in my eyes, it was only because I was crying with happiness. I've waited so long to come back… You wouldn't understand—"

"Of course I can understand. I went through exactly the same thing when I came, six months ago…" He let go of my arm.

"Oh, yes, I had forgotten. I can hardly believe you're English: you feel French to me. We were told about you, and Jean-Claude, and your chief."

"We call him the Patron. He sent me to receive you. Colonel Halsall will have to come back with me. He wants to talk to him."

"Mmmm… We'll have to talk about that," he replied, suddenly stiff. I felt there would be opposition. Yves seemed the actual leader of the party: or at last seemed to think he was.[9]

CHAPTER XVII

Madame Bérard clasped and unclasped her hands as our cumbersome group walked into the kitchen. Her mother retired into a corner and sat on a low stool; she viewed the scene silently, her eyes bright with emotion. Madame Bérard exclaimed:

"We saw it all. Yes, we saw it all; all the parachutes floating in the air, all the fires, and the plane above... It was so beautiful, I shall never forget it," she added, her hand on her cheek.

Yves de Changins threw his heavy rucksack to the floor and pushed his beret off his forehead. Then, with outstretched hand:

"Good evening," he said to her. "It is so kind of you to have us here."

Madame Bérard stepped back, giving herself time to wipe her hands nervously on her apron, and shook hands, her lips trembling. Her old mother wiped a tear rolling down her cheek.

"Ah, these brave boys, these brave boys..." I heard her mumble to herself.

Monsieur Bérard brought some *piquette* and we sat round the table, eating an enormous asparagus omelette with sausages and bread. Yves de Changins was a strong, tough-looking man with a wisp of hair sticking up childishly at the back of his head. His blue eyes stood out sharply in a sun-tanned, boyish face; they could be hard or tender, but never indifferent. Maupassant would have said of him: "He is no longer a young man, but he is a man who is still young."

He looked at me with a gleam of mischief in his eye, then, putting his head on one side:

"I've seen you somewhere before... Could it be at the Rembrandt Hotel, in London?"

"Stop, *stop*," Ross Halsall cried, jumping to his feet and placing himself between Yves and me. "That is his first line, Paulette. Be careful, I warn you, he's a wolf..."

"A wolf, me?" Yves protested innocently.

"Oh, stop it. Play is over now, and I'm just warning her to keep out of your way for her own safety..."

Yves, obviously flattered, turned his attention back to his omelette. Ross kept a watchful eye on him. He was very tall and very fair, with a hard, set face all built in horizontal lines. His eyes were his only youthful feature, blue and candid. When he smiled, he looked like a dog ready to bite. He was rather quiet, while Yves talked and babbled away endlessly. Bouboule sat silently in his corner.

De Changins wanted to have a small team of men to work closely with him and help his group to get settled. I told him of my four friends: Auguste, Jean, Raymond and Jacques. They were keen to start real fighting, and had felt rather frustrated under Roger's orders to save the small store of arms to support demolition parties. Auguste and Jean, who came in with the three parachutists' packages, agreed enthusiastically. The deal was settled then and there, with the help of a couple of glasses of *piquette*. The containers had all been found, the parachutes packed and loaded on a couple of trucks. Auguste and Raymond took charge of driving them to the depots; they started out, each with four men in the back and on the running-boards, armed to the teeth, and ready to fight out any interference.

After they had gone, Roger and I retired to the Bérards' other room for a conference with Ross and Yves. Yves made a rapid layout of his plans; he wanted to set up a *maquis* in the mountains immediately, contact and unite the other *maquis* around, and organise raids on enemy dumps, railway traffic and road transport. Roger and I looked at each other.

"And what do you expect to do that with?" Roger asked.

"The material? Easy... We're going to get as many *parachutages* as we want, and we shall soon be ready to attack a whole division."

"Aren't you afraid of being a little optimistic?" I asked. "I was told the same thing when I left London; we only had to ask, and we would get anything we wanted... But unfortunately, it was never so. Weather, lack of planes, other circuits to be fed, those were the reasons London gave us. We were more often disappointed than not..."

"Nothing of all that for us..." Yves waved his hand airily. "Your time is over. We are the special envoys of Eisenhower and the High Command; we're going to be looked after properly."

I was furious. "Our time is over? Thank you... You couldn't have come here if we hadn't prepared the ground for you."

Roger and I looked at each other again, with a mental wave of mutual solidarity and resentment. What did these fresh-from-the-sky windbags think they were? After we'd toiled for weeks and months, it was infuriating to be told we were no use. Like old orange skins. The conference went on stormily. Another violent argument developed when I declared that Ross Halsall would have to return to the

Lannemaignan *maquis* with me the next day. Yves asserted that they were an inseparable team – which was another way of saying that he didn't want anything to happen without his knowledge and participation.

"I'm sorry," I told him. "I have strict orders. Colonel Halsall can explain that to the Patron himself. I came here four times to fetch him, and I'm not going back without completing my mission."

"I shall see and we will decide later," Yves concluded importantly. You'd better make a positive decision, I thought, or there will be trouble. Madame Bérard announced that some coffee had been made; some of the coffee her son had picked up off the ground after the parcels had crashed. We all went back to the kitchen where Bouboule and Jean were in gay spirits; their natural and friendly atmosphere relaxed the tension created by our touchy dignities.

A car came to collect the three and we agreed to meet the next afternoon, after everyone had had some rest. Plucci was worried.

"We're already a whole day late. They're going to wonder where we are, back at Lannemaignan." But there was nothing to be done.

Jean, Plucci and I retired to the hayloft for a bit of sleep. At 8am, Auguste and Raymond had not returned. Jean shook me.

"Wake up. I'm sick of worrying alone… They ought to have been back long ago. I hope nothing's happened. I ought to have gone with them."

I tried to reassure him, but he shook his head. "Auguste told me yesterday that he had a feeling something would happen to him soon. He never bothers about his own safety…"

A couple of hours later he went off to meet them. He came back in the early afternoon, mounted on the back of a thunderous motor-cycle, with Auguste. I was pretty worried myself by then and heaved a sigh of relief at the sight of them. Auguste had had three narrow escapes: he had been chased right up the mountains by two German tractions and a small armoured car, firing continuously at him. He had driven his motor-cycle at such a speed up narrow mountain roads that he had finally lost them. He came to inform me that Captain de Changins had finally decided that Colonel Halsall was not to come with me.

I flared up in a fury. I jumped on the back of the motor-cycle and went off with Auguste. Jean and Plucci would follow in the car. We drove fifteen miles to a poor little farm in a valley run by a Spanish refugee family. I clung on to Auguste's belt for my life while we jumped over holes and bumps and skidded every turn at ninety miles an hour. But I was so enraged I had no time to be scared.

Yves de Changins was in a friendly mood after his rest and I burst into his room with such determination and in such a bad temper that he soon agreed to be magnanimous enough to allow Ross Halsall to return with me. Then he cooled me down by filling my pockets with toothpaste and chocolate. The final gift of two packets of Chesterfield cigarettes reduced my fury to a mere memory. He was a diplomat.

Jean and Plucci arrived a little while later. Jean had picked some information up on the way: it appeared that the Lannemezan Milice was looking for "the blonde woman in the grey car." The doctor who had created such a bad impression on me was a friend of the Commandant; he had noticed us returning several times to the Bérard farm and reported us. We would have to find another car.

We left at 5pm, Ross in full uniform, with his green beret pulled over his forehead, wedged between the seat and the bicycle, at the back of the car. On the way he told us how he had fought in France in 1940, then returned to the States, fought in the Philippines and at Guadalcanal; then again fought in North Africa, before being enrolled in the Special Force. He was tough and modest about it.

We arrived at Lannemaignan in the early evening.

"Well, we thought you were dead…" some of the staff officers exclaimed as I walked into the mess. Without surprise, either. That happened another time later on, too, when someone reported that our car had been riddled with bullets on the Pau road and that Plucci's body and mine had been identified, lying in a ditch. They called me 'The Phantom' from that day.

The *maquis* had been attacked that very afternoon, by half a dozen fighter planes which had wrecked a number of cars and killed one man. Alcazio produced a pair of my panties, to my great embarrassment, with four cannon-shell holes through them… In the evening I found my mattress pierced in three places: the house I lived in appeared to have been one of the main targets.

Two young, baby-faced Americans had arrived from a more northern *maquis*: Bud and Harold. They had only one thought in mind: to get a tooth-brush. Then go away. We couldn't get them off for some time: our usual Pyrenees guides had run into a German flying column and been shot dead in their car and we had no contacts for the present. A few days later, Bud and Harold ("We're both from Michigan, that's why we're buddies," they'd told me) started out on their own, without telling anyone. After wandering two days, they were picked up by the Germans and, although they were in uniform, shot point-blank in the back of the neck.

I spent the following day washing my few belongings: I had to wear one of Mike's shirts and a filthy old pair of dungarees, as I had nothing else to change into. Mike was learning French fast and having a wonderful time.

"Everybody is so good to me," he used to say. "They all rush and share everything with me. I don't want to go away. I'd be sure to reach England too late to do anything." And he went on living in his barn and cleaning parachuted arms.

I never saw him do anything else. While I had been away, the *maquis* had had several *parachutages*. Also, other *maquis* had joined us: we were nearly eight hundred by then.

In the evening, the Patron called me to his PC. I felt a little more like an orderly every time he did: ended were the days of chatting in the garden and allowing me to carry out my missions according to my own initiative. This time, however, we had an argument.

"Tomorrow morning, you'll go off with Halsall," he declared. "He will go as a sick person in the back of an ambulance, and you will be in front, as a voluntary nurse. You'll have papers."

I refused point-blank.

"I know the region like the back of my hand," I told him. "I know where and when the danger lies. If we run into an enemy column we would never have a chance. They would inspect the inside of the ambulance, find Halsall, his yankee accent and his uniform. Besides, I have a gruesome presentiment about this trip…"

The Patron was quiet for a while. I knew that he trusted personal instinct more than anything else, having been saved several times by his own.

"How do you want to go?" he said finally.

"I want to leave in the early morning, with a traction, in good working order, and take the roads I know. By eleven we would be there. And safely, I promise you…" The Patron said he'd think it over.

French *maquis* all possessed dozens of cars, but few were in working order. They had a habit of breaking down in lonely spots or at vital moments. Half the boys who drove them had learnt by themselves, and didn't know the first thing about an engine: the organisation of a *maquis* repair service always broke down in its first stages, the few mechanics finding themselves faced with the work of ten big garages put together.

The next morning, I was again summoned to the PC, by a motor-cyclist who took me there. The Patron had decided that Plucci would be given a traction, since the grey car had been betrayed to the Milice, and that we would start the same evening. A French police car would precede us and accompany us through the dangerous zone. The Patron was not in an argumentative mood and there was no point in making a fuss, this time. I told him, however, that I still had a gloomy presentiment and did not like the idea. He shrugged his shoulders and I walked out.

In the evening, I had a talk with the police lieutenant. We agreed on the road, different from our usual one, and on a red flashlight danger signal. One of the policemen belonged to a small *maquis* near the village of Simorre. They would come with us as far as there and we would finish the journey alone.

At half-past eleven we started out. Ross had had a slight attack of malaria, remains of his Guadalcanal days, and felt a bit sick. The "traction in good working order" had feeble headlights and puffed noisily. The petrol was getting short and petroleum had been added to it: the mixture choked the engine. We drove slowly. Nearing the town of Miélan, where German movements had been reported in the afternoon, the police car stopped and the lieutenant got out and poked his head through our window.

"This is a dangerous bit," he said. "You'd better put your headlights out and follow us at a distance. We'll go slowly."

I was irritated with the slowness of the trip. The quicker it could be got over, the better it would be. Plucci was irritated with the traction; it was difficult to drive and refused to gather any speed. Ross was asleep in the back.

We passed the dangerous approaches to Miélan without incident and started climbing up a hill. The moon was up and the road shone on Plucci's eyes, giving him a false sense of security. The road wound up endlessly. Suddenly Plucci missed part of a bend, gave a quick turn of the wheel, but too late. We went straight over a small ditch, overturned and rolled twice down the hill, until the car jerked to a standstill against a tree.

We were stunned for a few minutes: the car was on its side and I was sitting on top of Plucci. He rapidly cut the contact. I groped for the door.

"Those damned French drivers," Ross fumed suddenly. "They're all the same, they don't know how the hell to drive a car..."

"Are you okay?" I asked.

Yes, he was. But furious. Plucci was silent after apologising and explaining that he was used to his own Renault and to driving with headlights on, at night. We all clambered out as we could: the wheels went on turning in mid-air. The policemen ran down the hill, expecting to find us all dead. It was a piece of luck that the tree had been in the way, otherwise we would probably have rolled all the way down the hill and reached the bottom in a thousand bits.

The car would have to be pulled out and towed by one of the Simorre *maquis'* five-ton trucks; it was well sunk in the grass and one of the connecting rods was broken. Ross Halsall went on fuming as we climbed back to the road. After I had got over the first moment of nervousness, I wanted to laugh; it seemed so foolish to take all our precious precautions and finish up by busting the car down a hill... We all sat on top of one another in the police car and drove off to the Simorre *maquis*. We were stopped by three fierce-looking unshaven youths, pointing a Bren gun right into our faces. They recognised their police pal and allowed him to go up to the *maquis* PC while we waited.

It was after three in the morning by then. Half an hour later, we were accompanied to the PC by a liaison officer. The *maquis* was perched on the crest of a small hill; it seemed dangerously situated, with little cover, and surrounded by other hill-crests within easy reach. The eighty men in it lived in two disused and dilapidated houses. They used candles as means of lighting, slept out of doors or in the hay, and were fed by a neighbouring farm.

We were greeted by Dr Raynaud, a very amiable and intelligent man who was the head of the *maquis*.[1] Ross immediately established liaison contacts and promised them a *parachutage* in the near future. Dr Raynaud called the cook and asked him to prepare some food for us. He was a little Parisian student with a turned-up nose and fair hair falling all over his face. He was called Mimosa.[2]

"Watch how I cook," he said with a wink. He built a fire that must have been visible miles away, produced part of a container, and threw a large chunk of fat inside. A few minutes later, he presented us with tempting-looking beefsteaks which we devoured hungrily. Everybody loved little Mimosa; he sang and laughed all day long, preparing the meals and helping everyone.

A couple of hours later, Plucci arrived in the traction duly towed by the five-ton truck. It would have to be taken to Boulogne to be repaired. Dr Raynaud promised to lend us a car.

"Colonel Halsall will drive it to the Pyrenees," I suggested, knowing Ross's disapproval of French drivers, "and I'll drive it back here tonight."

Dr Raynaud, however, wanted one of his drivers to take it. We started out at six-thirty; Plucci stayed behind, in charge of the traction. The driver seemed highly inexperienced, as we bumped down the hill in a Peugeot 402, without avoiding the smallest ditch or hole. Ross, sitting in front, turned to me with a meaning look, his eyes raised to the heavens. We passed Boulogne without incidents and turned into small country lanes, to reach our destination by the quickest route.

"Don't drive so fast," Ross snapped as we sped at sixty miles an hour on the dusty road. The chauffeur[3] slowed down to fifty-five miles, and Ross crouched angrily in his seat. A large notice glared at us: "TAKE CARE – NARROW ROAD", but the driver paid no attention.

"Watch out, there's a bend coming," Ross yelled suddenly. The chauffeur obviously hadn't seen it, and jammed on the brakes: the car skidded in the turn, jumped over a gravel heap, and went straight into a tree at forty-five miles an hour. "This time, we're dead…" I thought.

The front seat backed into my legs and pinned me in my seat. I was dumb for a second, but shook myself and looked around. Ross's head had disappeared into the hood; he had gone clean through it and was knocked unconscious for a few minutes. The front window was broken to smithereens, the bonnet crashed to a shapeless finish. I sat back and laughed till tears rolled down my face: at three we roll down a hill, at seven we crash into a tree, what would happen at ten? I had begun to pull myself out, when Ross recovered his senses.

"Those bloody French drivers..." he yelled. "This is the last time I ever go in a car with any Frenchman. What the hell am I doing here anyway?"

I nearly collapsed on the ground with laughter. Ross's fair hair and puffed red face, sticking out of the hood and yelling his imprecations, was too much.

"Are you hurt?" I asked weakly.

"No, but how in God's name I'm not is more than I'll ever understand. And stop laughing, you grinning idiot over there..." he added, nearly choking with rage.

"I can't help it. You would too, if you saw yourself. This is all so silly... And since we're both okay, there's nothing to cry about."

"To hell with French drivers..." he went on to himself. "And to hell with all the French put together..."

That annoyed me. "You have nothing to say against the French. We've had bad luck, and that's all there is to it. You're pleased enough to be here, you know that..."

He began extracting himself. The driver was already out and unhurt: the poor little boy looked so embarrassed that I felt sorry for him. He was paralysed with fright at Ross's fury. Ross climbed out of his hood and over the debris of the car onto the road. His pockets were full of safety glass, broken into neat little squares, his forehead was cut and he was white with dust. Otherwise he was whole. My mirth finally communicated itself to him and we both sat down to laugh at our ridiculous adventure.

"Yeah, that's fine, but how the heck do we get there now?"

I took the map out of my bag and we studied the road. We were nearly ten miles from our destination. We would have to walk: this meant leaving behind a transmitter set lent by the Patron and terribly heavy, and various arms we had with us. We climbed up a wooded slope and buried the stuff under a tree.

The sun was already hot. Fortunately it was Sunday and the farmers were not in the fields: Ross's uniform was visible for miles. He took off his green beret and his tunic: there was less chance that he would be noticed in plain khaki and stripped of colourful badges. But Ross would be noticed anywhere in this part of France: tall and blond and extremely tough, he had the casual and dignified walk typical of Americans. People watched us curiously as we strolled past, trying to look like a couple on a romantic Sunday morning walk.

We were both tired and hot. After walking an hour, we stopped by a lonely stream, took our shoes off and paddled in the icy water. Halsall had his toilet case with him, and we managed a rapid freshening-up. We emerged from our respective bushes full of renewed energy but desperately hungry. As we passed a cherry tree, weighed down under a mass of small, ripe cherries, Ross suggested picking some.

He climbed up and threw them through the leaves, while I caught them in his beret. At one moment he poked his hard-boiled face, topped by a mass of tousled blond curls, through the branches, and remarked:

"If I'd known that three days after being parachuted into France I would've been picking my breakfast in a cherry tree, I'm damned if I'd have come…"

CHAPTER XVIII

We reached the Spanish farm under the torrid midday sun and found that Yves and Bouboule had already gone to join a *maquis* in the Pyrenees. Roger was waiting for Ross and took him there, while I waited for Auguste who would take me back to Simorre on his motor-cycle. I slept sixteen hours straight that night, my first peaceful and noiseless one for a long time, and only awoke in the evening for an enormous plateful of fried onions.

Auguste came in the late afternoon.

"Captain de Changins wants me to come all the way back to your *maquis* with you," he said. "All the liaison contacts are on your side and we have no way of getting in touch with you."

"In that case, you'd better leave your motor-cycle at Simorre and do the rest of the journey in the car with us. It would kill you to ride more than two hundred kilometres on a motor-cycle, and back…"

"All right. How far is Simorre?"

"About fifty kilometres."

"Fine, we'll be there in half an hour."

"Auguste, no… Please. You'll finish me off long before we get there: don't forget there are no feet supports on your motor-cycle and that I feel every bump and hole like a blow."

He laughed. "I'll give you a pair of glasses against the wind," he said, as a consolation.

We started off. At the first bend we skidded straight into a ditch, and I flew head-first into a bush.

"Look here, I'm tired of this… Yesterday, two car crashes, today breaking my neck with a nincompoop who can't drive a motor-cycle under ninety miles an hour. Please go slowly…"

I grabbed his leather belt and we took off again. Within five minutes I had lost all my combs and hairpins, the sole of my shoe had been burnt clean through when

I put my foot on the exhaust pipe, and I was blinded with the tears streaming out of my eyes, in spite of the glasses.

"Lean with me at the bends…" he yelled through the noise. We thundered past the Bérard farm, but Auguste wouldn't, or couldn't, hear my shouts to stop. I didn't want to see the Bérards so much as to give myself a few minutes' respite. After twenty minutes, I hit him on the head until he stopped.

"I must rest a minute," I said, climbing off. My knees knocked together and I felt as though I had lost my arms. Auguste thought it very funny. I didn't.

We arrived at Simorre at ten. It was too late to start out for Lannemaignan, and we decided to stay the night.

The traction had been repaired. Dr Raynaud was very apologetic about the bust-up on the previous day.

"Was Colonel Halsall cross?" he asked.

"No, not cross, enraged. Never mention cars or French chauffeurs to him. I think it would be wiser."

We laughed and joked while Mimosa prepared some food. But Dr Raynaud suddenly became serious.

"I'm worried about staying here," he declared. "I meant to leave today; we've been in this *maquis* a whole week now, and our policy is to be continually moving."

"Well, why don't you?"

"We hope to have a *parachutage* here soon. We want to stay near; we need the stuff so badly."

"Are you very short of arms?"

"Short? Do you know that our 'heavy' armament consists of four Brens with three hundred rounds each? And with that a few rifles and a number of Stens. But Stens are no good further than fifty yards. I'm afraid we would be in an awful mess if we were attacked. There are German columns patrolling the region. They're stationed at St-Gaudens."

His right-hand man was a major in the French army: the men adored him. He was very worried too.

"I hope you don't mind staying here?" he said.

I didn't. He took me to the neighbouring farm, where I spent the night. It was my first contact with a real feather bed for days: the combination of forgotten comfort, too short a bed and the endless chiming of the hours by a grandfather clock, made my night a restless one. We started early the next morning.

"Come back soon," said Mimosa. "We like seeing women here: you're the first one we've seen in months…" I shall never forget his twinkling blue eyes as he threw his long hair back with a rapid movement of the head, and laughed.

At lunchtime we arrived at Lannemaignan. On the way we had stopped at a couple of Gendarmeries, and I had introduced Auguste to the chief constables. They were kept informed as to the whereabouts of our *maquis,* and would take Auguste to us whenever he came.

I told the Patron about our car accidents. He mumbled something about people's instincts being always right. He had expected us to be back two days earlier and had obviously been turning my last words in his head all this time.

"Auguste ought to go straight back after lunch," he said. "There is no point in his hanging about. You'll take him, Paulette."

He prepared another complicated departure, giving us an escort of six armed men. The driver was the Condom jeweller with the club foot, who had sold my precious clock to the Cérensacs. As I got into the car, I realized the futility of another trip, and went to the Patron.

"Look: Auguste knows the way to Simorre. We've come from there this very morning. I'm rather tired after all these journeys. Would you mind if I didn't go?"

The Patron agreed.

The six men who left with Auguste did not return that night. Nor the following nights. Three days later, we heard what had happened to them.

When they arrived at Simorre, they found some old pals and decided to stay the night for a bit of celebration. They all went to sleep on the floor of the kitchen. At 4am, as dawn broke in a faint white line over the horizon, the Germans attacked them. Twelve hundred Germans. Twelve hundred against eighty – fifteen to one. The enemy approached silently, under cover of darkness: some *miliciens* were with them. They occupied the neighbouring hill-tops and opened fire simultaneously from all sides. They had eight 13mm machine-guns and a number of mortars, against the Simorre boys' four Bren guns with their three hundred rounds. A mortar shell fell on the ammunition dump, blowing up their small reserve.

The eighty men fought to their last bullet. Then they tried to escape through the high corn and the vines. They were shot one after the other. The Germans and *miliciens* then came on the scene of the *maquis.* They set fire to the disused houses in which the boys had lived, and blew up the remains with hand grenades. Just as they had done at Castelnau, and at other small villages in the region. The wounded men were dragged in front of the burning houses and finished off, some according to the enemy's favourite method, shot in the back of the neck; but mostly murdered savagely, their skulls bashed in with rifle-butts. The ones that had been caught unhurt were made to look on, then mowed down with machine-gun fire and finished off like their wounded comrades.

Four of the boys managed to escape. Two of them were mortally wounded and died in a fox-hole, two hours after the fight. The whole thing was over by 8am. The Germans and *miliciens,* proud of themselves, got back into their truck laughing and singing. But a last idea made them jump out again, rush to the farm where I had spent the night twenty-four hours before, murder the whole family and burn the farm down. The next day, the farmer's son was to come back from Germany, where he had been a prisoner four years, to find his home a smoking ruin and the bodies of his parents rotting in the front yard.

The massacre was complete.[1] Seventy-eight *maquisards*, out of eighty, killed and murdered, and added to them, a family of six, shot for having helped them.

Dr Driziers told me the frightful tale. What had happened to Auguste? He had left with a number of contacts to be established in the Pyrenees sector, and some messages for Halsall and de Changins. Had he spent the night at Simorre, or had he gone straight on? I rushed to the Patron, who knew nothing more than Driziers had told me.

"Jean-Claude has just arrived," he said. "I suppose you want to see him. But you will have to leave for the Pyrenees tomorrow, find out what has happened to Auguste, and carry out his mission, if he has been killed."

I was so pleased to see Jean-Claude that I momentarily forgot about the Simorre *maquis*. I found him resting under a tree; his hair had grown long and he was dirtier than ever. When no one was looking, we kissed each other.

"I'm so pleased to see you, Minou," he declared in his quiet, even voice. "We haven't seen each other for six weeks, have we?"

We had had virtually no contacts with the Dordogne sector since D-Day. Colomiers' men, united with other Resistance groups, had cut off the Dordogne and made it an impenetrable zone. They had even proclaimed the birth of the Fourth Republic.

"You should've been there," Jean-Claude said. "We had telephone communications from town to town: 'Hello? This is the Bergerac PC – Hello? This is the Sarlat PC' etc. The Germans haven't been able to use either of the main roads to Paris. We also cut the railway communications completely, by blowing up the bridges on the Dordogne and the Lot. I've been chasing around in tractions and having a swell time..."

"Yes, I can see that. But not time to wash your shirt."

"Me? Wash my shirt? Don't be funny. There is no one to do it for me, so I just don't bother."

"Why don't you wear it inside out, then?"

Without answering, he pulled a flap out of his pants and turned it over; it was stiff with grease, dust and just plain dirt. He smiled, and put on his best cherubic expression.

"Minou," he said, "I *always* have a clean shirt, because everything is relative in this world. When my shirt is dirty on one side, I turn it inside out. When it's dirtier on that side than on the first one, I turn it again. So I always have the cleaner side on…"

I have always said there was no arguing with Jean-Claude. We went off hand in hand and walked around the *maquis*. Two days earlier, we had moved out of Lannemaignan and gone further south in a great convoy. I had given up Alcazio and his assurances of lodgings, and found a comfortable room for myself in a small, occupied château. It was inhabited by an old lady and her housekeeper, who frowned on my dirty, dishevelled person, but didn't dare refuse me a room. They probably thought I would have begun to fire at all their precious vases and beaded lampshades. The next day, however, I got into their good graces by going to church with them, which must have convinced them that I was not a cannibal. They invited me to breakfast: Dr Driziers, who also lived in the château, was invited too, and both of us passed the sugar, and praised the coffee, and praised the jam, and praised the château, until the two old ladies confessed their relief. At night the housekeeper would bring me a jug of hot water – unbelievable luxury.

"How did you come, Jean-Claude, and why?" I asked him.

"I had to bring a parachutist to the Patron. One of those men who were parachuted in uniform; he's a nice guy too. His name is Captain Conte.[2] We started out yesterday by motor-cycle, but when we reached the Lot river; we found a barrage of *miliciens* on the bridge, so we had to hide the motor-cycle and swim."

"Swim? And then what?"

"We walked… We had to swim the Dordogne too; there was another barrage there, and we walked the rest. That's about sixty kilometres of walking."

"How will you go back?"

"The Patron promised us a car as far as the Garonne. We won't have to walk so far that way."

I suggested going back with them as far as Condom, and spending the night at Nasoulens. I was getting too badly off for clothes and wanted to collect a suit. The Patron agreed.

Captain Conte was young and quiet. He was a great friend of Yves and Ross; they had all trained together in England and North Africa. The three of us started out the next afternoon. Before I left the Patron said:

"You can't have the car any further than Condom. I can't go on risking cars like this. You'll have to go by bicycle."

Two hundred kilometres and back by bicycle? I told him I didn't know when I would be back.

"Never mind… Take your time…"

It was wonderful seeing the Cérensacs again. I waved at them from far off; they were in the fields, cutting the corn.

"We're so pleased to see you, Petite," they said, as I passed from arm to arm. "We've had no news of you since the Castelnau fight."

"Goodness, and how worried I've been about you. I was so afraid the Boches might make reprisals on Nasoulens."

"They came damn near it. They burnt four farms further up," Henri Cérensac said. "I had already buried all my money. I tried to send Odilla away, but she wouldn't leave me. Fortunately we're all right. André is back too, and much better although still quite weak. He has such a strong constitution that he got through. In fact, he astonished the doctors, because they expected him to have a purulent pleurisy, but he didn't."

André was very pale and thin; he had only been up two days.

"I'll never rest until I've paid my debt to those *miliciens*," he said, clenching his fists. "I have all those boys to revenge. And I will, ah yes, I will…"

His parents looked at each other and said nothing.

I understood that they didn't want to get into an argument and hoped that he would forget about it. Madame Driziers was still living at the farm. Since the Castelnau fight, the Gestapo had sealed her house in Condom and was looking for her. I went all over Nasoulens, smelling the good smells and playing with the cat, Ketty, and Sirrou; both of which had had families. We all talked way into the night before I retired to sleep, in the hayloft: in the middle of the night I woke up with a terrific row going on under my bed. Three large rats were fighting for my shoes. I rescued them, shooed the rats off, and went back to sleep. Rats were small fry now, and didn't bother me.

The next morning I went down to Condom and took the bus to Auch. Then I cycled to Seissan, on the Nationale 129, and stopped at the Chéniers' just in time for lunch. The sun was cruel; it blazed on the long straight road, hitting me on the back of the head. I was terribly hot: all I had left to wear was my old tweed suit, the one I had jumped in, in the middle of the winter. The Chéniers' house was cool.

"But you don't intend to go to Simorre this afternoon, do you?" I nodded. "It's uphill and very hard going all the way. It's about twenty kilometres from here, and the hills are in the full sun, without any trees on the edge of the road. You'll get sunstroke…"

"I have to, nevertheless. I must find out if Auguste is alive."

Chénier had made a masterful understatement about the road to Simorre; it was deserted, and the sun burnt pitilessly every living thing. I walked for miles, pushing my bicycle up the steep country roads, my shirt sticking to my back and my feet swollen in a pair of *espadrilles*, or canvas shoes with rope soles. In Simorre, I contacted the grocer who used to feed the *maquis* and whose name had been given to me as a liaison. He was a kind, fat man with three beautiful daughters. They showed me to their back-shop.

"The Germans were here this afternoon; they seem to be all over the place. I don't know anything about Auguste or the boys who came with him, but I can tell you where to find one of the survivors. He is in a frightful state of nerves, but I suppose he will be able to help you."

After ice-cold shandies, he showed me the way to Saramon, another village, ten miles off. The baker there would be able to tell me where Christophe was. The baker was suspicious, however.

"Christophe? Don't know him."

I explained who had sent me. He shook his head and insisted that he knew nothing about Christophe.

"Now look," I said impatiently. "I've come a long way to see him. I shall go and sit in the village square. Tell him that Paulette is here, and you can come and warn me when and where I can see him."

He shrugged his shoulders and went in. A few minutes later he caught me up.

"I'm sorry I was so rude, but Christophe is in such a state that he's terrified of anyone approaching the house. When I told him you were here, however, he said he wanted to see you right away."

Christophe had been one of Dr Raynaud's closest associates, and we had talked to each other quite a lot, at the *maquis*. I found him pacing up and down in a darkened room. He looked at me for a minute, then collapsed in a chair, and burst out sobbing, his face in his folded elbow. I shook him gently to try and calm him down.

"My-my father was taken away by the Milice two weeks ago," he gulped. "The other day I saw my brother being killed. They fired a gun right into his face. It blew away in all directions, all red, a mass of red blood gushed out like a torrent... I can't stand it, I can't stand it..."

Then he was silent for a while and grew a little calmer.

"I suppose you want to know about Auguste, don't you? He was a good friend of yours. He's dead. I saw him myself. He had two bullets in the thigh, but they murdered him. They bashed his skull in: you wouldn't recognize him now. I knew him because of his green checked jacket. His black hair was all stuck together and brown with blood."

I sat down. Tears rolled down my cheeks: I suddenly realised that I had thought all along that Auguste was safe. I had not even worried. And he had been killed, less than twenty-four hours after we had been there together. What was it he had told Jean? "I know something will happen to me before long..." God, I would have to tell Jean myself, his best friend. I couldn't prevent a sob. Christophe looked up, his face red and swollen. For a moment he forgot his own misery and put his hand on my shoulder.

"He fought wonderfully. He caught hold of a rifle and fired every one of his rounds slowly and precisely. But we hadn't a chance, you know… The others who came with him are all dead too. So are Dr Raynaud and the Major."

Then, after a while: "Mimosa too. Poor little Mimosa; he had an arm shot off, tears running down his face with pain. They shot him in the neck. He looked them in the face as they were doing it."

Mimosa too… I had hoped he would have been saved: I hadn't even imagined that the ones I liked could have been hurt. And they were all dead… Murdered. How could this story be told to the world? Eighty against twelve hundred. And the Germans laughed as they left…

"I hid in a small hole in the corn with two others. We covered ourselves with branches. The Germans and *miliciens* were running all around, shouting 'Here's one; don't let him go,' or 'They'll learn better than to try and intimidate us…' Yes, we learned, we learned fifteen to one. But we learned that we can't stop fighting them, until the last one is dead… The two others with me were terribly wounded. I nearly had to choke them to stop them from screaming or groaning. They both died there, under my own eyes. I couldn't do a thing: the enemy was still about."

It was dark outside when I left Christophe. The baker filled my little bag with fruit. I came back by a different road, up and down hill again, lost my way twice, but eventually reached Seissan at one in the morning. I threw stones at Chénier's bedroom; I couldn't risk shouting to wake them up, because the curfew was at eleven.

I didn't even bother to undress, and fell into a heavy, dreamless sleep. The next morning I started out early: I had nearly a hundred kilometres to do. I went straight through Montréjeau in the afternoon and went on to St-Gaudens. There I was told to go to a small village, Izaut, at the foot of the Pyrenees: Halsall and de Changins had set up their *maquis* there. I reached Izaut at 9.30pm and contacted the grocer there, as I had been told.

"The *maquis*?" he cried, throwing his arms to the ceiling. "But it's up in the mountains… You don't want to go there now? It's a three-hours' climb."

My legs were wobbly and my posterior sore from the riding. I sat down, discouraged. Then I remembered Jean, who still thought Auguste was alive and was waiting for him. I couldn't let him down.

"Yes, I'll have to go tonight."

"Very well, my nephew will show you the way. But stay and have a little food, won't you?" I accepted gratefully. All I'd eaten that day was bread and sausage and a few peaches that Madame Chénier had put in my bag before I left. Everyone was so genuinely generous and helpful.

The grocer's nephew, Petit-Paul, suggested we should take a short cut. "It'll be only two hours if we do. And you look as though you can take it…"

"Mmmm… What do you mean, 'take' it? I've cycled a hundred and four kilometres since this morning, you know…"

He waved a casual hand. "I only mean that we won't be going straight along an easy road… But it's so much quicker."

The night was as dark as ink. I soon saw what Petit-Paul had meant… At first we climbed through fields and over fences. Then through woods: the climb became steeper. Finally, we had to pull ourselves over rocks and through thick undergrowth.

"Petit-Paul, are you sure you know where we are?" I asked, after one hour of silent climbing.

"Don't worry. I've been in this *maquis* since 1943. I know every stone and every tree on the way. It was terrible in the winter; we could be seen right down in the valley, because the trees and bushes were bare. During the day, we had to remain shut up in our house. Sometimes the snow was higher than the roof. We came down at night for our food, but it was very hard. Two of my friends died of pneumonia. We were ten up there, all wanted by the Gestapo."

"Why did they want you?"

"That's a long story," he said, after a pause. "And it's a waste of energy to talk during a climb." I didn't insist.

We arrived at the *maquis* after three. I was led to the hayloft where Ross and Yves slept. Yves was away. Jean lived with them.

"Is it you, Paulette?" he asked, poking his head through the opening. "What the hell are you doing here at this hour of the night?"

He came down the ladder. "I came to see you, Jean," I said.

"Me? Something's happened to Auguste… I knew it all along."

"Yes, Jean. Auguste was killed three days ago during a fight."

"A fight? Where?" Ross shouted from his hayloft. He jumped down.

"At Simorre. They were waiting for a *parachutage*, and the Boches fell on them." I told them the whole story. Jean sat on the ground, his chin on his bent knees, and said nothing. After a while Raymond Mautrens and Jacques joined us. I saw tears shining in Raymond's eyes, and suddenly he put his arm around Jean.

"Auguste was a brave boy," he told him. "We'll avenge him, I swear…"

"He was the best friend I ever had," Jean said. "We did so many things together. And he knew that he would be killed… It is all my fault, all my fault. I should never have let him go alone."

He turned away and climbed back to the hayloft. We followed him. Ross gave me Yves' sleeping-bag and we all lay in the hay. Jean dragged his sleeping-bag next to me; he kept his eyes wide open all night, making an occasional remark. I fell asleep as dawn broke. When I awoke, Yves had returned. He had been in Tarbes. He already knew the story; he came and sat next to me.

"I've got some chocolate for you," he said, smiling. "We're friends now, I hope?"

The chocolate did it. I saw Ross shrug his shoulders and look to the sky: "Yves, you're incorrigible."

Yves turned his face to me: somehow there was a frankness in it.

"No, I mean it," he said gently. He put his hand out and brushed my forehead, then jumped up and emptied his pockets of chocolate and Chesterfields.

"I've got a tooth-brush for you," said Bouboule, climbing the ladder. "I thought you might want it…"

Outside, the boys were washing in a doubtful well. I joined them and tidied up. Jean came up to me.

"Paulette, I'm going back with you. I want to say thank-you for having come and told me yourself. You were a friend of Auguste's too, and I would've felt awful if I'd heard it just casually. But will you show me how to get to Simorre?"

I didn't dare refuse, but I had a gruesome vision of trying to keep up with a tough and impatient cyclist on the sun-drenched road to Simorre. We had lunch outside the barn. The view from the *maquis* was magnificent: green valleys curling gracefully down to the plain, which stretched endlessly to merge in a purple horizon of mist.

In the afternoon, Jean and I were taken by car as far as Montréjeau. Jean had no bicycle, so, in true *maquis* fashion, swiped a stray one parked by the side of the pavement. *Piquer*, they called it… Just outside Montréjeau, a black car came speeding along the road behind us.

"Let's hitch," said Jean, and waved. The car passed us, and stopped a little ahead. A short German stepped out. Jean and I looked at each other aghast.

"Vot de hell do you tink you're doing?" he asked Jean.

"I'm sorry. We thought you were a French car and we wanted a lift."

The short soldier stamped his foot. "Not at all, you wanted to boder us." Jean frowned. He was getting mad and things threatened to end badly. Two German sergeants sat in the car. I approached it and gave them a syrupy smile.

"Can you explain to your friend that we didn't mean to bother you? We thought you were an ordinary French car. The sun was shining on your front pane and we couldn't see inside. We're very sorry."

The short German had begun to yell and Jean's fists were clenched.

"Friedrich," one of the sergeants called out of the window, in French, "come back. Don't make such a fuss…"

Then he looked at me and smiled. I smiled back: maybe *you* killed Auguste, I thought behind my grin… God, how I'd like to bash your face in!

They went on and turned a little further up the road into the drive of a beautiful château, occupied by a German divisional General.[3] Jean was fuming.

"Dirty double-crossing swine… I came damn near to pulling my gun out. If you hadn't been there I think I would have. Only there was no point in getting you caught."

"No point in getting yourself caught or shot, either. We got rid of them easily enough without all that bother. Next time, keep your temper, that's all."

"I couldn't. I was thinking of Auguste."

Chapter XIX

The next morning, we cycled all the way back to Simorre. It was as bad as I had anticipated: Jean climbed tirelessly up the hills and waited for me at the top, bored and impatient. Then his front tyre blew out: every fifty yards or so we had to stop and pump it up. Then I got bitten by a dog while trying to borrow a pair of pincers from a farm. Finally, we reached the old emplacement of the *maquis*; it was lunchtime and the sun blazed. We dragged ourselves up the narrow hill. The dry blades of grass crissed as the slight breeze bent them down.

Rubble, broken glass and broken bricks met our eyes. The once-green trees now stood black and bare as though struck down by pitiless lightning. We picked up a few torn and bloody berets still lying on the ground. We even found stray bits of bones from bashed skulls.

"Look, Auguste's motor-cycle…" Jean said. Burnt and twisted by an explosion, it lay stripped of small parts, obviously stolen by the Germans.

"And the car he returned in," I said. Burnt and twisted too: the sides of the door were thick with melted glass.

Jean and I stood together before the common grave of our friends. A small cross had been erected in the middle, covered with blue, white and red ribbon. Burnt helmets and shattered arms lay on top.

"It's awful not to know where he is," Jean whispered.

The sun went on blazing and the soft breeze gently blowing the tricolour ribbons. The world went on while a few feet away from us, our friends lay dead. Only a few days ago little Mimosa was singing, Dr Raynaud planning the future and the Condom jeweller looking forward to his approaching wedding. The silence was heavy.

"I must do something…" Jean said suddenly. "Please take me to Christophe."

We went to Simorre, then on to Saramon. We found Christophe a little rested.

"Ah, am I glad to find someone ready to help me in my revenge…" he exclaimed, after Jean had told him what he wanted to do.

They agreed to meet in Auch and try to kill a few *miliciens* there. Their ultimate design was to blow up the Milice headquarters.[1] Those headquarters were a sickening sight: the entrance was barred with captured containers filled with sand and the *miliciens* sentries marched ferociously up and down with parachuted Stens and guns poking out of every pocket. They were terrified of the Resistance because they knew that everyone of them was destined to be killed.

Jean and I returned to Seissan the same night and arrived after midnight.

"Which way did you come?" Chénier asked anxiously. "We've come straight from Saramon."

"Miserable children. There's been a fight on that road, hardly an hour ago. We thought you'd been caught in it. Paulette, you have an uncanny luck overshadowing you… But never give me such frights again. You were crazy, both of you, to go to the Simorre *maquis* anyway: Germans are hanging round the whole time to catch pilgrims like you. I can't understand how you didn't run into them."

"Oh well, we'll always be okay, won't we, Paulette?" Jean concluded, sententiously.

The next day Jean went off to Auch while I returned to the Patron's *maquis*. It was in a general state of commotion. We were moving to a new *maquis* the same night, a little village further south: Avéron-Bergelle.

The displacement of eight hundred men was no small affair. Commandant Parisot organised everything. I could never quite make out what the Patron was doing: Parisot seemed the definite head of the *maquis*, since he was a professional soldier. Everyone loved him; his gay and sparkling personality, his constant good-humour and obvious ability as a leader made him the most popular character in the *maquis*.

As night fell we started out. The men climbed into trucks, the leaders into cars, and reconnaissance parties went ahead of the convoy led by motor-cycles. As we passed through villages, shutters and windows burst open and people cheered with cries of "*Vive la Résistance!*" and "*Vive la France!*" We reached Avéron at midnight.

"This time I've got a room for you," one of the staff officers said. "It's the best in the village."

And so it was: all blue plush and blue satin, with the usual pompously covered cushions and newly varnished suite of bed, wardrobe and chairs. The house was owned by the village grocer and my room reserved for the newly married daughter. The grocer was slightly mad.

"Get the hell out of here…" he yelled when I went in. His wife ran to my rescue.

"Don't mind him," she explained in embarrassment. "He doesn't understand what the Resistance is and doesn't like to have people in his house."

"Get out, get out!…" he shouted again. I ran to my room and barricaded myself inside. He went on shouting all night.

Avéron-Bergelle was an attractive village on a hill-top. It was on the edge of wooded country and carefully chosen for its advantageous situation in case of attack. The *maquis* itself was spread over four or five miles. The various companies were in charge of fortifying certain sectors for defence. The PC was, as usual, in the middle of the village.[2]

"You can have a few days' rest," the Patron declared. "I have no mission for you for the moment."

I relaxed gratefully. I spent long hours lying on the PC's front lawn reading and resting, or discussing things with the young staff officers. Most of them were students or graduates from the Toulouse and Paris faculties. They were gay and intelligent and most of them had long records of underground activities. But I found that social relations with them were no simple matter: young men, frustrated of the company of women for long periods, are not easy to deal with. It was difficult to be both amicable and distant, friendly to all and very friendly to none. I liked one of them in particular, a Toulouse medical student, but he had to suffer the constant jeers of his friends. His name was André Bonnay; he had black hair and black eyes and a black outlook on life.[3]

"How old do you think I am?" he asked me one day.

"I don't know, André. About twenty-four?"

"No, I'm only just nineteen. People always think I'm older than my age."

"That's because you're such a cynic. It's ridiculous at your age to talk of being sick of life and of humanity being fundamentally bad. You have faith in yourself, there's no reason why you shouldn't have faith in others."

"That's just what is the matter," he cried. "I haven't faith in myself. I began medicine because I thought I could help people to suffer less. But one man can't do that… Doctors are all out to get what they can out of their patients, not to cure them for the sake of relieving pain. I'm sure I'll get like them. I hate people. I hate them all… Come and pick some plums with me."

We came back with our pockets bulging. It began to rain.

"I don't understand why you're like that," I said, for the hundredth time.

"Let's take shelter under this tree, and I'll tell you a few things I've seen," he said, dragging me by the arm. We sat under a large oak tree and chewed our plums.

"You don't know what my job in the Resistance was, do you?" he said, tearing handfuls of grass out, with jerky movements. "I was in the Gestapo, a double agent. I shouldn't think there could exist a more awful job. See? Even you shrink from me…" I had made an involuntary movement of shocked surprise.

"No, don't be silly. Go on."

"Yes, I belonged to the Gestapo. I worked in the prison of St-Michel, in Toulouse. There, I collected all the information I could and passed it on to the Resistance. But only one or two people knew what my real job was, and whenever I went out, I was in constant fear of my life. Paulette, I heard people screaming under torture night after night. Sometimes I saw them go into a special chamber: the floor was made of asbestos and underneath was an electrical heating system. They were shut in there and the heating was turned on: I could hear them scream and jump about. When they became silent, they were fetched out, their feet and bodies covered with burns. I can still smell the odour of burnt flesh. They were revived, and if they still did not talk, put back in… How can I forget things like that?" he added. Then he was quiet. The rain cracked against the leaves.

"One day, my best friend was caught," he went on. "He didn't know what I was really doing. He looked away from me, and as he passed me he spat in my face without a word. I couldn't stand it. I prepared his escape. I had already succeeded in making a few people escape by passing keys and details to the Resistance. But this time, I decided to get away myself. I couldn't prevent him from being taken to the heating chamber though; he never uttered a sound while he was in there. He was brought out frightfully burnt. The same night I carried him over my back and we escaped together… I wonder how many people still think I'm a traitor?"

"But, André, we've been fighting because we don't believe in those ways of existence. The very fact that millions and millions of people have sacrificed everything to fight against that is a proof that humanity isn't bad."

He shook his head. "No, you haven't seen men take pleasure in all this. You haven't heard what some Frenchmen had to say about their compatriots. I saw and heard all that when I was seventeen and eighteen: you'll never get it out of my system. You've been away so much, Paulette. You don't know everything that goes on, even in this *maquis*. When men are pushed to a certain pitch, they do anything. All men are like that."

How many young men are like André Bonnay? Young men who have been faced with atrocities, with vice and dishonesty, with sadism and treachery. Young men who have learnt to hate and to get their way, whatever the means. Their hurt is deep. Their youth gone.

A couple of days later, Alcazio came to Avéron. He had moved to a *maquis* some way from us after finding that his men did not get on very well with the French and preferred to remain separated. His latest trick was to remove the exhaust-pipe from his car so that he would be heard coming miles away.

"I've come to fetch you, Paulette," he declared. "I'm going on an expedition to collect cars and I haven't enough people who can drive. And we always sing when you come with us; it's more fun…" I was getting a bit bored, so went off with him.

It was a typical *maquis* expedition: Alcazio driving at a crazy speed, three men standing up in the back of his open car, Stens in hand and hair flying in the wind. At every crossroads they cocked their Stens, and after we'd passed put them back at 'safety'. Alcazio's gun was stuck, barrel down, between his seat and mine. We sang at the top of our voices.

> *Yo te quiero mucho,*
> *Mucho, mucho, mucho,*

was Alcazio's favourite song. Like most Spaniards, he sang with a deep, hoarse voice. We all had tricolour armbands, with 'ARMAGNAC' and the Cross of Lorraine painted on the white.

"I've heard there are some cars hidden in a château near here," Alcazio informed me. "I want to get them out. But I have an idea the people are Fascists, so we shall have to act as collaborators to get into their confidence."

"Alcazio, I don't like that."

"All right. You can stay in my car then." But he grinned, because he knew that I wouldn't miss the party for a fortune. We arrived at a beautiful seventeenth-century house.[4] Alcazio sent his men to keep all the issues of the park, left his car outside the heavy iron gate and walked in with me. We rang the bell. No answer. We rang again. Tiptoes and whispers were heard behind the door, but still no answer. Alcazio became impatient and knocked loudly. A fat old woman half opened the door and poked her nose through.

"What do you want?" she said, her voice trembling.

"Information…" said Alcazio.

"Information? Come on, open up, Emilie," said a voice inside. Emilie opened the door and a small, white-haired woman dressed in purple appeared. "What information?"

"We'd like to know if you have any details about the *maquis* round here. We don't want to be caught by them…"

"Don't you belong to the *maquis*?" she asked, astonished. "What are those then?" she went on, pointing to our armbands.

"We wear them for safety."

"Come in, then, come in," the little woman went on. She led us through a wide hall to her dining-room. The parquet floor was shining and old paintings hung on the walls. The draught from the door gently swung the chandelier to and fro, and its crystal pendants clinked with a musical sound.

"Is that an original?" I asked, looking at one of the paintings.

"Yes. How did you know that?" she replied, looking me up and down. I suddenly realised the wild note I made in her elegant dining-room. My white blouse was covered with grease stains, my hands dirty and my hair dishevelled and my shoes torn. I looked like a gypsy in a china shop: no wonder she distrusted me... Alcazio sat down like a duke in a Louis XV chair.

"Well, there are *maquis* all around here," the little lady began. "They are absolute savages, these people; they steal things, rape women and destroy everything. You must be careful..."

"Don't worry," Alcazio said. "Our friends the Germans will soon reduce them to nothing..." I had great trouble in repressing my laughter. Alcazio was as steady as a judge.

"Oh, I hope so, I hope so," she said, clasping her hands. The housekeeper, Emilie, approved, nodding repeatedly.

"Have you any cars and things, to help us fight them?" Alcazio said.

"No, oh no. You've already taken all our tyres. We've only got a few litres of petrol, and we're so afraid the *maquis* might come and get it..." She and Emilie exchanged a glance. So did Alcazio and I. She was lying.

"Well, thank you for your information," Alcazio said, getting up. "Mind if we look round a bit?"

"No. Do, by all means. We like the Germans, you know," she informed us. "They have their good points. My son works with them."

"Oh, yes? What does your son do?" I asked her.

"He's a banker."

We all went out. The wide hall was lined with white marble statues. Heavily framed paintings of the family ancestors hung in the staircase. We left the two women and went into the garden, where Alcazio found the gardener.

"Do you like the *châtelaine*?" he asked him.

"Me? I can't bear her. She hasn't paid my wages for two years now. I can't get her to do it."

"We may help you," Alcazio replied quickly. "We belong to the Resistance, and you could give us some information. Has she got any cars?"

"Cars? She has three. In the garage. The tyres are hidden away: I know where they are, and if you get her to pay my wages, I'll get them for you."

We made it a deal. The gardener fetched the key and opened the garage: an eight-cylinder Packard and a super-luxury Hudson limousine.

"I've never seen anything so beautiful," Alcazio whispered. "Those aren't cars, they're aeroplanes..." He stroked them and looked them over; they were practically new. He brought a couple of batteries out of his car, put them in, and poured a little petrol into the reservoirs. Within two minutes the engines turned, with a soft purring sound. The two women rushed out of the château.

"What are you doing?" they cried.

"I see you lied to us," Alcazio replied quietly. "We lied to you too, so we're square. We belong to the *maquis* you were so graciously telling us about."

The women clasped their hands on their mouths with a horrified gasp.

"She's English," Alcazio said. I was annoyed. But the women gathered a little hope. The *châtelaine* in purple spoke excellent English and tried to appeal to my better sentiments.

"You, mademoiselle, you must understand that we're two frightened old ladies. We're—"

"Would you mind speaking in French?" I interrupted. "The Spanish major cannot understand what you're saying."

"We're – we're really great friends of the English," she went on. "My son knows a lot of English people. He's a great friend of the manager of the Lloyds Bank, and of the manager of the Barclays Bank, and of the manager—"

"Look, we're not really interested in the friends of your son. We are not going to do anything to you, because in spite of all you may think, the *maquisards* do not destroy everything in their wake, or shoot everyone they see. It will be the role of the French justice to deal with you. Meanwhile, we shall simply take whatever we need here. So, to begin with, we shall inspect your whole house."

An hour or so later we left. I drove the third car, discovered camouflaged in a back garage. Alcazio had filled his own with petrol tins, two small motor-cycles and a barrel of wine. The two old ladies, dismayed and anguished, watched us go from their antique doorstep, while the gardener waved us goodbye gaily.

The following day the Patron called me in.

"You'll have to leave this afternoon and contact Halsall in the Pyrenees. You must also contact General Ch— and make a rendezvous for me with him. Then you have to bring back Captain de Changins with you: I have to see him. You must be in the Pyrenees by Saturday." It was Thursday then. "It's urgent," he added, after giving me long explanations.

"Okay, Patron. I'll be there tomorrow, then."

"How will you do it?"

"Well, I'll cycle all night; it's the only way."

He shrugged his shoulders. That meant "You're talking through your hat." I'll show you, I thought. One of the village girls lent me a pair of pink shorts, because I couldn't stand my thick tweed skirt in the torrid July sun any more.

Thus equipped, I reached Seissan in the early evening. The worst bit was over: the Gers department was nothing but hills and vales. Madame Chénier was as amiable as usual, her little curls bubbling merrily on top of her head.

"You're mad to go off by night, Paulette. You know you can't ride after the curfew."

"Yes, I can. I can see the headlights of cars for miles and will have ample time to hide." She again lent me her bicycle, as she had done all the previous times. My own had a hard and uncomfortable saddle and no gears.

I left her at 9pm and rode off. Night came down: the road was long, lonely and silent. I began to feel heroic, and gruesome thoughts came into my mind. The night was soft and cool, but terribly quiet. I went fast, but as I sped down a small hill, my front wheel began to wobble. I got off and looked at it: my tyre was punctured. And not a house within miles… I had no instruments to remove the wheel, although I had everything necessary to repair the tyre. I pushed the bicycle for two or three miles, then caught sight of a farm by the roadside. It was just after eleven, just after curfew.

"Can you lend me a spanner to remove my wheel, please?" I asked the farmer. He looked at me suspiciously.

"What are you doing out at this hour?" he snapped.

"I'm going a little way further, as far as Mauléon. My bicycle broke down some way back, and I've been walking quite a while."

He gave me the spanner, and stood beside me watching me like a lynx. I sat down, trying to remember how on earth to repair the thing: I hadn't repaired a bicycle since my schooldays. I recalled something about blowing up the inner tube and plunging it into water. After toiling half an hour, I found the hole, stuck a piece of rubber on top and gleefully put the wheel on again. The old farmer had not moved an inch or put out a finger to help me. I thanked him for his spanner and left.

It was well after midnight. I felt more and more heroic on the long, black road. But I hadn't gone five miles when my front tyre burst again. I sat by the side of the road and wept with fury and discouragement. It was too late to go to another farm: the people would be asleep and would throw me out. The whole region was on edge: the Germans patrolled it all day, and not a day went by without some farms being burnt and people shot in village squares. The enemy tried to terrify the peasants in the hope of paralysing the *maquis'* food resources. But their action did not stop the *maquis* from getting food, any more than tortures had stopped the activities of the underground.

I unhooked my skirt and *canadienne* from the back of my bicycle, slipped both of them on, lay down in a ditch and went to sleep. I was so used to sleeping anywhere by then, that a ditch was as comfortable as any other place. I woke up a few hours later, at the crack of dawn, cold and stiff. I walked a few miles to warm up and stopped at another farm run by Spaniards this time. Spaniards have been good to me all along: these farmers showed me to their kitchen, gave me a breakfast composed of warm wine and cold rabbit, while their small son fixed my tyre for me.

"You had a nail in it," the little boy said. "And four holes too."

In the afternoon, I reached Montréjeau and went down to Mazères.

"Hello, Paulette," Miette said gaily. "Fouffi has just had kittens; come and see them – they're perfectly white."

Miette was ever the same: kind, helpful and happy with her cats. Roger came in, barked a bit, and suggested taking me up to Halsall's *maquis*.

"It's a good thing you came to Mazères; they've moved. They're above St-Bertrand-de-Comminges now. It's a long climb…"

I felt terribly tired: all the way along the Nationale 129 the wind had blown in my face, making the ride twice as hard… But I suddenly remembered the Patron's shoulder-shrugging. He would see…

Roger and I climbed up narrow mountain paths, through bushes and undergrowth, in woods and rocky fields. The sun painted gold on every leaf. Sometimes we slipped deep in mud, on paths where it could never penetrate.

"Roger, how the heck do they get their stuff carried up there?"

"Mules,"" Roger answered, pointing to mule-pats on the path.

At last we reached the *maquis*. The men had built a small, wooden hut for the three paratroopers and put up a couple of tents for themselves: they were fifteen in all. A small kitchen was built – stones and a hole in the ground – and a brilliant orange parachute had been stretched above it to keep the cooking dry in case of rain.

"Hye, Paulette," Jacques and Raymond Mautrens said gaily. "Is Jean with you?"

"Jean? No. Isn't he back? He went to Auch a few days ago, but he ought to be back by now…"

We looked at each other uneasily. As a matter of fact, Jean was all right. On his way back to Auch, where it was reported he and Christophe had shot two *miliciens*, he had had an accident and gone home for a rest.

Yves threw his arms to the sky when he saw me. "Paulette, what do you think you're doing here in those pink shorts?"

"It's too hot cycling in my skirt…"

"My dear girl, do you know that a *maquis* is a place where women are not meant to be, as a rule? And what do you think the men say or think when they see you trotting past in shorts?"

I told them why I had come. Yves bounced about angrily: how would he get to Avéron-Bergelle?

"I cycled all the way… You can do the same."

"Nothing doing. I'm not crazy. What other way can we go?"

"Have you any papers and civilian clothes?"

"Yes, I have papers, and Raymond would lend me a suit."

"All right, we'll go to Tarbes by train, take the bus to Auch and find some means of getting from Auch to Avéron."

"You'll have to go down to Montréjeau, now, before it's dark," Ross said.

I had begun to feel queer as soon as I'd sat down on one of their pine-branch beds.

"Oh, Ross, for God's sake don't send me down," I cried. "I can't stand up any more. Besides, my head feels heavy and my legs are wobbly: please let me stay here."

"Hate having women in *maquis*," he mumbled. But Yves had extracted a thermometer from one of the innumerable boxes that composed his equipment.

"Take your temperature," he ordered peremptorily. I obeyed: it was a new and agreeable feeling to be ordered about for your own sake. The thermometer read 102...

"Of course she can't go down. You little nut, you've been overdoing it," Ross bullied kindly. "Look, have my pyjamas and my sleeping-bag."

"Ross, you and I will go down and leave her here," Yves said. "Raymond Mautrens will sleep on my bed and help Bouboule with the night *émission*. Tomorrow, if you're well again, we'll start off for Tarbes."

Both of them tucked me up and filled me up with pills and drugs. In the middle of the night I woke up hot and thirsty. On the pine-branch bed next to mine, Bouboule was quietly emitting a long message. His set was worked with a hand-generated battery: Raymond, his chin on his chest and half asleep, turned it with a regular and rhythmic gesture. Outside, the air smelt of pines and damp trees. One of the men could be heard snoring in the distance.

Bouboule turned his knobs, took his ear-phones off and shut his set with a click. Raymond looked up, opening one eye, let go of the handle and fell on his bed, instantaneously asleep. Bouboule turned round and offered me some chocolate.

"Nobody knows I still have this bar," he smiled. "I kept it for you..."

CHAPTER XX

On the station the following day, with Yves and Jacques, I resumed my old Gestapo-consciousness: two men were standing next to us talking in fluent German. One was a fat, fair man in civilian clothes, the other a French captain in uniform. French officers walking about freely in uniform were definitely suspicious at that time. I nudged Yves.

"Look out for these two. Don't forget that men of your age must have a good excuse not to be in Germany."

"Now, now, don't worry…" Yves cut in.

The fat civilian climbed into our carriage, as the train pulled out. I took the only free seat in a compartment while Yves and Jacques stood chatting in the corridor. From the corner of my eye, I saw the fat man approach them.

"War going well, isn't it?" he began, in perfect French this time. I tried to catch Yves eye in vain.

"Depends what you mean," Yves replied, his head on one side.

"Well, the Germans will soon be finished in Normandy—"

"Finished in Normandy?" Yves interrupted. "What do you mean? They don't seem to be doing so badly; in fact I shouldn't be a bit surprised if they finally threw the Allies back into the sea."

I observed, with growing annoyance, the people in my compartment looking at each other and frowning with shocked surprise: the conversation in the corridor was easily audible. I wanted to tell Yves to keep quiet and avoid the argument, but his eyes purposely kept avoiding mine.

"Well, I don't think you're right," the fat man went on. "But even if you were, the Russians would soon finish them."

"I don't think you're right there either…" And to prove his point Yves began drawing maps of the Russian front on the dusty carriage window. I leaned back in my seat and gave him up. My neighbours were whispering imprecations at him: I could see the moment when we would be thrown out of the train… At

Lannemezan, two people got off and Jacques and Yves came and sat opposite me. I shrugged my shoulders at them and looked out of the window.

"Some people care for their country more than for anything else," a middle-aged man remarked casually behind his newspaper. I looked up: Yves was watching me with satisfaction written all over his face. He said nothing.

"Yes," said another, all dressed in blue, "but others, big and strong, would never bother to do a thing for it."

Yves and Jacques exchanged a glance. "Excuse me, but are all these little hints aimed at me?" Yves put in innocently. The man-in-blue did not reply and went on:

"Yes, some courageous young boys go into the *maquis*. They give up everything for their country. Indeed, I have wonderful boys under my orders," he added, talking to the middle-aged man, and obviously inferring that he headed a *maquis*. But people who head *maquis* know how to keep quiet in trains.

Yves took my hand and looked tenderly in my eyes.

"Jacques why should I give up everything when I have a good job and a sweet little wife like this? Don't you agree, darling?"

The darling gave him a wry smile and tried to hold down her growing rage.

"It doesn't matter," the middle-aged man said, talking to the man-in-blue, without looking in our direction. "Millions of worthy young men have done their duty. In fact, it's just as well that the weeds should keep out. Rot spreads."

Yves went on shooting syrupy smiles in my direction while he and Jacques praised the wise people who stayed at home and refused to indulge in the crazy and uncomfortable life of the *maquis*. The middle-aged man and the man-in-blue continued praising the patriots who sacrificed all to *la Patrie*. My anger was cooled down only weeks later, when Yves told me how he had run into the man-in-blue who turned out to be the proprietor of a small café and not a *maquis* chief at all. Yves was in full uniform, parachute wings, Special Force wings, Croix de Guerre and all: the man had disappeared into his café at the sight of him, and had never been seen again.

Yves and I walked along the streets of Tarbes while he told me how he had lived in the city for a while, before the war.

"I left a car near here, and I hoped to collect it when I came back. But the Germans requisitioned it two years ago…"

"Poor Yves, you and all your beautiful illusions when you came back: thousands of *parachutages*, smart cars, fights and uniforms…" He was looking pretty ridiculous in Raymond's suit, at least three times too big for him. Suddenly he grabbed my hand, and made me cross the road.

"Do you see that woman over there? The one with the check dress? I used to know her…er' – quite well. I don't want her to recognise me. Hide my face, will you?"

I did my best to conceal his large person. The woman looked at us with a where-have-I-seen-you-before expression; she certainly had doubts. But we passed on. A few minutes later, on the Place de Verdun, Yves suddenly stopped dead and dug his nails into my arm.

"Ouch, stop it…you're hurting me."

"My car…" he said hoarsely.

A long, white Buick was gliding silently by: at the wheel, a German General, looking thoroughly pleased with himself.[1] Yves was trembling from head to foot. He put his hand on his hip-pocket.

"I'll shoot him down and get it back."

"Yves, don't be a crazy idiot: the Kommandantur is right here, on the corner. You wouldn't get ten yards in your car… You'll get it back later…"

"I can't bear it…" he cried. "A damned German General sitting in my stolen car…"

"Never mind – bear it this time… You won't be of any use in a prison cell."

To flatter Yves was the only way of getting anywhere with him. He watched, white with fury, as his Buick came to a smooth stop in front of the Kommandantur. Three weeks later, he caught the General and recovered his car.

We took the bus and arrived at Auch after dinner. I went to the police station, found the lieutenant who had accompanied us to Simorre, and pulled a long yarn about Allied parachutists who were urgently expected at Avéron.

"All I can offer you is a prisoners' van," the lieutenant said. Then excitedly: "Are they Americans?"

This would give us unlimited help. "Yes, one of them is," I lied. Yves spoke English with an ear-grinding mixture of American slang and French idioms.

"Good, I'll practise my English on him…"

All the way to Avéron, hot and jolted about in the van, we were obliged to speak English. It was so dark by the time we left that we couldn't see each other. Yves put his arm round my shoulder.

"How do you say *boussole*?" he would whisper, inaudible to all but me.

"Compass," I'd whisper back.

"What does compass mean, Mademoiselle Paulette?" the lieutenant would ask.

"*Boussole*," I'd inform him.

And so it went on. I could hear Jacques laughing softly to himself. As for Yves, he delighted in creating awkward situations, just to show how well he could get out of them. We arrived at Avéron well after midnight, after passing through four consecutive guard posts. Every time I had to get out to be recognised.

"Hello, Paulette," people would say. "How are you? I haven't seen you for a long time…"

I had no idea who they were, but I said Hello, and no, I hadn't seen them for a long time either.

Yves walked about importantly the whole of the next day and went off on a fight, somewhere. The Patron called me in.

"I have news for you, Paulette. I don't know if you're going to like it. You must go off to England."

"Oh no... You can't do that... Not so near the end..."

"I'm afraid you must. You must take a detailed report to London for me, and as quick as you possibly can."

I sat down miserably and conceived black projects of revenge on the Patron.

"You'll go with Mike and three Americans and a Dutchman who arrived here yesterday. Johnny will also go with you." Johnny was a South African 'darkie', as he called himself. He had been at Avéron a few days and helped in the cookhouse. He had been captured at Tobruk in 1941, had escaped from an Italian prison camp, then from a German one, and had finally made his way to France and been rescued by the *maquis*. He never said a word. The Dutchman, Henry, had fair hair and a humorous face; he sat quietly on the PC lawn, all day long, reading a fat book.[2]

I ran into the three Americans, a short time after seeing the Patron: Nick, tall and fair and kinda stupid; Bill, quiet and composed; and Elmer, small and dark with a long nose.

"Hye, we're going off over the Pyrenees together, you know," I declared sullenly. They looked at each other with annoyance.

"Well, you don't look too pleased about it," Nick said, being pleasant. Nick tried to be pleasant all the time.

"I'm not a bit. I didn't want to go before the end of everything here."

"Think you can make it?" Elmer asked.

"What do you mean, 'make it'?"

"I mean the mountains and the walk and all that. I guess you'll slow us down, but it doesn't matter..." he declared magnanimously.

I went round looking for Mike. "I-I know what you're going to say," he put in, before I had time to open my mouth. "We're off and you're mad about it."

"Yep. That's just it. I knew you'd understand, Mike."

"I feel pretty sad myself. I like the chaps here... But never mind, we'll see Spain, and we wouldn't have had a chance to do so otherwise."

Mike knew the right thing to say. I was so miserable that I had not thought of that. We were to go off with Yves as soon as his talks with the Patron were over.

Just as we finished lunch a motor-cyclist thundered to a stop in front of the door. We used to have our meal in the corridor of the PC, at a long table presided over by Commandant Parisot.

"Who's that bearded individual?" he exclaimed. The silhouette was familiar. Suddenly I recognized it: Jean-Claude. I had to stop myself from running to him: I was so relieved to see him before I left. He had grown a massive brown beard. He sailed in, casting a quiet glance at everyone. His eyes smiled as they crossed mine, but he said nothing. I knew that he hated crowds of strangers. Without a word, he sat down at the far end of the table and chewed a few peaches. He had come on a liaison mission.

"I'm leaving for England, Jean-Claude," I told him, as soon as we were alone.

"Minou, you're not... What shall I do without you to talk to any more?"

I couldn't help bursting into tears. "I don't know... I don't know what I'll do either, knowing that all this will be going on without me. After all this time, waiting for the end and working for it... Going away just for a bit of a report... I'm so unhappy, you have no idea."

Jean-Claude hugged me affectionately. "Never mind, it'll soon be over anyway. But I can understand how you feel."

We picked a few plums and ate them in silence. The air was full of the sweet smell of ripe fruit.

"Jean-Claude, what are you doing with that hideous beard?"

"Don't you think it's smart?" he said, stroking it happily. "It's the latest fashion..."

"You mean that you can't be bothered to shave."

"Minou, you're hopeless. Why can't you recognise art when you see it?" This, looking super-cherubic.

"I suppose that shirt of yours is art too? Thank goodness I got one for you the last time I was at the Chéniers'." Jean-Claude's shirt was stiff with dirt.

"Well, that will be my first change of shirt in two months..." he declared, unmoved. "I don't know why you talk so much, you little prig. You haven't anything on me.... What's this?" he said, pointing to grease marks on my blouse. "And this?" pointing to a hole in my canvas shoe. "And this hair?" pulling at a dry and strawy curl falling on my face.

"I've been working," I said weakly.

"Just what I thought you'd say. What do you think I've been doing? Writing poetry?"

Things were not so easy as during the first days. The Dordogne was too important to the Germans as a communication centre. They had besieged the department with a couple of SS divisions, and carried out ceaseless attacks on the *maquis*. Within a short time, the *maquis* had run out of ammunition and had dispersed. The *parachutages* had become rare: the Allies' first task was to arm the circuits immediately behind the front, to enable the Resistance to destroy German reinforcements on their way to Normandy. In Dordogne, the Fourth Republic had fallen, and the population suffered pitiless reprisals. It was at this time that the village of Oradour-sur-Glane was razed to the ground, the men mowed down with machine-gun fire and the women and children burnt alive in the church.

People were getting discouraged and morale had dropped lower than at any time during the days of the underground. This was not peculiar to the Dordogne alone. The fighting on the distant beaches of Normandy seemed to make no progress. The airborne landing in the southwest was definitely not going to happen. The war in Western Europe seemed to threaten to be a long one. The Germans had gathered renewed daring and terrorised the population with their savagery. Ammunition and supplies were getting short. The men had no boots and no clothes; their families lived with difficulty without their daily earnings. Yves, so full of enthusiasm the first day, had not had a single *parachutage* within the first month of his arrival. The best-served *maquis* seemed to be ours: more neighbouring groups had joined us, and the Armagnac Battalion now counted twelve hundred men. Most of them were equipped with the green uniforms of Pétain's Youth Camps, with tricolour armbands. Many months later, the Armagnac Battalion was to be the one to besiege the Germans at the mouth of the Gironde and to liberate Royan with General Leclerc's division. It was named after one of the most famous regiments of the French Army: the 158th Infantry.

Jean-Claude left at dawn the next day: I was going to miss the feeling that he might turn up at any moment. In the afternoon, we prepared to leave. The Patron handed me his report. I learnt it by heart in case it had to be destroyed in Spain. The Patron had no contact or safe-route to reach Barcelona, so the report had to be smuggled through. Alcazio was heard coming five miles away, his free exhaust shaking the countryside. As usual, everyone took cover in ditches and behind hedges, as he tore through Avéron, and stopped abruptly inside the PC, raising a cloud of dust.

"We've come to say goodbye to you, Paulette," he said. "You'll have to kiss us all…" Five of his inseparable dare-devils got out of the car.

"Alcazio, I can't. What will people say?"

"If you don't, we'll know that you've let the Spaniards down…" With Alcazio, I was always faced with moral problems. He had tried several times to make me stay in his own *maquis*, and I had had great trouble in explaining that I was under the Patron's orders, and couldn't spend my time chasing around in fast cars with him. He had declared, very well, it was obvious I didn't like the Spaniards any more. But the Spaniards still liked me, he had concluded, going all holy.

So I had to submit myself to being kissed by six hard-bearded Spaniards.

"Here's my address in Barcelona," one of them said. "I haven't seen my wife for

seven years. Don't tell her where I am, but tell her I'm alive and thinking of her."
I did.

I was heart-broken at not seeing the Cérensacs before I left.[3] "Germans in the
neighbourhood, I can't risk a car," the Patron had said. Dr Driziers, Privat, Robert
Laroche, Commandant Parisot, André Bonnay, Plucci, Scharks and others came
to shake hands.

Yves drew me apart. "The Americans say they won't fight; they intend to be
made prisoners of war if we fall into an ambush, and nothing will make them
believe that the Germans won't take that much trouble. I've talked to Mike, Henry
and Johnny; they'll all fight. So will Granger." Granger was the owner and driver
of the car we were going in. He was an armagnac dealer and brought along six
bottles of old armagnac, as a present for Ross.

The nine of us packed into his large-size traction: hail poured thick and heavy,
thumping on the roof. We took four hours to cover a hundred kilometres, because
the engine choked and the carburettor had to be cleaned about every five miles.
At every stop the men clambered out, took defence positions on the open road
while Granger blew into his pipes and swallowed a few mouthfuls of petrol, and
clambered in again after he was through. This little operation took a quarter of an
hour each time. Yves became impatient and restless.

"Next thing that will happen is that we'll be chased by German cars in a traction
which breaks down every five minutes. What a picnic!…"

In fact, the dirty carburettor saved us. We arrived at Vic-en-Bigorre, our first
relay, just after a number of Germans and *miliciens* had been having a fight.
Raymond Mautrens had a house in Vic.

"But why were the Germans fighting the Milice?" Yves asked Raymond's wife.

"Don't you know that they hate each other? The Germans say that the *miliciens*
are traitors and never miss a chance to pick a quarrel with them."

We spent the night in Vic.[4] The six men had to be left in a barn outside the
village; they were all in parachuted battle-dress except Henry, and couldn't be taken
within sight of the population. Before getting out of the car, they swiped a couple
of Ross's armagnac bottles, got copiously drunk in their barn and rowed gaily. Nick
practically chipped Mike's ear off, inadvertently pressing the trigger of his Sten.
Oddly enough, nobody heard them. Henry sat disapprovingly, reading his fat book.
He was a Rotterdam lawyer.

The next day, Granger having returned to Avéron, we were lent a fast Peugeot
truck by the local Resistance. Mike, his shirt unbuttoned as usual, sat calmly in
the back holding his Sten menacingly. Johnny sat by his side without a word; he
and Mike had become inseparable pals. Henry methodically folded his raincoat
and settled it under the side seat, then sat behind Mike, his fat book under one

arm, his Sten under the other. The six men were separated from us by a board with a small glass window in the middle.

"Damn this car," said man-of-the-world Yves. "Why the hell won't it go faster?" Nothing could induce the Peugeot to do more than 30mph. "Doesn't a single Resistance car *ever* work?" A knock on the back window made me turn around: Nick's nose was flattened against the glass, and he was signalling something with his hand. Suddenly I understood.

"Your hand-brake, Yves..." Yves went pink in the face: this did not suit his sophisticated personality at all. He shoved the brake off just as the smell of burnt rubber began to tickle our nostrils. The truck jerked forward.

"Never mind, Paulette. I'll show you that I'm more proficient in a sailing boat," he declared lightly, catching hold of my hand. "I'll take you round the world one day..."

Jacques, who had joined us at Vic and was sitting on my other side, sneered mockingly.

"I bet you I do, Jacques. I'll take her to Mauritius first. You can tag on, if you want..."

Yves talked gaily of the small island where he had spent his childhood. I wondered what had become of one of my best friends, Maurice, a boy from Mauritius who had trained with me in England. I heard later that he had been killed, a few days before that.

"We'd better watch out now," Yves said, as he turned the truck onto the Nationale 117. We drove silently along, watching the road ahead. Just before turning off on the St-Bertrand-de-Comminges road, we passed five German soldiers, taking a little bicycle ride, with turned-up shirt-sleeves and independent airs.

"Why should those Germans be allowed to go about as though they owned the place?" Yves said. "Jacques, shall we make an ambush?"

"Yes, let's," Jacques said quickly. Yves stopped the car three hundred yards or so from the main road. Mike and Johnny jumped out.

"We're making an ambush, are you coming?" Yves said.

"Why, sure we are. I saw those five Germans too," Mike replied.

"Ambush?" Henry exclaimed, laying down his fat book and jumping out of the truck. "I don't want to miss it."

The Americans followed. "We're not on this," Elmer declared.

"Are you scared?" Yves threw impatiently.

"No, we're not scared," Nick said. "We just have orders not to fight the Germans. We're fliers, not soldiers, can't you understand?"

Yves shrugged his shoulders and turned to me. "In seven or eight minutes' time, you'll back the truck to the road. Then we'll chuck the Germans inside and drive off without wasting any time."

They all scattered through the fields. At the given time, I turned the engine on.

"You're not driving this car to the road," Elmer said, jumping on the running-board.

"I'll do just what I have to do. You keep out of this."

"Like hell we will," Nick said, climbing next to me, and turning the ignition off. "We're trying to get back to flying, and that's not the way to do it."

A few minutes later, Yves and the others returned with empty hands. "Things never seem to turn out as you plan them, he grumbled. "They must've smelt something; they were nowhere to be seen. There's no point in wasting any more time: there may be a garrison somewhere, and we couldn't tackle that."

We started off again. "Why didn't you back the truck?" Yves asked mischievously. "Scared?" I told him the story.

"You'd better be careful with them in the mountains. Why on earth won't they believe that all the Germans will bother to do with them is to put a bullet into them? It makes me mad: thank goodness all Americans aren't like that."

"As a matter of fact, it's a well-known thing that fliers don't mind hell and fire when they're flying, and are scared when they're faced with the smallest thing on the ground," Jacques put in sententiously.

We arrived at St-Bertrand-de-Comminges in the early evening. Jacques went up to the *maquis* with the boys: Yves had more work to do.

"Are you coming with me, Paulette? I have to go and collect stores of rifles and stuff up in the mountains." I loved those car expeditions: somehow they were fantastic and unreal, as well as exciting. Petit-Louis came with us. Petit-Louis had a baby face topped with ash-blond hair, but he was the big tough of the *maquis*; they called him 'The Killer'. We went off after midnight with full headlights on. Yves drove up winding, rocky mountain roads. Four *maquisards* were in the back and Petit-Louis sat quietly next to me, his gun between his knees. The arms were hidden in a desperately complicated place, under rocks and stones inside a cave. Yves patiently pulled me up as my *espadrilles* slipped on the damp stones around the cave.

"I'll have to get some boots for you: you can't cross the Pyrenees in those… You'd be barefoot by the time you'd get to Spain."

"I'll need a pair of pants too: my skirt is too hot and the thorns will reduce my legs to shreds…"

Yves promised to obtain everything for me. Meanwhile, he lent me a pair of army gym shoes four times my size, and grey army socks to allow them to hold on. We returned to St-Bertrand just after two in the morning. The boys had found a room but I had nowhere to go.

"Stay with us," Petit-Louis declared. "We can manage. We're not in the Victorian days any longer…"

They had a small room with a double bed and mattresses on the floor. They generously allotted the bed to the Capitaine and Mademoiselle Paulette, while they lay around on the floor. Yves removed his boots but I didn't even have the strength to do the same and fell asleep all dressed while they laughed and chatted. Yves shook me four hours later.

"For goodness' sake, not yet…"

"Yes, we must go: there's a three hours' climb to the *maquis*. I have to see Ross and rush off to Tarbes. I won't even be able to see you off: I have too much to do."

Yves had become a monument of patience and helpfulness; he dragged me up over rocks and brambles and even carried me over muddy, slippery bits, which was poor training for trekking over the Pyrenees.

"I've been thinking of something, Paulette. Do you think you could go to Algiers on a mission for us? I have a long report to send to HQ and Bouboule has too much work to pass it on by radio."

"Of course, but I don't know if London will agree: I couldn't go to Algiers without their consent. I would know in Barcelona."

"It's very urgent. I would like this report to be there before the 15th of August. How would it work with your mission for the Patron?"

"His report will go through the Embassy anyway. That's quicker than I ever would be."

"I would like you to go to Algiers yourself though: there's a lot of stuff I don't want to risk writing down and you'd have to learn it by heart."

We reached the *maquis* just before the sun had become unbearably hot. Ross had been decoding messages; now he was observing something through field-glasses. These parachutists' equipment was an endless source of admiration to everyone, and especially to the agent who had been dropped armed only with a gun, a spade and false papers. They had two sets of uniforms, packed in practical rucksacks, medical supplies reduced to the minimum of space, field-glasses and detailed maps, warm and comfortable sleeping-bags, tinned food of all description, including American K and C rations, and fascinating, small .32 carbines. Raymond, cleaning Ross's, lost one of the small pieces one day.

"My God," he had said, "I'll never dare farce Ross again. Nothing is more precious to him than his carbine…"

But Bouboule, who was his friend, had given him the spare part. "I'm only the radio operator here," he had explained bitterly. "I'm not allowed to fight and I'll never need my carbine…"

"What are you looking at, Ross?" Yves asked as we walked in.

"At the château over there, where the German General lives.[5] I can see right into his room. It drives me nuts. Do you think we'd be able to reach it with a bazooka?"

Yves looked out and shook his head. "I doubt it. But later on, when we're well armed, there will be no harm in trying. Paulette is going to Algiers for us; she's going to ask for material. If she succeeds, you can shoot your General out of his room…"

"Paulette, why, my little Paulette… Have some chocolate. I still have a bar," Ross said, jumping to his rucksack.

CHAPTER XXI

W e decided to leave on August 1st. Yves went back to Tarbes, where he had to meet two Generals.

"Wish I didn't have to leave you, but very important this meeting, you know," he declared with his indispensable-to-the-Resistance air. Ross laboriously typed long and detailed reports of his activities. I sewed them up in my shoulder pads.

"Would you mind sewing mine up with yours?" Henry asked. Henry was on a mission for the Dutch underground. "The Spaniards might throw me into jail and discover those papers. In Madrid you can hand them in to the Dutch Embassy."

Ross produced needles and thread out of his precious rucksack and I pulled the stuffing from the shoulders of my suit and concealed the papers in them. The men who had promised to find boots and long pants for me had vanished: I had to go off in Yves' size-10 rubber shoes and my narrow tweed skirt. Ross gave us each a tin of bully beef and Henry methodically packed a kilo of cube sugar in his small bag, next to his fat book. I had a small case with a nightdress and a sweat-shirt given to me by Jacques: the boys put our small supplies inside it and promised to carry it.

We were taken by car to the Col des Ares, where we met the guides. They were not very sure of the way; they had only followed our route once. Bouboule had radioed Algiers that we would arrive at Canejan, a small village just over the Spanish border, on August 2nd.

"Colonel Halsall said that a truck would be waiting for us there," Elmer declared.

"Elmer, don't be silly. We're lucky if the Consulates even know we're on the way."

"'I'm sure we'll find a truck…" Elmer persisted. He talked of nothing but this truck the whole way. Or maybe this is an injustice; he also talked of hamburger steaks: "What wouldn't I give for a nice fat juicy hamburger, and a Scotch…"

The guides were annoyed at having to cross towards Canejan because of the radio message: but they promised to do their best. It seemed an easy matter, then. They cut out a long, smooth stick for me, and we started out at 10am. The sun was hot and already high. At first we all joked and chatted gaily, but after an hour of solid climbing through woods, we grew silent. I tied my jacket round my waist and became hotter and hotter. The guides were weighed down under heavy rucksacks with food.

"The last time we took anyone over, we lost ourselves in the fog on the way back and went without food for four days. That's not going to happen again."

At four in the afternoon, we reached the Pic du Gard, some eight thousand feet up. We stopped for a rest, lying on the soft grass stretching towards the point of the rocky peak. The three Americans had small rubber flasks; they filled them with the limpid cold water of a small stream. Below us, far in the distance, spread the Lannemezan plateau and the Garonne plain. The day was so clear that we could see nearly as far as Auch: the long straight Lannemezan road on which I had cycled so often, and the Nationale 117, ribboned white and narrow across the green landscape. Montréjeau and St-Gaudens stood like small dots of mist.

I sat far from the others to hide my tears: how hard it seemed to have waited so long for the end, to have shared so many hopes and disappointments, and to have to leave so near their conclusion! I already missed my friends: Cérensac coming back from the fields with his instruments on his back; Jean-Claude chasing about in filthy shirts and beard; Yves discussing big plans importantly; Jean planning thoughts of revenge; André Bonnay, turning black depressions in his young head; Alcazio terrifying the population with his car; and the friendly companionship of the *maquisards*.

"Come on, we'd better go on," one of the guides suggested. "We have to reach the neighbourhood of Boutx at nightfall. There's a German garrison there, so we'll have to cross the road near it at night."

I looked a last time at the France I knew, peaceful and beautiful, with its flowing rivers and green hills. Mike put a hand on my shoulder.

"Come on, Paulette," he said gently. "I didn't want to go either. But you'll be back soon…"

We went off again, following the crest through birch woods. On one side of us, the mountain was a vertical wall of rocks. We walked an hour or two, then the guides stopped.

"We're damned if we know the way. Somewhere around here there's a grassy slope leading down to Boutx, but we can't find it. You'd better all stop here while we go on a reconnaissance."

That was a bad beginning. They dumped their heavy rucksacks and went off while we lay in the grass. My legs were getting weak and my back hurt. I had to pull my skirt high above my knees and hold it up with Johnny's leather belt. Otherwise I couldn't take big steps. After a time the guides returned.

"We've got to go back. We've taken the wrong direction."

Henry shrugged his shoulders and checked up on the packing of the box of sugar. We walked back past the peak and found the path after a two-hour search. It was nearly 8pm.

"What about getting to Spain tomorrow?" Henry asked.

"Don't think you'll be able to make it," the guides said.

"But the truck…" Elmer moaned.

"I think you'd better get used to the idea that there won't be a truck anyway. This isn't a week-end picnic, you know…" Henry said impatiently.

The guides motioned us to lie low. "Boutx is down there, can you see it? We're in full view, we must be careful."

Boutx hung on the edge of a white road near the bottom of the valley. "People down there can hear every sound in the mountains, so you'd better not talk." We crept down the steep slope one at a time, so as not to attract attention. It took a long time. We all gathered at the edge of a thick wood, a few hundred feet above the village. The calls of the peasants to their cattle grazing in the mountains echoed from crest to crest. The guides put an urgent finger on their mouth and we followed them, carefully avoiding stones that might roll down and attract attention. We stopped some time before crossing the road while they went on a reconnaissance. It was now past 10pm. We had walked for twelve hours without any appreciable interruption. My feet ached in Yves' rubber shoes and we were all tired.

The guides came back and said the road was clear. We crept up to it, then ran across one by one to the cover of bushes on the other side. The night was already dark. We crossed a small torrent in Indian file; it seemed to make a deafening noise in the silence of the night. We climbed a few hundred feet on the other side and stopped for the night. The air had become cold: Henry drew his pants over his home-made shorts, wrapped himself up in a raincoat and settled down. He seemed prepared for everything. I slipped my nightdress on and attached it below my skirt; it would save my bare legs from the innumerable mosquitoes buzzing wildly around.

After eating bread and bully beef we lay down to sleep.

All this had to be done in utter silence; we were still within earshot of Boutx.

"We'll have to leave at daybreak, before the Germans have a chance to send patrols out."

"Patrols?" Bill cried.

"Shh… Yes, they send patrols out in the mountains all the time. With dogs too, if you must know…"

Dogs seemed a gloomy menace: the Patron had refused to let me take my small gun with me and I wondered what in heaven's name I would do if one of the vicious Gestapo dogs started chasing me. The ground was hard and damp and none of us had found a flat space to lie on. Every time I began to doze off I felt myself slipping away and awoke with a start. Every time one of us fell asleep, he began to snore because of the uncomfortable position. Mike had to be shaken in case he was heard in Boutx.

"Really, that's exaggerated," he grumbled furiously.

At 5am, the guides said it was time to start again. We were all stiff cold and stiff with weariness. The climb up the second mountain was much steeper than the Pic du Gard. We pulled ourselves over rocks and followed muddy strips of path that soon disappeared under impenetrable undergrowth. Then, the guides stopped and scratched their heads.

"Lost our way again…"

"Look here, how often is this going to happen?" Henry and I said together. "We only have food for today…"

"We're doing our best. We told you that we'd only done this route once, but you insisted on going to Canejan."

There was nothing to say to that. We followed them as they tried to find small landmarks. Suddenly one of them cried:

"Look, that cress growing on the edge of that path. I remember stopping here to make sandwiches with it. This is the right track. Near the top of this mountain there's a shepherd's cottage. We'll have to wait until it's dark."

"Why do we have to stop at all?" I asked.

"Our next objective is Melles. At Melles we have to cross a bridge: the Germans patrol it and pass over it approximately every ten minutes. We'll have to run across after a patrol has passed, and we can only do that at night."

The sun was terribly hot: our hair stuck to our foreheads and our clothes to our backs. We reached the shepherd's cottage in the middle of the afternoon: a small grey house standing in a clearing. We added our names, next to a number of others, on the walls of the house. A gurgling stream ran across the high grass of the clearing: after the boys had washed, I took my turn and let the water run over my sore feet for a long time. It was cool and clean. What were they doing at Avéron now? What were they doing at St-Bertrand? I stayed lying in the grass for a long time, with my face in the sun. It all seemed so futile: the Patron's report would be out of date by the time it got to London. And how would I impress a lot of stern staff officers in Algiers with the fact that the three parachutists needed arms and material? By my head, the grasshoppers and the crickets had become trusting and played in the long swaying blades of grass. Everything was so calm and beautiful around, so little in harmony with the immensity of my misery at having to go. I went to sleep.

"Wake up, we're going now," Henry said, shaking me gently. I stood up, stiffer than ever: every bone in my body seemed to ache and my legs wobbled.

"Yes, we're all feeling like that," Henry said.

We began groping our way downhill again: going down was much more tiring then climbing – the effort to stop yourself from running down, more painful than the effort to pull yourself up. Elmer, Bill and Nick spent their time trying to be at the top of the column and childishly catching each other up: with this system we went faster and faster.

"There's no point in hurrying like this," the guides declared. "We'll only have to stop again before approaching Melles." This quiet and stubborn race to head the file continued all the way to Spain, and eventually the malady caught all of us. Mike and Johnny were the only ones who didn't care, carrying on a continual and inaudible conversation at the rear. At 10pm we reached the neighbourhood of Melles and had to stop again; it was still not dark enough. I wrote a long letter to Yves, whom I had promised to keep informed on every moment of the journey; it reached him four months later, in London, after passing through a few hundred hands. Elmer whined about his truck.

"It'll never wait for us…"

But the most serious thing was food. We started out with enough for one and a half days. We had one tin of bully beef left and half a loaf of bread. Henry had sparingly distributed his sugar; it was the only thing we'd have on the rest of the walk.

"You ought to reach Spain tomorrow morning," the guides said. "That's if we find the rest of the way…"

So far we had only got lost twice and both times found the road again: but the prospects were getting darker, for the guides got more doubtful as we went further. At half-past eleven the night was pitch dark, and we started silently down again, one behind the other, tiptoeing on the grassy patches of the paths. Like the night before, we crept over the road near Melles, and gathered in a group between the road and the river.

"We'll have to crawl to the bridge," one of the guides whispered.

We stooped and crawled and got wet and muddy. Near the river, thundering in the night, we stopped again. The guides went forward: German voices could be heard some way away, mingled with the sound of the water. If they had dogs, we wouldn't get across. But the voices receded in the distance and a short low whistle from the guides warned us to follow them. We all ran across the bridge in a file, as noiselessly as possible. On our left, on the other side of the bridge, a path ran straight up into the mountains. But the guides didn't take it and disappeared in the dark thickness to the right; they probably knew where they were going…

The climb became very difficult; we couldn't talk as we were still too near Melles. We had to follow very close behind one another so as not to get lost. The undergrowth got thicker, the night blacker, the climb steeper. We fought our way through dense blackberry bushes, catching on to anything that came under our hand: blackberry branches, holly trees and cutting blades of something. I never found out what. The branches swept across my face and caught into my hair. Within a short time I felt blood running down my bare legs where the scratches hurt with a sharp, burning pain. I couldn't close my hands for fear of digging the thorns further into my palms.

"Where the hell are we going? I'm not going another step," I declared, after nearly an hour of this.

The column stopped.

"Shh… We must climb a little further up. We're still too near Melles," the guides replied.

We started again, climbing what seemed to be a vertical wall of thick bushes and murderous thorns, pulling ourselves up with the strength of our arms: my feet slipped off the damp footholds I found. Rubber shoes four times your size are no recommendable footwear for crossing the Pyrenees. As we went on I bit my lower lip to keep quiet: nothing would induce me to stop again, after Elmer's allusions to slowing the party up. But Henry put a stop to this sinister battle through the night.

"We're far enough from Melles now," he declared, stopping dead. "We'll be so tired tomorrow that we won't be able to move. Besides, I bet you don't know where we are," he told the guides. "We may be near a precipice of some sort."

We didn't think he was so near the truth. We stopped and the guides volunteered to get some water. After a considerable absence, they returned.

"Do you know that we're about sixty yards from a real precipice? We nearly fell down a vertical wall covered with damp and slippery moss. Thank God we didn't go any further…"

We passed the flasks around. The water had a sharp taste of earth. The guides were rather touching in their efforts to please us and make up for the waste of time during the day. I was determined not to sleep on a slope again. I found a horizontal patch about a yard long, built it up with stones, covered it with soft leaves and branches and fell asleep instantaneously. Mike slept with his legs dangling both sides of a tree-trunk, which stopped him slipping downhill. The others did not sleep much more than the first night. At 6am, Nick shook me.

"C'mon, we're off. But look at that…" A thick grey cloud of fog was slowly rolling down the slopes towards us. Already the dampness had penetrated right through our clothes.

"I'm hungry. Let's eat something," I suggested. By now the bread was so hard that we had to soften it down with water. No bully beef was left.

"No, not yet. Let's get still further from Melles before we do."

We started up once more: the slope was covered with wet leaves; for every three steps, I slipped back two.

"Poor Paulette, by the time she reaches Spain she will have walked five times what we have," Mike remarked, patting me on the back.

We were hidden from Melles by thin trees: at times we must have been visible to anyone watching the mountains. It was imperative to get out of sight as soon as possible. At the top, we sat down and cut up the bread into seven shares. The guides produced cold pork and cold chicken, laid thick butter over their slice of bread, and tried to make us share their food with them. But we refused. They still had the journey back. The fog closed in thickly.

We walked for five hours along the crest of the mountain. The fog clung thicker and thicker to the pine trees and muffled the sound of our footsteps. We lost all sense of direction. I had grown so used to walking that I was no longer tired and followed the boys like an automaton. Then suddenly the mist lifted. Below us lay a deep and beautiful valley: the Garonne glittered in the brilliant sun. We were in full view of the town of Fos and well off the route to Spain. One by one we ran to the cover of woods, sat round Nick who produced a pilot's silk map, and a small compass. We decided to go on alone. The guides left us after warm handshakes and returned on their long journey home, while we headed south, towards the Spanish border.

Before starting up the last mountain, we gathered branches of huckleberries and improvised a meal with handfuls of them and bits of sugar. Voices could be heard shouting in the distance. Who were they? Shepherds or German patrols? But sounds in the hills are completely out of proportion with distances.

The last climb was the hardest and steepest of all. The sun scorched our backs and grasshoppers swarmed by hundreds under our feet. We followed the principle that the shortest distance between two points is the straight line, so we headed dead for the summit, which was like swimming against a rapid current. The vegetation came up above our knees.

At four we reached the top and ran over the crest, without paying the smallest attention to field-craft and outlines. It seemed that, on the other slope of the mountain, German bullets could no longer reach us, that the Gestapo could no longer catch us, and that the war no longer existed. It was only the next day that we heard that the actual border was only fifty yards above Canejan and that the slopes we had slipped, rolled and run down without cover were usually heavily patrolled by the Boches.

It was well after six when, weak with hunger and numb with weariness, we caught sight of Canejan in the distance. Dark stones and pointed roofs, it cuddled on the side of the mountain as though afraid of falling down. An old woman ambled slowly towards us along the narrow path. Her hair was tied up under a black scarf and her old hands knotted by years of toil and labour. She stopped as I approached her and her eyes looked up, although she didn't move her head.

"Is this Spain?" I asked, feeling suddenly that we might well be a hundred kilometres from it.

She nodded slowly and smiled. "*Si, señorita, Ustedes están en España...*" Then she went on her way.

The seven of us resumed our trek towards Canejan. Far away, behind the rocky mountains we had just come over, the fight went on in France; the gay and uncomfortable life of the *maquis*, with its perils and its hardships, with its happy comradeships and the heart-warming contentment brought about by the accomplishment of patriotic duty.

And over the crest of the blue Spanish Pyrenees, the setting sun painted the pale sky with long stretches of tropical gold merging into arctic crimson.[1]

THE END

POSTSCRIPT

I have always been disappointed that *Moondrop to Gascony* finished so abruptly with Anne-Marie Walters' arrival in Canejan and with no mention of what happened to her during her journey through Spain to Algiers and afterwards. I became interested as to why she was so suddenly despatched by George Starr on a seemingly unnecessary mission, with a report about the current political situation in southwest France at almost the moment of complete success for WHEELWRIGHT. I also wondered what became of her in later life, as she appeared to have severed her connections with southwest France and her former colleagues in SOE.

That Anne-Marie had "worked courageously and shown personal courage and willingness to undergo danger" was public knowledge, and evidenced in the recommendation signed by Major General Colin Gubbins on 27 April 1945 "that this FANY officer be appointed a Member of the Order of the British Empire."

She had given an account of some of her experiences in a BBC interview broadcast to coincide with the statement made to the House of Commons by Sir Archibald Sinclair, the Secretary of State for Air, on 5 March 1945. In this he made public for the first time that "several members of the WAAF had been to the fore in helping the Resistance groups in Europe before the landings on D-Day, either as liaison officers or couriers or radio operators."

She had also contributed, anonymously because of wartime security restrictions, an article for *The Daily Telegraph*, published on 14 February 1945. This gave an abbreviated account of what was to appear in *Moondrop to Gascony* the following year.

It was only with the gradual release into the public domain of the remaining records of SOE Western Europe, which began in 2002, that a lot more information became available about Starr, Anne-Marie and WHEELWRIGHT. In this connection, the most important were the release in 2004 of the personnel file of Starr (HS 9/1407/1) and in 2006 that of Anne-Marie (HS 9/339/2). In addition, a copy of the confidential report which Anne-Marie wrote to Lieutenant Colonel

Buckmaster in December 1944, of which there is no copy on her file, was made available to me by her family.

From these sources, the picture became clearer. Anne-Marie had indeed crossed the frontier into Spain near the small, hillside village of Canejan, perched just below the summit of the Pyrenees, which forms the border with France. The whole group were taken into custody by the Spanish police and transported via Sort to Vielha, where they were held for four days while the local British Consul was informed. He was able to make the necessary arrangements for her release and onward travel to the British Consulate in Barcelona and the good offices of the Consul General, Harold Farquhar, a solid supporter of SOE and its agents, many of whom passed through his hands while on the run.

During her stay in Barcelona, Anne-Marie was able to make contact with Ana Marie Ensesa, a fellow-pupil at the International School in Geneva, who quickly reported the news of her arrival to the school and thus to many of her friends.

Two days later, now under the guise of 'Miss Fitzgerald', Anne-Marie left by train for the British Embassy in Madrid. Here she was forced to wait another four days while arrangements were made for her onward journey to Algiers, so that she could deliver the message she was carrying on behalf of Lieutenant Colonel Fuller, the commander of the JEDBURGH BUGATTI team. Her passage from Madrid to Algiers was sanctioned by SOE headquarters but, strangely, without the knowledge or agreement of Lieutenant Colonel Buckmaster and F Section.

On arrival in Algiers, Anne-Marie delivered Lieutenant Colonel Fuller's message to Major H N Marten of the Northamptonshire Yeomanry, who was responsible for the despatch and administration of JEDBURGH teams in France. He suggested she should go back to France for JEDBURGH and work with a party under his command. As Anne-Marie described it later, her mission would have been "to help rounding up the JEDBURGH teams, which I could easily do in southwest France, and help in their debriefing. After that was done, we were to start a new plan of re-contacting all the contacts we had (both F Section's and the JEDBURGH's) in order to build up, from that very solid base, new and better post-war relations between the French and the British."[1]

To her surprise, what could have been considered a logical and sensible idea was quickly vetoed by F Section, and Anne-Marie was ordered to return immediately to London. Unbeknown to her, on 31 July 1944, the day of her departure from Avéron-Bergelle, Starr had sent his message no. 48 to SOE F Section, stating

"Have had to send *Colette* back because she is undisciplined in spite of my efforts to train her since arrival. Most indiscreet. Very man-mad, also disobedient in personal matters. She constitutes a danger to security, not only her own but of everyone. On other hand she does not lack courage, never hesitated to go on any mission. Totally unsuitable for commission. She should never be sent back to France to work for our organisation."

With such a message from one of their most distinguished commanders, the attitude of F Section can be understood.

As to what prompted it, it seems that since D-Day and the formation of the *maquis* at Castelnau-sur-l'Auvignon, relations between Starr and Anne-Marie had deteriorated. Until this time, Anne-Marie had acted as courier between Starr and de Gunzbourg in the Dordogne, which meant she could keep in touch with Arnault, who was then de Gunzbourg's second-in-command. Starr now decided that Maguy Merchez should replace Anne-Marie as courier, much to Anne-Marie's annoyance.

Things apparently got worse. Back in London, in an undated confidential report addressed to Lieutenant Colonel Buckmaster, which does not appear on any SOE file, Anne-Marie Walters wrote that, on her return to Avéron-Bergelle at midnight on 25 July 1944

"I was pushed in a room by Buresie (*Hilaire's 'garde du corps'* – a Russian ex-legionnaire) and shown a paper declaring textually: *prière d'arrêter et d'incarcérer Mademoiselle Colette dès son retour*... I was thrown in prison with the captured *miliciens* and collaborators (including their fleas and lice) and a guard was ordered to sleep by my side... The whole *maquis* knew of this and decided I must be a Gestapo double-agent..."

According to Anne-Marie's report, at noon the next day Starr had her brought to his command post and accused her of having an affair with a member of the Battalion, of spreading scandalous stories concerning his relations with another woman agent and of being undisciplined. Accusations which she vigorously denied. Anne-Marie continues:

"It was obvious that after the humiliations and insults I'd publicly received, I could no longer work for [Starr]. He despatched me to England with a small report and declared that 'if I got there quickly, he would mention nothing of all this.' I replied that I would, in view of the flagrant injustice of it all, but refrained from doing so at the last minute...

Before I left, Captain Monnet (now Col. Monnet), called me and told me, in the name of Commandant Parisot and his men, that they had been sorry about the ridiculous ordeal I had been through and that they had tried to stop *Hilaire* but could not do much as I was under his direct orders. But they all wanted me to know that they knew I was wrongly accused and did not want me to go away with the awful idea that men I admired and esteemed had the wrong opinion about me.

Captain Guy de la Roche told me later that *Hilaire* told him he intended to shoot me, '*lui foutre une balle dans la nuque*' to quote his own words, but that he was afraid of my father. Upon which, Captain de la Roche strongly advised him against it and said he would not leave the *maquis* without me and without making sure I was safe. *Hilaire* repeated and admitted this assertion to me in London."[2]

On her return to London in 1944, Anne-Marie was first interviewed on 14 September by F Section Security Officer Vera Atkins, who found her

"to be in a highly excitable and unsatisfactory frame of mind. She seems to have an idea of the unfavourable reports received by us and is in a most aggressive mood. She says that we are responsible for preventing her going on a most useful mission to France for 'Massingham' [the JEDBURGH base in Algeria]. I know she was taken to Algiers for reasons which I fail to understand."

Five days later Anne-Marie was debriefed on her mission to France. Her seven-page report is detailed and accurate, with few exaggerations and much useful information about WHEELWRIGHT, its local contacts and its achievements. In it she is generous with her comments about Starr: "He is a first-class agent. He has excellent principles of security... He is very courageous, very patient and a very disciplined person." She also, however, adds her criticisms where she considers them necessary:

"We got along very well up to D-Day as long as we were leading an ordinary agent's life, but after it suddenly became difficult, he went for days and nights without sleeping one minute, was very worried and concerned with the first *maquis* organisation and very much over-worked. Thus it was that he simply followed blindly his impulses (and sometimes some shrewdly given advice) without stopping to think of the consequences they might bring.

A small example: he adopted a Russian as '*Garde de corps*' (which was hardly necessary in a *maquis* of 1200 men). That Russian, Buresie, was an ex-Foreign Legion soldier, a dangerous and blood-thirsty character, also slightly mad; he suggested and carried out absolutely horrible tortures on captured *miliciens*. At the beginning of July, I was asked by *Chainette*[3] to arrange a meeting between *Hilaire* and himself. The rendezvous was only 15 kms from our *maquis* but *Hilaire* refused to come in spite of the fact that *Chainette* moved some 100 kms to come and see him. He sent me on to fetch him and told Buresie to come with me and bring him at the point of the Sten if he refused to come. That order would certainly have been carried out had *Chainette* refused to follow me and quite naturally would have caused most serious trouble for us. *Hilaire* had just not stopped to think.

It was also quite wrong in my opinion to lower ourselves to the standards of the Gestapo by torturing *miliciens* and collaborators to make them reveal the whereabouts of their colleagues – some were beaten until the blood spurted all over the walls, others were horribly burnt; one man's feet were held in the fire 20 minutes and his legs slowly burnt off to the knee; other tortures are even too horrible to mention. A good number of people were also shot. Had *Hilaire* not been influenced in all this (and Buresie played a great part in suggesting, encouraging and carrying out those tortures) I am sure he would never have started it."[4]

Whatever F Section or others may have thought of this report, nothing appears to have resulted from Anne-Marie's comments about Starr and the torture of prisoners until Starr was asked, as a 'returned agent', to visit the SOE finishing school at Beaulieu, Hampshire, on 30 October 1944 to give an after-dinner talk in the Officers' Mess about his experiences in France.

Two days later Colonel Stanley Woolrych, the Commandant at Beaulieu, wrote a letter to Air Commodore Archie Boyle, the head of the SOE personnel board:

"This week's 'returned agent' who came down to see us was Lt. Col. Starr. I do not think that there is much doubt that he has done a magnificent piece of work in organising S. W. France during the last two years and has done a very excellent job personally, for which one is glad to see that he has been rewarded. At the same time I feel that his record has been somewhat marred by a streak of sadism which it is going to be extremely hard to ignore when one comes to assess the work of his particular mission, more especially as there already exists a protest in the report of one of his junior agents (Miss A. M. Walters) of which I attach an extract.

There is no doubt, both from Miss Walters' report and from Lt. Col. Starr's own narrative on Monday, that they tortured prisoners in a fairly big way. It might be answered, of course, that this was the work of the F.F.I. which Lt. Col. Starr was powerless to prevent. He recounted to us, however, with considerable relish, the episode of a capture he made personally and for which, of course, he must accept responsibility...

Starr's recital caused something like consternation amongst my officers who felt it was hardly worth while winning a war on these terms."[5]

Consternation was also caused in the highest echelons of SOE, who, following the receipt of this letter and a demand from Starr for an enquiry to clear his name, convened a top-secret court of enquiry on 26 January 1945 on the orders of Brigadier Mockler-Ferryman, head of SOE London Section. The terms of reference were "to investigate the conduct of Lieut/Colonel G R Starr, General List, employed on SFHQ Mission WHEELWRIGHT towards any enemy prisoners that may at any time during the course of the said mission have been under his control or under the control of troops or resistance forces under his immediate command or control."

The enquiry commenced at Norgeby House on 5 February 1945.[6] During the following ten days, evidence on oath amounting to 213 manuscript pages was assembled from the many people who had been involved with WHEELWRIGHT, including Anne-Marie, Yvonne Cormeau, Lieutenant Colonel Maurice Buckmaster and Starr himself. Surprisingly, pages 18 to 172, which included the main body of Anne-Marie's evidence, have been removed from the file. One can only guess what they contained. However, when recalled on 15 February and still on oath, Anne-Marie stated:

"I didn't write my report with any intention of making an accusation against *Hilaire*. I did not know he was not head of the *maquis*, in spite of the fact that I was his personal courier. I therefore considered him responsible for allowing these tortures. When I said 'he would not have started it' I was referring to *Hilaire*, but I really meant he would not have 'allowed it to be started'. In the paragraphs in which these words occur I did mean to say that *Hilaire* was responsible for not trying to stop the tortures. I wish to stress that I thought he was head of the *maquis*...

I agree that what I said may easily be construed as an accusation against *Hilaire*. As one of his people '*de confiance*' I feel I ought to have been told that *Hilaire* was not head of that *maquis* and about administrative changes."

In fact, after the battle of Castelnau-sur-l'Auvignon on 21 June 1944, Starr had put Maurice Parisot in command of the combined *maquis* of Panjas and Castelnau, which now formed the Bataillon d'Armagnac. As Starr explained in an interview with Major Angelo on 20 November 1944, "Parisot had all the qualities needed in a leader, and a French unit fighting in France should not be commanded by a foreigner." It was therefore as Commandant of the Bataillon that Parisot issued his '*Décision*' on 27 June 1944 about members' rates of pay.[7] At the court of enquiry, Starr cited this '*Décision*' as evidence that he himself had not been in command of the *maquis* at that time or subsequently, when tortures were alleged to have been carried out on prisoners.

Anne-Marie seems to have mistakenly assumed that Starr was in command and therefore responsible for the tortures to which she refers in her report of 18 September 1944, and which Starr also mentions in his interview with Major Angelo: "Torture of all sorts was used extensively. Other methods used would include a salt diet, being left in a dark cell and then interrogated in the blinding light and the placing of a stool-pigeon with a man in solitary confinement or putting microphones in a cell where two people knew each other well, threats were used of even worse treatment, and so on."

Despite all these references to torture, by 28 February the court had reached its conclusion that

"there is no justification whatever for any imputation against Lieut/Colonel Starr of inhumanity or cruel treatment to any enemy prisoner at any time under his control or under the control of troops or resistance forces under his immediate command or control. The Court is satisfied that not only is this the case but that Lieut/Colonel Starr made every endeavour to ensure that enemy prisoners should be treated fairly and correctly. On more than one occasion he went to the length of incurring adverse criticism from men under his command or with whom he was working on account of his endeavours to protect enemy prisoners against ill-treatment by resistance forces, and his rigid insistence that brutality against them was not to be allowed. Undoubtedly, Lieut/Colonel Starr was aware, as a matter of general knowledge, as were other organisers and resistance leaders, that on occasion enemy prisoners were ill-treated and even subjected to torture in various *maquis*. He himself, however, was never party to, nor did he authorise, approve or condone such ill-treatment or the inflicting of torture."

So ended the affair and Starr's career with SOE. He received the Distinguished Service Order in addition to the Military Cross he had already been awarded, and was regarded by F Section as "one of the most distinguished officers they ever sent to the field."

By 1946, Anne-Marie had returned to Paris and in December of that year married Jean-Claude Comert, her childhood friend from Geneva who had also attended the International School. Like her father, her father-in-law, Pierre Comert, had joined the Secretariat of the League of Nations at its inception in 1919, as head of the information department. He had previously been a correspondent for *Le Temps* in Vienna and Berlin, and in 1940 he founded the independent Free-French paper, *France*, in London with Charles Gombault.

In 1950, Anne-Marie and her family, which now consisted of a son and daughter, moved to New York, where Jean-Claude was appointed head of information of the French Section at the UN. On their return to Paris in 1955, Anne-Marie found work as a sub-editor at *France-Soir*, working under Charles Gombault. She remained there for ten years until, in 1965, she established herself as a translator.

At the same time, Anne-Marie was perfecting her Spanish with a tutor, with whose help she found herself among a group of friends including actors and intellectuals when, in 1968, she moved to live in Barcelona. (Anne-Marie was always much attracted to Spanish culture and had made a long visit to Mexico during her time in New York.) In Barcelona, Anne-Marie worked for a Spanish publisher, Argos, as literary director, before founding her own literary agency, liaising between British and French authors and publishers and their Spanish counterparts.

She finally returned to France in 1990, when she bought an apartment in Montpellier. By this time she was already suffering from the early symptoms of Alzheimer's disease. She died in a nursing home at La Baume-de-Transit, in the Drôme, on 2 October 1998 at the age of 75.

In recognition of her "personal courage and willingness to undergo any danger," *The London Gazette* announced on 17 July 1945 that Ensign Anne-Marie Walters of the FANY had been appointed a Member of the Order of the British Empire (Civil). (FANYs who survived the war were not eligible for the Military MBE since they were regarded as having belonged to a civilian organisation.)

NOTES

INTRODUCTION (PP 11–24)

1. By coincidence, the VIC escape line was set up and run by Giliana Gerson's husband, Victor, under the overall control of Lieutenant Colonel Leslie Humphreys. It was one of SOE's most successful lines, responsible for the escape through Spain and Gibraltar of many SOE and other agents.

2. "Travel is no longer a pleasure, but a grim undertaking, not to be embarked upon lightly. It is devastating for the weak and exhausting even for the strong. Trains are crowded beyond belief and look like a Walt Disney brain storm, with passengers filling all the windows of compartments and corridors alike and packed on to the entrance platforms so that often the doors can not close." (HS 9/647/4 Virginia Hall in an article for the *New York Post*, 8 October 1941.)

3. Brian Stonehouse parachuted to a dropping ground near Tours in July 1941 to work as a radio operator for Philippe de Vomécourt (*Gauthier*). Soon he was in such demand by several agents that he began to operate too often and for dangerously long periods. This led to his being discovered by 'Direction Finding' (DF) equipment and arrested on 24 October 1942. Taken to Germany, he was imprisoned in Mauthausen and then Dachau, from where he was freed by American troops on 29 April 1945.

4. Rouneau returned to France in April 1944 to lead the highly successful RACKETEER circuit in Brittany, which was responsible for cutting many main railway lines and which provided much information for the American forces.

5. Following her arrival in England in 1943, Denise Bloch (*Danielle*)

underwent full SOE training, before returning to France to work with Robert Benoist (*Lionel*) and his CLERGYMAN circuit near Paris. She was captured with other members of the circuit on 19 June 1944 and executed in Ravensbruck camp early in 1945.

6. A scholar at Eton and editor of the *Eton College Chronicle*, Frank Walters had already in 1913 been elected a Fellow of University College Oxford at the age of 25 and appointed to teach Latin and Greek. At Eton he excelled at games, where one of his closest acquaintances playing "that most mysterious and unrewarding of Eton's sports, the Wall Game", was Stuart Menzies, later to become the war-time head of MI6 and Churchill's spymaster.

7. Frank Walters later wrote the official history of the League: *A History of the League of Nations* (2 vols), Francis P Walters, Oxford University Press, 1952.

8. Among the influential people Frank Walters numbered as friends were Sir Alexander Cadogan, Permanent Under-Secretary at the Foreign Office, and Edward Wood, later Lord Halifax and Foreign Secretary at the outbreak of war. Although living in Geneva and deeply involved with the League, Frank Walters also kept in close touch with his contemporaries from Eton and Oxford and his erstwhile friends who now held important positions in London and Washington.

9. "After the defeat of the Spanish Republicans, I had cried when I saw the news reels showing streams of refugees arriving in France. To enlist, therefore seemed to me the most natural thing to do at that time. I didn't do it out of any sort of patriotism; it was above all a stand against Fascism." (Anne-Marie Walters quoted in *Des Femmes dans la Résistance*, Nicole Chatel, Julliard, 1972.)

10. At his debrief in January 1945, Arnault remarked that, in towns, active help was more forthcoming from the small business community, such as mechanics and engineers, but that the greater part of townspeople were simply watching and waiting. Although they may have had anti-German feelings, most were unwilling to do more than listen to the BBC broadcasts. In the country, on the other hand, he found that many farmers were nervous about undertaking dangerous work but were sympathetic to the Resistance. He also considered that, on the whole, the Gendarmerie was well-disposed towards the Resistance. When Arnault attacked the Empalot gunpowder

factory, for example, a police inspector working for the Resistance helped carry the explosives through the control at Toulouse station. Earlier, following the break-out from the prison at Eysse, a *gendarme* accompanied the escapees through the road blocks around Agen.

11. Château Ferron, near Tonneins, was requisitioned by the Vichy authorities from Madame Vanderheyden (the widow of a French officer killed in 1916) to be used as the headquarters of the local *miliciens* under their chief, Pierre de la Rochère. (Archives Départmentales de Lot-et-Garonne, Agen, COTE 1W445.)

12. The HOPKINSON mission, commanded by Lieutenant Colonel G F Hopkinson MC, had its origins in operation PHANTOM, which was launched in November 1939 to provide up to date ground information for the Commander of British Air Forces in France. This information was collected by two troops of armoured cars from the 12th Lancers, a platoon of picked motorcyclists from the Queen Victoria Rifles and an Intelligence section consisting of a further six subalterns and six junior NCOs, all of whom could understand and speak French. In due course, the HOPKINSON mission was also tasked with keeping GHQ British Expeditionary Force fully briefed on the quick-moving withdrawal to Dunkerque. PHANTOM later developed into a separate regiment, one squadron of which worked with the SAS in 1944.

13. Imperial War Museum Sound Archive (IWMSA) interview with G R Starr in France, 24613.

14. IWMSA interview with G R Starr in France, 24613.

CHAPTER 1 (PP 28–38)

1. Claude Arnault. See Introduction p20–22.

2. Many sorties flown by 138 and 161 squadrons of the Royal Air Force to infiltrate agents also carried packs of leaflets known as "nickels". The size of a leaflet was approximately 20 cm by 25 cm and the packs were about 30 cm thick, and therefore of considerable weight. They were often released some distance from the agents' dropping zone in order to draw the attention of the local authorities away from the real purpose of the sortie. During one month in 1942, nearly eight million of these leaflets were dropped over France.

LE COURRIER DE L'AIR

Propriété Publique

APPORTE PAR LA R.A.F.   *LONDRES, LE 3 FEVRIER 1944*

Sombre week-end en Allemagne

LA GUERRE D'USURE À LAQUELLE EST SOUMISE LA LUFTWAFFE ATTEINT DE NOUVEAUX DEGRÉS D'INTENSITÉ.

La R.A.F. opérant de nuit et de jour, et la U.S.A.A.F. par ses attaques diurnes méthodiques, imposent aux pilotes allemands une lutte ininterrompue dont les premiers effets se font déjà sentir sur l'efficacité de la défense du Reich.

Pour se faire une juste appréciation de la guerre aérienne dans son stade actuel, il faut tenir compte du fait que l'Allemagne, rejetée sur la défensive, a attelé son industrie aéronautique presque intégralement à la construction d'avions de chasse. Ces avions, dont la force de première ligne est de l'ordre de 2.000 environ, sont tenus en réserve pour être jetés dans l'assaut final.

La Luftwaffe contrainte au combat

Le problème se posait donc pour les Alliés : forcer la *Luftwaffe* à livrer l'air et ainsi affronter les escadrilles massées de bombardiers et de chasseurs alliés; détruire les avions qui, par leur production, alimentent les groupes de chasse de l'ennemi.

Dans les quarante-huit heures des 29 au 30 janvier, la R.A.F. et des États-Unis ont lancé des attaques extrêmement lourdes sur Francfort, Brunswick et Hanovre.

De bonne heure dans la matinée du 29 janvier, des bombardiers en formations très puissantes ont bombardé Berlin, causant de vastes explosions et allumant de nombreux incendies ; quarante-sept appareils britanniques ne sont pas rentrés.

Cette opération faisait suite au bombardement de Berlin, exécuté dans la nuit du 27 janvier, quand des centaines de *Lancasters* jetèrent sur Berlin en 20 minutes mille cinq cents tonnes de bombes explosives et incendiaires. Les pertes britanniques se sont montées à 34 appareils.

Débarquement américain en territoire japonais

Les Américains ont débarqué dans les îles Marshall, qui sont sous mandat japonais depuis la dernière guerre. Les Marshall, à environ 350 kilomètres au nord des îles Gilbert, occupées par les Américains, constituent un des bastions extérieurs de la sphère de domination japonaise dans le Pacifique.

On dit officiellement à Washington que les premiers débarquements ont eu lieu dans les atolls qui entourent les îles de Roi et de Kwajalein, stratégiquement les plus importantes de l'archipel. Après un bombardement aérien intense, les forces d'invasion, protégées par la flotte américaine, ont réussi à établir des têtes de plage, malgré une forte résistance japonaise. Les opérations se développent. Elles sont parmi les plus considérables entreprises par les Alliés à ce jour dans le Pacifique.

Pertes justifiées

Comme on s'en rend compte, ces opérations sont coûteuses, mais elles justifient pleinement les efforts de la R.A.F., qui passe malgré les multiples et ingénieux moyens de défense mis en action par l'ennemi.

De son côté, la *Fighter Command* de la R.A.F., au cours des coups faits au-dessus du nord de la France et de la Hollande, remporte des succès éclatants. C'est ainsi que dans la journée du 30 janvier des *Typhoons* ont abattu,

Suite à la page 3

LES CHEFS ALLIÉS EN CONFERENCE AU Q.G. SUPREME

De gauche à droite: (assis) Air Chief Marshal Tedder, le général Eisenhower, Commandant-en-Chef suprême, et le général Montgomery ; (debout) le lieutenant-général Bradley, l'amiral Ramsay, Air Chief Marshal Leigh-Mallory et le lieutenant-général Smith.

Les Allemands se cramponnent à la "Ligne Gustav"

Tandis que dans le secteur Nettuno-Anzio les Alliés consolident leurs positions, débarquent de l'artillerie lourde et des chars et repoussent les contre-attaques, le gros de la Ve Armée exerce une pression continue sur la ligne Gustav, qui s'étend sur les rives nord du Rapido et du Garigliano.

Celle-ci a été rompue en plusieurs points.

Les Allemands semblent attacher une grande importance à cette ligne Gustav. Un ordre de Hitler daté du 24 janvier, dont un exemplaire est tombé entre les mains des Alliés, montre que le Führer ordonne de tenir à tout prix les positions de la ligne Gustav.

En attendant, les troupes françaises continuent de se distinguer au nord-est de Cassino, dont la chute semble imminente. Elles attaquent sur une altitude de 1.000 à 2.000 mètres une série de positions-forteresses dont déjà ont d'importantes conséquences, comme le fait remarquer le général Clark dans son message au général Juin.

Quant aux autres unités de la Ve Armée qui ont débarqué sur la côte de la mer Tyrrhénienne au sud de Rome, elles n'ont rencontré l'ennemi en force qu'au sixième jour. Elles livrèrent leur premier engagement sérieux le 27 janvier au sud-ouest de Littoria, à une vingtaine de kilomètres des têtes de plage de Nettuno.

La contre-attaque, lancée par des troupes de la division Panzer *Hermann Goering* prélevées sur le front de Cassino, fut

Suite à la page 2

LES TROUPES FRANÇAISES A L'ŒUVRE

Le général Clark, commandant la Ve Armée, a adressé le message suivant au général Juin, commandant les forces françaises en action en Italie :

"Je tiens à vous exprimer mon admiration et ma reconnaissance pour la façon splendide dont votre corps remplit sa mission en facilitant le succès du débarquement de nos forces au voisinage d'Anzio.

"L'heureuse exécution du débarquement de nos forces et l'établissement d'une importante tête de pont dans la région Anzio-Nettuno ont été dues pour une large part à l'efficacité de l'action menée au moment même par votre corps.

"Par un plan d'opérations uniquement préparé et coordonné, vous avez lancé et soutenu une série d'attaques qui ont atteint avec un succès remarquable leur but principal, à savoir fixer par de durs combats le plus grand nombre possible de forces ennemies et les empêcher ainsi d'intervenir contre notre débarquement et contre l'établissement de la tête de pont d'Anzio."

"De retour du front d'Italie, le général Giraud a déclaré à la radio d'Alger :

"Je suis fier de l'Armée française depuis le dernier des hommes.

"Je comprends les félicitations chaleureuses que le général commandant la Ve Armée adresse au corps d'armée français qui combat sous ses ordres."

TRES BIEN

"Au nom de Laval, le chef de la milice, Darnand, vient de proclamer :

'Il faut vaincre ou mourir.'

"Très bien ! Très bien puisqu'il ne reste aux Boches et à leur valetaille aucune possibilité de vaincre."

Libération 9.11.43.

F.12

ABOVE: *Le Courrier de l'Air*, 3 February 1944, printed in London and dropped by the RAF.

ABOVE RIGHT: Report of the discovery of *Le Courrier de l'Air* in Auch, 3 March 1944.

S.R. N° 745

PRÉFECTURE DU GERS
-6 MARS 1944
CABINET DU PRÉFET

AUCH, le 3 mars 1944.

OBJET: découverte de tracts d'origine
anglaise à AUCH.
SOURCE: contrôlée.

NOTE DE RENSEIGNEMENTS N° 181

J'ai l'honneur de vous rendre compte, qu'une quantité assez importante de tracts, d'origine anglaise, ont été découverts à AUCH, dans les
premières heures de la matinée du 2 courant.

Ces tracts, imprimés noirs, sur fond blanc, à double feuillets,
sont de format 27 X 21 et ont pour titre "LE COURRIER DE L'AIR". Ils
portent, en outre, en tête de chaque premier feuillet, dans les coins
une cocarde aux couleurs britanniques et plus bas, les inscriptions ci-
après "APPORTE PAR LA R.A.F." - "LONDRES, le 3 février 1944".

Ces documents ont trait à la guerre sur tous les fronts. Aux opérations aériennes sur l'ALLEMAGNE; Evènements d'ESPAGNE et d'ARGENTINE;
Conférence africaine. En première page, est reproduite une photographie
représentant sept officiers en uniforme, avec les titres suivants: "LES
CHEFS ALLIES en CONFERENCE AU Q.G. SUPREME".

Le plus grand nombre de ces tracts a été découverts dans la partie
Nord de la ville, par paquets de 10 ou 20. Ils ont été ramassés par les
Services de police de la ville et la population n'en a pour ainsi dire
pas eu connaissance. Aucune réaction n'a été enregistrée.

Des avions ont survolé la ville d'AUCH, entre le 23 et zéro heures,
dans la nuit du 1 au 2 mars et il y a tout lieu de supposer qu'ils ont
été lancés par ces appareils.

L'alerte n'a pas été donnée.

3. Pigeons were able to carry small maps and drawings quicker than by other methods, except wireless. There were limitations as to how far they could fly, however, and they lost the homing instinct if not used soon after they were dropped. Feeding and exercising them was also difficult in occupied France.

4. Anne-Marie was called for interview by F Section on 4 June 1943. She would have been interviewed by Captain Selwyn Jepson, usually known to potential agents as "Mr Potter". Jepson was a successful crime writer before and after the war.

5. 56 Queen's Gate, Kensington, was the main place where an agent's clothing was 'aged' to help make his or her cover story ring true. Care had to be taken to ensure that the tailoring of clothes gave no hint of British origin. Initially, enough genuine clothing was obtained from refugees, but eventually this source dried up and SOE had to start its own tailoring process. This was achieved by UK companies employing refugees who made clothes in their

national styles, without being told why they were doing so.

6. 'The *Patron*': Lieutenant Colonel George Reginald Starr, DSO, MC (*Hilaire*, *Gaston*). See Introduction, p22–24.

7. The WHEELWRIGHT circuit, under F Section of SOE.

8. A small town on the borders of the Landes and Gers departments, where there was an important Resistance group forming part of the WHEELWRIGHT circuit.

9. Although Anne-Marie was allocated the field name *Colette*, she gives herself the name *Paulette* in her book.

10. Lieutenant Colonel Maurice Buckmaster, OBE. Educated at Eton, Buckmaster worked as a journalist at *Le Matin* and then, from 1923–1929, at the merchant bank J Henry Schroder, before joining the Ford company's French operation. He eventually rose to become head of its European Division in 1938. When war broke out, Buckmaster was commissioned into the Intelligence Corps and was one of the last British officers to be evacuated from Dunkerque. His linguistic skills – he had by then also perfected German – made him a natural candidate for the highly specialised work of SOE, where he served as head of F Section from 1941 to 1945.

11. RAF Tempsford was the home of 138 and 161 squadrons of the Royal Air Force. These two squadrons were principally concerned with infiltrating agents into France for both SOE and the Secret Intelligence Service. The 'departure school' was situated at Hazel Hall, a large house near the airfield, which had been requisitioned from the Pym family.

12. Gibraltar Farm Barn, still well preserved, has a plaque commemorating its wartime use. Here the containers were stored and agents strapped into their parachutes by their despatchers, helped by their conducting officers from SOE or other organisations.

13. "Halifax bomber DK 206 MA-V, piloted by Flight Lieutenant S N Gray, took off on 17 December 1943 at 2034 from RAF Tempsford on operation WHEELWRIGHT 50 and set course for France. Poor weather forced an early return and while attempting to land at RAF Woodbridge, Suffolk, the

12846

Can you have this checked up [handwritten]

then Walter's file [handwritten]

W. W. [handwritten]

17 December 1943.

A.M.W [handwritten]

REPORT FROM HAIRDRESSER AND MILKMAID.

Hairdresser and Milkmaid were interviewed by FM/US at Orchard Court today around 12:30. The following is their report:-

The trip to the grounds by Halifax-V where they were to be parachuted was uneventful. On arrival over the pinpoint the pilot saw the signal letter flashed but could not see the red lights; also the eureka of the plane was not functioning.

Forty miles further they saw another reception committee signaling the same letter. The plane was flying at 6,000 feet over the landing ground. There were a lot of clouds and it was slightly misty over the ground. After circling for over twenty minutes the pilot decided to return.

Several carrier pigeons and tracts were released at about twenty kilometres inland from the French coast. On the return trip it was foggy everywhere over England. Near Woodbridge the pilot communicated with the airfield. The Commanding Officer of Woodbridge asked permission of the Commanding Officer of Tempsford to have the passengers bail out, but this was refused. The Commanding Officer of Woodbridge gave all possible assistance. This was admitted by all remaining members of the crew.

The plane crashed in trees near the airfield at 5:10 A.M., at which time Arnault's watch stopped. (Woodbridge is near Ipswich in Suffolk County.) Three members of the crew were killed; Hairdresser and Milkmaid believe them to be the pilot, the navigator, and either the engineer or the aid-despatcher. The other three members of the crew were wounded, one sustaining broken ribs, another a broken arm, and the third a broken leg. Both Hairdresser and Milkmaid suffered shock and concussions. Major Ireland, the Medical Officer, examined both of them and stated that Milkmaid had a cut on the scalp, a bruise behind the right ear, and was suffering from shock. Hairdresser has an abrasion over the right eye and slight sprains of the ankles, plus shock. The Medical Officer recommends complete rest for both, and will see them again tomorrow at their homes. Milkmaid was taken to Mrs. Winser, 17 Devonshire Close, W.1., and Hairdresser to Mrs. Williams, 20 Cranley Place, S.W.7.

Both are in very good spirits and express the wish to be able to return soon to their jobs.

ABOVE: Report of the crash of the Halifax bomber after Anne-Marie's ('Milkmaid') and Arnault's ('Hairdresser') first attempt to parachute into southwest France, 17 December 1943 (HS 9/339/2).

Halifax flew into trees and crashed at 0505 in Tangham Forest near Capel St Andrew. 3 members of crew, including the captain were killed and 3 injured. Strangely enough, the two passengers got off without injury and were able to proceed to London the same day." (Operational Record Book, 161 Squadron RAF, AIR 27/1068.)

CHAPTER II (PP 39–45)

1. Pilot Officer James ("Jock") Buchanan flew WHEELWRIGHT 50 to France on 4 January 1944. "Near Angoulême they saw a twin-engined aeroplane with its navigation lights on. After pinpointing Langon (Gironde), 10 kilometres from the target, they picked up 'Rebecca' and, in clear skies and good visibility, dropped from 700 feet, in addition to Claude Arnault and a WAAF, Anne-Marie Walters, 15 containers and four packages. The site appears to have been situated near Gabarret (Landes), 40 kilometres east of Mont-de-Marsan." (Operational Record Book, 161 Squadron RAF, AIR 27/1068.)

2. "I wasn't afraid. In fact it was the only time in all the jumps that I have made that I really wasn't afraid at all. There were so many things to do and think about and it was our second trip. The pilot had circled some time in the region before being able to contact the people on the ground and we had a horrible moment that we should have to go back once more. And when the pilot declared that he had contacted the people and we were made to go to Action Stations and jump, I felt so relieved at the idea that we wouldn't have to go back again to England it was really quite a pleasure." (BBC interview with Anne-Marie Walters by Vera Lindsay, 19 January 1945.)

3. 'Le Terrain de la Vertu', between Créon-d'Armagnac and Gabarret, is at the edge of a vast clearing in the forests of Les Landes, and well serviced by all-weather tracks. Map reference: Michelin sheet 79, 43mm E250–45mm N4880.

4. Le Grand Canal du Marais, which runs along the eastern boundary of the dropping zone.

5. 'Scharks': Théodore ("Théo") Levy, born at Saarbrücken in 1917, was a refugee from Alsace who settled in Vic-Fezensac, in the Gers, with his mother. He was a furniture dealer and was sheltered by Madame Lac-

Ferblanterie, an accountant in Vic-Fezensac, through whom he made the acquaintance of the St-Avit family. The St-Avits were large farmers and much involved with the local Resistance. It was through Théo that Starr first met Maurice Parisot, later to be commander of the Bataillon d'Armagnac. (Archives Communales de Condom, February 2009.)

6. 'Morel': Gabriel Cantal, a master carpenter who lived in Gabarret and organised the local Resistance. He lent Starr/WHEELWRIGHT FF200,000 (£1000). Cantal was later captured and deported to Germany, where he died. His son Albert, also a member of WHEELWRIGHT, was captured at Gabarret during a *rafle* and deported to Germany under the Service de Travail Obligatoire (STO). He returned to Mont-de-Marsan, where he still lives.

7. Between April 1943 and August 1944 there were 143 *parachutages* to WHEELWRIGHT, comprising 2066 containers and 548 packages.

8. "There were no cars to be used during the curfew time. The containers were like huge metal cigars weighing about 400 pounds each, which had to be got as far away from the dropping zone as possible in case the drop had been noticed. All horses had been requisitioned, so they had to fall back on carts drawn by working cows who used to do the work in the fields." (IWMSA interview with Yvonne Cormeau, 7369, Reel 4.)

9. Maison Pelon, the family home of Louise Fiton, near Gabarret. "She was young and asleep and unaware of what was happening." (Interview with her granddaughter, Lydie Fiton, July 2007.)

10. René Barbères, who worked as a foreman for Gabriel Cantal. He lived at Lapeyrade, where he was responsible for the village telephone box.

11. Joseph Darroux. Joseph and his wife Alice owned the combined café, grocery shop and forge at Fourcès, which had become a centre of resistance. The family was responsible for many reception committees which handled *parachutages* in that area. They also sheltered many SOE agents and escaped prisoners of war on their way to Spain. Their son, Robert, who was only 12 years old at the time, also helped by carrying parcels and messages concerning impending *parachutages*. He still lives in Fourcès, where his parents' café is now the restaurant Tournepique. Alice Darroux, author of

Mémoires de la Résistance à Fourcès, died in 1997 at the age of 92. (Interview with Madame Robert Darroux, May 2009.)

CHAPTER III (PP 46–56)

1. 'Monsieur Laroche': Albert Bordes, who lived at 43 rue Gambetta, Condom, with his wife, three daughters (Gilberte, Andrée and Suzanne) and son Robert.

2. 'Nasoulens': Mamoulens, the farm belonging to the Castagnos family, and where they still live. It is in the commune of Caussens, which in 1944 comprised a population of 519, most of whom were farmers.

3. "My London-issued identity card was no use to me as it had been made in Cannes and *visé* in Paris, which meant that I had crossed the demarcation line '*en fraude*'. *Hilaire* gave me a Gers card right away, registered in Auch. Later on I got two Lot-et-Garonne and the Hautes-Pyrénées departmental cards. I had no cover story, except a very local one, as *Hilaire* had declared they were useless once really in the hands of the Gestapo." (HS 9/339/2 Report by Anne-Marie Walters, 18 September 1944.)

4. 'Privat': Olivier Prieur, the brother-in-law of Albert Bordes, was a butcher in Condom whose shop was also in rue Gambetta. As a butcher, he had permission to keep a vehicle and travel around the local area.

5. The 'Cérensac' family: The Castagnos family consisted of Henri, his wife Odilla and their son André, who was wounded at Astaffort on 13 June 1944 in a fight between the Milice from Agen and the *maquisards*.

6. The independent, Free-French paper *France*, published daily, was founded in London in 1940 by Anne-Marie's future father-in-law, Pierre Comert, and her future employer, Charles Gombault.

CHAPTER IV (PP 57–65)

1. Francs-Tireurs first appeared as irregular military groups, somewhat akin to guerrillas, during the Franco-Prussian War of 1870–71, when they gave the Germans a nasty fright. During World War I, they acted as sharpshooters

in the French infantry. Later, Francs-Tireurs et Partisans (FTP) described the Communist elements of the Resistance movement in France.

2. "I was never captured – the only one I think I told was Anne-Marie Walters. I told her that I had been captured and tortured to impress the little bitch. Not true." (IWMSA interview with G R Starr, 24613, Reel 2.)

3. 'VanderBock': Antoine Merchez. One of the original founders of *réseau* VICTOIRE and Starr's lieutenant in Agen, where he owned the Garage Agenais at 2 cours de Belgique (now avenue du Général-de-Gaulle). Merchez repaired Wehrmacht vehicles and so was able to move about freely.

4. A popular card game invented in the early twentieth century.

5. 'Marie': Marguerite ("Maguy") Merchez, later Reber, was the daughter of Antoine Merchez. She succeeded Anne-Marie as courier between Starr and Philippe de Gunzbourg, the regional chief of the Resistance for Lot-et-Garonne.

6. SOE agent R M Sheppard (*Patrice*) landed on the roof of the Gendarmerie at Anse near Lyon in June 1942, where he was immediately arrested. Eventually, after escaping from the Gestapo and being recaptured near the Pyrenees, he was imprisoned in Dachau, from where he returned in 1945. (HS 9/1353)

7. "The Gestapo Headquarters in Agen is in a private house in rue Louis-Vivent. In a small town such as Agen it is very easy for French collaborators to denounce patriots and this is the cause of many arrests. There are many French agents with the Gestapo – in fact, source only knew 6 real Germans in the Gestapo at Agen. He heard that the collaborators were paid 5000 francs a month." (HS 9/62/2 Interrogation of Raymond Aubin MC, 17 May 1944.)

8. 'Cyprien': Albert Cambon. A shady character who had been in prison before the war, Cambon worked initially to Philippe de Gunzbourg, for whom he received the first *parachutage* in the region, at the end of 1942. In addition, he later joined the COMBAT group based near Marmande, in Lot-et-Garonne, but remained officially under the command of Starr, from whom he received so many weapons that his area was one of the best equipped.

He continued in liaison with de Gunzbourg until 7 November 1943, when they disagreed and parted company. By now his ideas of assuming command of all the Resistance in Lot-et-Garonne had become too grandiose and he gossiped too much. Cambon was killed in a gunfight with the Gestapo while having lunch with Raymond Cosculuella, the Police Inspector at Agen, at the Restaurant Vert, rue Sentini, Agen.

9. 'Monsieur Chénier': Marius Sorbé was a Communist and the owner of outfitters shops in Seissan (4 place Carnot) and Boulogne-sur-Gesse. He was an ardent supporter of WHEELWRIGHT and often supplied clothes for those attempting to escape over the Pyrenees. He lent Starr/WHEELWRIGHT FF200,000 in September 1943. (HS 6/456 FP to D/FIN, 23 Decmber 1943.)

10. 'Roger': Roland Mansencal (*Roger, Castex*). Born in 1904, Mansencal had been an officer in the French Air Force. Following the arrest of Starr's local chief, Monsieur Labeyle, in June 1943, Mansencal assumed his responsibilities. He lived in a big house with a large garden in the village of Mazères, near Montréjeau. Here he received many visitors, so no undue attention was caused when members of the circuit arrived and departed. He controlled six small reception committees based at Tarbes, Bagnères-de-Bigorre, Tajan, St-Gaudens, Cazères and Montréjeau. Claude Arnault was initially based at his house and it was from here that Arnault carried out his attack on the Toulouse powder factory. Mansencal was also responsible for arranging '*passeurs*' for those needing to escape to Spain via the Pyrenees.

11. C J Duchalard (*Denis*) (HS 9/452/7; and HS 9/1285/7 Interview with M H Rouneau, 3 February 1945.)

CHAPTER V (PP 66–71)

1. 'Colomiers': Baron Philippe de Gunzbourg, MBE (*Philibert*). The son of a Russian banker (whose father was one of the founders of Royal Dutch Shell) and a French mother, de Gunzbourg was educated in Paris and at Oxford. When the French army demobilised in 1940, he rejected all thoughts of emigrating to safety and chose instead to buy the Château Pont du Casse, near Agen, in a part of the country to which he became deeply attached: "*J'ai sauvé Antoinette et mes fils d'une vie faussée à New York!*"

In November 1942, at the time of the Allied landings in North Africa, de Gunzbourg made contact, through his cousin Raymond Leven, with

Maurice Pertschuk, the head of SOE's PRUNUS circuit in Toulouse. Later, after the collapse of PRUNUS in April 1943, and by now under the command of Starr, he became active in the Gers, the northern sector of Les Landes, Lot-et-Garonne and the Dordogne. Here he proved himself to be an outstanding organiser, who contributed greatly, with other SOE and *maquis* organisations further north, to the successful 17-day hold-up of the 'Das Reich' Panzer Division on its move to the Normandy battlefield from its previous base in Toulouse. During his time in command, de Gunzbourg estimated that he had covered 20,000 kilometres on his bicycle carrying messages and explosives.

After the war, de Gunzbourg devoted himself to agriculture and food production, especially plums/prunes, and became the first President of the company France Prune (Obituaries in *The Times* 23 July 1986 and *Sud Ouest* 18 July 1986.)

2. 'L'Asperge': Francis Peyrot.

3. 'The Lantrets': Bertrand Alessandri and his wife were wine-merchants at Eymet and were close helpers of de Gunzbourg. "Monsieur et Madame Alessandri were both arrested and horribly beaten, neither gave anything away. One son, Jean, was in the *maquis* for 1½ years and Bertrand, the other son (only 17), sabotaged nine locomotives all by himself and worked directly for *Philibert*." (HS 9/339/2 Report by Anne-Marie Walters, 18 September 1944.)

4. 'Schark's brother': Louis Levy, brother of Théodore Levy (see Chapter II, note 5). Louis was born in Weinsheim, Germany. He was arrested on 19 August 1943, imprisoned at St-Michel, Toulouse, and subsequently at Buchenwald, but survived and returned to France after the war.

5. Château de la Clotte, near Castelculier, the home of Maurice Jacob, leader of the Alsace-Lorraine group of resistants and also head of the Service des Réfugiés at the Prefecture in Agen. The Alsace-Lorraine group formed part of *réseau* VICTOIRE and subsequently WHEELWRIGHT. Jacob had requisitioned the château ostensibly for housing refugees, but used it to store arms. The Germans took 165 sub-machine guns and many other weapons when they raided the château to arrest Jacob following his betrayal by Fernand Gaucher. He died in captivity in Germany.

6. 'Dr Driziers': Dr Jean Deyris of Condom. He attended to any medical

ABOVE: Temporary movement order for Dr Deyris, 27–28 October 1943.

problems suffered by members of WHEELWRIGHT and other *maquis* organisations in the area.

CHAPTER VI (PP 72–82)

1. "On the evening of 3 January 1944, [Philippe de Vomécourt] was able, with the connivance of the keepers, to escape by overwhelming the guards with chloroform stolen from the prison hospital. This was accomplished by five men absenting themselves from roll-call on such pretexts as going to the dentist or reporting sick. The gaoler who was working with them got into conversation with the other gaolers and with the help of these five men tied up the gaolers and took their uniforms. When the rest of the prisoners were being marched back from roll-call in groups of seven, each group was accompanied by a 'friendly' gaoler who took them through the gate, whereupon they all separated and ran, making for a fixed meeting point. The sentries on the walls were completely taken by surprise and when they had started firing it was getting dark and they lost sight of the prisoners." (HS 9/1539/5 Interrogation of Philippe de Vomécourt, 25 January 1945.)

2. Major Charles S Hudson, DSO. Parachuted into the Puy-de-Dôme department on 24 September 1942 to lead the HEADMASTER circuit, he was arrested two days later in Le Crest at the home of the man responsible for his reception committee. Hudson was initially imprisoned at St Paul's prison in Lyon and then transferred to the Maison Centrale at Eysse, near Villeneuve-sur-Lot, where he met Philippe de Vomécourt and helped to plan the escape. Hudson returned to France in 1944 to carry out a more successful mission with the HEADMASTER circuit, which he re-established around Le Mans.

3. 'Raymond Mautrens': André Coulom lived at 4 rue Bertrand-Barrère, Tarbes, where he was head of the Tarbes sector of PRUNUS/WHEELWRIGHT, responsible to his uncle, Roland Mansencal. He worked in Tarbes as a contractor for electrical and sanitary installations. Coulom was in touch with the Services des Prisonniers Français Rapatriés at Tarbes and organised escapes for them.

4. 'Janine': Juliette Coulom.

5. 'Maryse': Françoise Coulom (later Campardon). 'Francine': Annette. She was christened in honour of Yvonne Cormeau (*Annette*), who had spent some time with the family in Tarbes.

6. 'Miette': Juliette Mansencal.

7. 'The Agen bus driver': Louis Prouadère. He lived in Condom and was taken prisoner by the Germans during the battle at Castelnau-sur-l'Auvignon on 21 June 1944. He was executed in Auch on 23 June, accused of having killed a German soldier during the battle.

8. 'Thévenin': Raymond Aubin, MC. In May 1944, Aubin was denounced and forced to escape, with the help of the WHEELWRIGHT circuit, via Spain to Britain, where he joined SOE. He subsequently returned to France as organiser of the AUDITOR circuit near Lons-le-Saunier, in the Jura, for which he was awarded the MC in September 1945.

9. "Just outside the town of Agen, a charming newcomer joined our cramped party in the back – an English girl called Anne-Marie Walters, who had dropped into Gascony and was operating under the code-name of *Paulette*. She had cycled ahead to make sure the way was clear of Germans.

The atmosphere in the back of the vehicle was tense. The black maria was a good cover, but we felt so helpless shut up in the darkness, not knowing what dangers lay on the road ahead. *Paulette* helped to relieve the tension. One of the other two British officers, called confusingly for her, Hudson, swapped stories with her about SOE in London.

Farther on, another girl stopped the van on the road to Nérac to tell us there was a barrage of *gendarmes* ahead, searching all cars. Our *gendarme* in front dealt with them with complete confidence, although the silence in the back, for the two minutes we stopped, was taut with tension." (*Who Lived to See the Day*, Philippe de Vomécourt, Hutchinson, 1961.)

10. Besides Charles Hudson and Philippe de Vomécourt, the group included five other escapees. After resting at Mazères, they crossed the Pyrenees on foot near the Hospice de Rioumajou at the head of the Vallée d'Aure (with the help of Mme Labadie, *Daniele*) and arrived at Gibraltar via Barcelona on 23 February 1944 (HS8/178.)

11. 'Colonel B—': Lieutenant Colonel M J Buckmaster, Head of F Section. 'B.P.': Major R A Bourne-Patterson, Head of Planning at F Section. 'Vera': Vera Atkins, F Section Intelligence Officer.

12. Inspector Raymond Cosculuella.

13. "The black maria took us to a farm just outside Fourcès. There we bedded down for the night in a barn – but not until we had eaten largely of ham and bread, and we had learned that we had just missed a much bigger crowd of *miliciens* on manoeuvres in the area.

For a few days we were able to relax, eating well at the farm and enjoying freedom from alarms. All of us were the fitter at the end of it. Then a truck and a car, both running on illicit petrol, came to take us to our next stop – the small town of Montréjeau, southwest of Toulouse, and only about thirty miles from the Spanish frontier." (*Who Lived to See the Day*, Philippe de Vomécourt, Hutchinson, 1961.)

CHAPTER VII (PP 83–92)

1. Capitaine (later, Colonel) Fernand Pagès, Croix de Guerre.

2. 'François de Tranches': Pierre Fauré, a police inspector who by mistake shot

and killed André Delacartie, the young leader of the FTP, at Agen on 9 October 1943. Starr insisted that Fauré leave the country for his own safety.

3. 'Picolet': Paul Dufazza. He lived with his wife Marie in a large house with large barns in the village of Mazères, near Montréjeau, where the Mansencals also lived. Dufazza worked with Roland Mansencal hiding and helping Allied aircrew on their way over the Pyrenees. He also assisted at *parachutages* and helped with the transport of weapons. Dufazza and his wife were arrested by double agents. He was deported, but survived and returned to France after the war. Marie was released after two months in the prison of St-Michel in Toulouse. (Interview with their daughter, Josette Durrieu, 30 August 2006.)

CHAPTER VIII (PP 93–101)

1. Although Starr forbade the groups to carry out any sabotage before the Allied invasion, he did give Arnault two large targets to attack before D-Day. These were to stop production at the Empalot gunpowder factory at Toulouse and to destroy the Lorraine-Dietrich factory at Bagnères-de-Bigorre (see Chapter XII, note 5).

The first task was carried out with the help of an engineer employed at Empalot, who gave Arnault plans of the site and showed him the most important machines to destroy. He also obtained false papers for Arnault and organised entry to the factory for him as a visiting engineer, so that he could make a thorough reconnaissance. The engineer then smuggled all the explosives into the factory over about a week, helped by the fact that engineers were not searched.

When everything was ready, Arnault entered the factory in the evening and worked in his friend's office until it was dark. He then placed all his charges. Unfortunately, no fire broke out, but production was stopped for about a month. (HS 9/53/5 Interview with Claude Arnault, 22 January 1945.)

In the attack on Empalot, Arnault was assisted by an engineer who smuggled 60 explosive charges and five bombs into the factory, concealed in the haversack which contained his packed lunch. (Interview with Pierre Péré, 8 May 2006.)

The initial police report, written on the day of the attack (28 March 1944), states that there was "a series of explosions, thought to number 31 in the factory, between 0315 and 0730. The explosives were placed on the very

TOULOUSE   28 mars   4

ATTENTAT POUDRERIE NATIONALE TOULOUSE

Note de renseignements N°I :

Le 28 mars 1944, à 3h15, une série d'explosions
a eu lieu à la POUDRERIE NATIONALE à Toulouse, Secteur C.P.E
(coton-poudre).

Les éclatements se sont poursuivis de 3h15 à 7h30,
au nombre de 31? Les dernières explosions ont eu lieu à 6h40,
6h55 et 7h30.

Il n'a été possible de se rendre compte des dégâts
que dans la matinée.

Les explosifs ont été placés sur les moteurs électri-
ques à grosse puissance qui actionnent les meules destinées à
brasser le coton-poudre. Sur 31 moteurs, 30 ont été détruits.

En outre, un nombre important de bombes incendiaires
avaient été placées sur les charpentes des deux bâtiments abri-
tant les moteurs. Ceux qui ont placé les engins n'en connais-
saient sans doute pas le fonctionnement car la plupart n'étaient
pas déclenchés. Ce sont des engins d'origine anglaise groupés
Ils comportent deux dispositifs semblables à acide et magnésium
et un troisième en aluminium. En outre, deux nourrices d'essen-
ce étaient jointes à ces groupes.

Il n'a pu être retrouvé aucune trace des engins explosifs, mais les dégâts témoignent de leur puissance.

En outre, une explosion a complètement détruit la
vanne d'alimentation d'eau.

M. le DIRECTEUR nous a déclaré qu'il disposait d'
autres moteurs et d'une autre vanne; l'interruption ne dépasse-
rait pas 3 jours.

A 6h40, le lieutenant allemand LUCKE, chargé de la
réception et de la sortie de la poudre et l'Oberleutnant GLEICH
mann ont voulu pénétrer dans les locaux des moteurs. Ils se
trouvaient a proximité de l'un d'eux quand une xplosion l'a
détruit sectionnant la jambe droite du 1° et blessant griève-
ment le 2° au pied gauche. Le lt LUCKE a été amputé au dessous
du genou.

Les premières investigations ont permis d'entendre

les 12 ouvriers et ouvrières qui étaient seuls en Service à l'
Usine, cette dernière ne travaillant plus la nuit.
En outre, les gardes de surveillance à la Poudrerie n'ont apport
aucun élément utile à l'enquête

La 8° Brigade poursuit ses auditions.

ABOVE: Police report of the attack on the Empalot gunpowder factory, 28 March 1944.

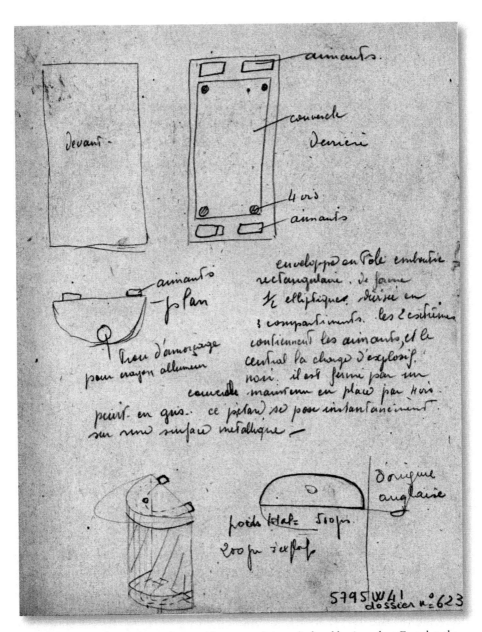

ABOVE: Diagram of an explosive device with magnets (*aimants*) placed by Arnault at Empalot, the only one which failed to detonate. (Police report, 29 March 1944.)

powerful electric motors which served the grinding machines used to mix the gunpowder. Thirty out of 31 motors were destroyed. In addition, another explosion has completely destroyed the main water supply and sluice. At 0640 Leutnant Lucke, the German responsible for movement of gunpowder in the factory, and Oberleutnant Gleichmann wanted to enter the area where the motors were. They were close to one of them when an explosion completely destroyed the right leg of the former and seriously wounded the latter in his left foot. Lt Lucke's leg had to be amputated below the knee." (COTE 5795W41, Dossier 623, Archives Départementales de la Haute-Garonne.)

The partially successful attack by Arnault to destroy the factory at Empalot was followed later by four aerial bombardments on Toulouse and the surrounding area by the RAF. Among these, the two most significant were an attack on 5/6 April 1944 against the aircraft factories at Blagnac and St-Martin-du-Touch, during which 22 civilians were killed and 45 wounded, and an attack on 2 May 1944 against Empalot, which completely destroyed the factory but caused 45 civilian deaths and 65 casualties. (*Ville de Toulouse*, Bulletin Municipal, Numéro spécial consacré à la libération, October 1944.)

2. Ghislaine Nicole Jeannier, whom Arnault married in December 1944.

3. La Frégate, 1 rue d'Austerlitz, Toulouse. "We dined with (inter alia) the proprietor of the restaurant 'La Frégate' and his English wife." (R A Bourne-Patterson in HS 7/134, JUDEX report on visit to Toulouse, December 1944.)

CHAPTER IX (PP 102–108)

1. 'The jeweller': Honoré Cazaubon. "I must also add the name of Cazaubon, jeweller at Condom, who was murdered at Simorre. He was an invalid and yet asked to go on all sorties and was indefatigably devoted and courageous." (HS 9/339/2 Report by Anne-Marie Walters, 18 September 1944.)

"Honoré Cazaubon volunteered as a liaison officer despite his right leg being permanently crippled by infantile paralysis. He concealed petrol and weapons in his house at Condom and placed his car and motorbicycle at the disposal of the Resistance without any charge." (*La Tragédie de Meilhan*, François Chevigné, Imprimerie Moderne, Toulouse, 1947.)

2. In 1944, Castelnau-sur-l'Auvignon had a population of just under 200.

3. Starr's radio operator: Yvonne Cormeau, MBE, Légion d'Honneur, Croix de Guerre (*Annette*). She was born Beatrice Biesterfeld in Shanghai, to a Scottish mother married to a Belgian consular official. Educated in Belgium and Scotland, Yvonne Cormeau was truly bilingual. She was dropped by parachute on 22 August 1943 at Château Maugarny, near St-Antoine-du-Queyret in the Gironde, to be radio operator to WHEELWRIGHT. During the next 15 months she sent more than 400 clandestine messages without being caught. Once she was stopped by the Germans, but successfully maintained her cover story of being a district nurse.

"I'm very nervous but patient. It's a funny mixture really and you need that for radio work. You need the patience to do the coding and de-coding. You need the resourcefulness of nervousness to be able to decide to go on if you think somebody's listening in, or to cut off and ask for another 'sked'. I can only say that the result seems to have been good because only one man beat me as regards the number of messages and he had stayed longer than I had." (IWMSA interview with Yvonne Cormeau, 7369, Reel 1.)

4. The Germans possessed sophisticated goniometric, or direction-finding (DF), equipment to help identify the exact position of a wireless transmitter during transmissions. It was usually fitted in small, grey Wehrmacht cars (known as 'gonios') carrying telescopic aerials. Usually these cars were disguised as Red Cross vehicles, although sometimes the apparatus was carried in commercial vehicles.

5. With the approval of Roger Larribeau, the mayor of Castelnau-sur-l'Auvignon, Starr lived in the kitchen of the village school, where Madame Rouneau (Jeanne Robert) was the schoolmistress. (Interview with Alain Geay, Archiviste, Archives Communales de Condom & President, Amicale Réseau VICTOIRE, June 2009.)

6. The Molesini family. The brothers, Aldo and Edward, who were both born in Italy, owned a wood merchants' business in Tonneins. In January 1944 they lent Starr/WHEELWRIGHT FF1.5 million. (HS 6/456 To D/FIN from FP, 17 January 1944.)

7. 'Lépine': Inspector Raymond Cosculuella, son of the Police Commissioner in Agen. He was later arrested and deported to Germany, where he died.

8. At 5 boulevard de Strasbourg, Toulouse, now the restaurant L'Entrecôte.

9. Le Capoul, place Wilson, Toulouse, which still exists today.

CHAPTER X (PP 109–118)

1. Maître Paul Pialoux, 4 rue des Armuriers, Condom. He often lent his office to Starr for meetings. As a busy *notaire* in a large country town, there were always many visitors to his office and therefore the comings and goings of Starr and his associates went unnoticed.

2. 'Suzanne Laroche': The youngest daughter of Albert Bordes.

CHAPTER XI (PP 119–127)

1. 'Auguste': Auguste Gerdessus. A law student hiding from the Service de Travail Obligatoire (STO), who joined the Resistance in January 1944. He was sheltered by Laurent Fourquet at Boila, near St-Laurent-de-Neste in the Hautes-Pyrénées, where he guarded the arms dump. He helped to organise liaison between Fuller (the commander of JEDBURGH's BUGATTI team) and Starr, and was also responsible for protecting Fuller and transporting Anne-Marie. (*La Tragédie de Meilhan*, François Chevigné, Imprimerie Moderne, Toulouse, 1947.)

"He showed particular courage after D-Day in saving *depôts* after they were betrayed to the enemy, protecting [members of the BUGATTI team], doing very good instruction and carrying out dangerous liaisons and missions. He was murdered after being wounded fighting the Boches in a *maquis* at Simorre. He is now buried with 75 of his comrades on the devastated site of the *maquis*." (HS 9/339/2 Report by Anne-Marie Walters, 18 September 1944.)

CHAPTER XII (PP 128–136)

1. 'Galles': Maurice Henri Rouneau MBE. A journalist by trade, Rouneau was

forced to flee from Lille because he was being hunted by the Gestapo for his known pro-British feelings and for distributing newspapers to the British Expeditionary Force before June 1940.

Rouneau moved to Pau, where he found work as a printer, and then to Agen in the same trade. It was here that he met several former NCOs of the 150ᵉ Régiment d'Infantrie who had been demobilised following the Armistice and who shared his opinions. At Easter 1942, with Pierre Wallerand he decided to start the VICTOIRE circuit, but only with NCOs he knew could be trusted.

As VICTOIRE was a locally formed organisation, it had neither contact with London nor access to arms or sabotage equipment. Through Monsieur Leurquin, the Belgian consul at Agen, they were put in touch with Henri Sevenet and Philippe de Vomécourt. Thus they eventually made contact with Starr, to whom Rouneau became deputy, bringing with him a large, well-organised circuit.

Forced by Starr to leave France for his own safety in November 1943, Rouneau escaped across the Pyrenees on foot with his wife and child. Passing through Gibraltar, he reached London, where he was recruited by F Section, trained by them and returned to France to organise the RACKETEER circuit around Rennes and Morlaix in Brittany.

2. 'Janet': Janet Bouchon, the daughter of Pierre Comert and sister of Jean-Claude, Anne-Marie's future husband, who was living in avenue Suffren, Paris 15ᵉ. Jean-Claude had been arrested 18 months previously and deported to Mauthausen, while their mother had also been arrested and sent to Ravensbruck. Janet was married to Fernand Bouchon who, after the war, became a dentist of some renown.

3. 'Georges VanderBock': Georges Merchez, son of Antoine Merchez, and brother of Maguy.

4. At 11 rue des Saussaies, in the eighth *arrondissement*.

5. "The factory at Bagnères-de-Bigorre fabricated parts for tanks and aeroplanes. There were no Germans in the town and informant was able to enter one night with a team of four, arrest the guards, take their keys and destroy all the machines. They then took the train to Tarbes and escaped without difficulty." (HS 9/53/5 Interview with Claude Arnault, 22 January 1945.)

6. The "suspicious people" turned out to be Jacques Poirier (*Nestor*) and members of his SOE DIGGER circuit. There was some rivalry between Starr and Poirier over control of the Dordogne and very little cooperation between the two organisations. (HS 9/53/5 Interview with Claude Arnault, 22 January 1945; HS 9/1196/9 J R E Poirier; *The Giraffe has a Long Neck*, J R E Poirier, Leo Cooper, 1995.)

CHAPTER XIII (PP 137–148)

1. There were many rumours and much speculation about possible Allied landings in southwest France, which even reached the ears of Hitler: "On 27 May Hitler … said that he himself thought that, after carrying out diversionary operations in Norway, Denmark, the southern part of the west coast of France and the French Mediterranean, the Allies would establish a bridgehead in Normandy and Brittany and, after seeing how things went, would then embark on the establishment of a real Second Front in the Channel." (*The Guy Liddell Diaries*, Vol II, 31 May 1944, Editor Nigel West, Routledge.)

2. The main prison in Toulouse, controlled by the Gestapo, where appalling tortures were carried out.

3. Most targets to be attacked by WHEELWRIGHT after D-Day were notified to the circuit during the last week of April 1944. A number of additional targets, including the Dax–Tarbes–Toulouse road (Route Nationale 117), were ordered on 5 June 1944. (HS 8/292 F/Plans to DR/Plans, 5 June 1944.)

4. 'Mike': Flight Sergeant Leslie J S Brown. He was shot down over northern France in April 1944, while serving as Flight Sergeant in a Stirling bomber belonging to 620 Squadron from RAF Fairford, a squadron used for supply drops and training glider pilots. Brown was awarded the Military Medal – a rare award for an airman to receive – for his valour during the battle at Castelnau.

   "A New Zealander who has been in the *maquis* since April. He was famous in the whole Gers for his courage and his shooting of the Bren at Castelnau-sur-l'Auvignon." (HS 9/332/2 Report by Anne-Marie Walters, 18 September 1944.)

5. Château de la Clotte. (See Chapter V, note 5.)

6. L'Abbé Boë took up his post as *curé* of Blaziert, near Castelnau-sur-l'Auvignon, in 1932. A professor of theology, former priest of the Vatican, a poly-glot and water-diviner, he was well known throughout the Gers. In his sermons he exhorted his congregation not to listen to Vichy: "The truth comes from London; we must fight with them." Boë joined the Resistance after the total occupation of France and subsequently became a recruiting agent and courier for the *maquis* at Castelnau.

7. 'Alcazio': Tomas Guerrero Ortega (*Camillo*). Born in Madrid in 1912, by 1931 Ortego was fighting with the Spanish Legion of King Alfonso XIII, which was then engaged in the Rif Campaign in North Africa. In 1933 Ortega, whose sympathies lay with the left, returned to Madrid and became involved in politics. On the outbreak of the Spanish Civil War in 1936, he was engaged as a regular soldier, gaining promotion and fighting in the battles around Barcelona in 1938, where he lost a leg.

    By February 1939 Ortega had arrived in France, after the Republican cause had lost hope. He was interned in various camps, ending up at the notorious Camp de Vernet, between Toulouse and Foix, which was reserved for those detainees considered by the French government to be the most dangerous and recalcitrant.

    The Quakers helped Ortega to get his discharge from the camp and to find employment at Montauban, where he was contacted by former comrades from the Union National des Espagnols (UNE). Before long he had joined the resistance movement in Lot-et-Garonne, and by July 1943 had arrived in the Gers to assemble his group of Spanish resistants who were to fight so gallantly with Starr in 1944.

CHAPTER XIV (PP 149–157)

1. 'Commandant Parisot': Maurice Parisot. A veteran of World War I, Parisot spent the inter-war years as an agricultural engineer improving the production of wheat in French North Africa. In 1941, he returned to France and bought and managed, on behalf of Monsieur Frick, director of a Swiss bank, the estate of Saint-Go, at Bouzon-Gellenave in the Gers.

    After joining SOE in January 1943, Parisot supervised no less than 24 reception committees, many of them at Saint-Go. He organised the transport and storage of weapons and explosives, instructed men in their use and made arrangements for 'safe houses'.

    On 6 June 1944, Parisot formed a *maquis* at Panjas, which was joined after 21 June by that of Castelnau-sur-l'Auvignon to form the Bataillon d'Armagnac, which Starr placed under Parisot's command.

Amongst the successful operations carried out by the Bataillon in the area were the battles of Estang on 3 July 1944, Aire-sur-l'Adour on 12 August and, following the surrender of the German garrison in Auch, L'Isle-Jourdain on 19/20 August.

Commandant Parisot was accidentally killed during a pick-up operation at Francazal, near Toulouse, on 6 September 1944.

"By his continued gallantry, devotion to duty and leadership of his men, the Bataillon became a terror to the German forces in the region." (SOE file of operations in southwest France.)

2. Château de Bascolles at Toujouse, to the west of Panjas, the property of Madame Cousseilhat.

3. It appears that, during the battle on 21 June, out of a total of 200-230 resistants who were in the village of Castelnau, seven Spanish and four French men were killed and four Spaniards wounded. It is generally accepted that five German soldiers were killed from a total force of 540 attacking Castelnau. The village was totally destroyed during the battle, except for the church and a tower. It was later rebuilt using the original stones. There is now a fine memorial commemorating the French and Spanish resistants who lost their lives on that day. (Interview with Alain Geay, Archiviste, Archives Communales de Condom, June 2009.)

CHAPTER XV (PP 158–168)

1. 'Plucci': Amedeo Scuttari, a stonemason from Condom.

2. This is the first intimation of the arrival of a JEDBURGH team in the WHEELWRIGHT area. The JEDBURGH operation was formulated in the late summer of 1942 by Major General Colin Gubbins, then Deputy Director of SOE, shortly after the landings at Dieppe. The aim was to parachute behind enemy lines, at the same time as the landings in Normandy, small groups of officers and soldiers with the mission of rousing and arming the civilian population to execute guerrilla attacks against enemy lines of communication. There were to be 70 such groups, each comprising two officers and a radio operator, and all wearing uniform, who would be parachuted into safe areas and met by SOE agents already on the ground.

Each team was to have only one or two missions to carry out and all members were trained in guerrilla warfare, the use of explosives and demolitions and in exercising command.

3. Situated near the hamlet of Tajan, east of the D929 between Castelnau-Magnoac and Lannemezan.

4. 'Choulac': Léon Abadie was dismissed as mayor of Tajan by the Vichy authorities. He fled to Toulouse but later returned and hid the entire contents of the first *parachutage* at Tajan in his own barn. (Interview with Monsieur Lacoste, Tajan, September 2006.)

5. Boulogne-sur-Gesse.

6. 'Bérard': the Petitjean family at Villeneuve-de-Lecussan. "William Fuller was first hidden by my cousin in Villeneuve-de-Lecussan. He was then taken in a truck to the underground Resistance group of St-Bertrand-de-Comminges, in his uniform so that he would not be accused of being a spy if ever he was caught." (Interview with Madame Luce Porthé, Montréjeau, November 2006. Madame Porthé, at the age of only 16, acted as courier for Maurice Pertschuk until his PRUNUS circuit collapsed in April 1943, after which she worked as a courier for Starr.)

CHAPTER XVI (PP 169–179)

1. *Piquette* is made by mixing grape *marc* with water in a barrel and leaving it to ferment for eight-to-ten days.

2. A memorial in the main square of Castelnau-Magnoac records that Maurice Cassagnabère, Juan Sanchez and Raymond Le Devedec were shot by the Germans on 21 June 1944.

3. 'Jacques': Pierre Cortezziani. (Interview with Madame Coulom, Tarbes, September 2006.)

4. 'Ross Halsall': Lieutenant Colonel Horace ("Hod") William Fuller, US Marine Corps. Officer in charge of the JEDBURGH BUGATTI team.

5. 'Yves de Changins': Capitaine Guy de la Roche. He grew up in Mauritius

and lived, before and after the war, at Tarbes, where he committed suicide in 1979. (Interview with Madame Coulom, Tarbes, September 2006.)

6. Fuller made a complaint about this in the BUGATTI debriefing: "Cardboard-composition containers usually broke in the air before landing, and their contents fell out." (HS 6/490 BUGATTI Team report.)

7. 'Bouboule': Michel Guillemot.

8. The Halifax carrying the BUGATTI team took off from Blida airfield in Algeria, where many of the JEDBURGH teams were based. (HS 6/490 BUGATTI Team report.)

9. "From 20 July onwards it was decided to divide our operations into two separate parts. Capt de la Roche was to take charge of organising and directing the FFI [Forces Françaises de l'Intérieur] from their HQ in Tarbes, while I was to direct the *maquis* groups in our camp and those in the valleys of Nistos and Luchon and as far east as St-Gaudens. Capt de la Roche provided himself with a full set of false papers and spent most of his time circulating among the Resistance groups in the 4th FFI region [approximately 150 km around Toulouse] in an effort to make them concentrate their efforts against the Boches and to forget their political differences until the war was won. He succeeded admirably in this work due to his tact and determination and was fully accepted by Davoust (*Chainette*), *Ravanel* and *Hilaire*, all of whom had the greatest confidence in him." (HS 6/490 Interview with Lieutenant Colonel H W Fuller, October 1944.)

CHAPTER XVII (PP 180–188)

1. Dr Joseph Raynaud. Born in 1911 at Chalabre, in the Aude, Raynaud studied medicine at Toulouse, where he won the "*prix d'excellence*". With this qualification he could have joined either the naval or army medical services, but chose instead to enter a civilian practice in Lombez, in the Gers. At the outbreak of war, he was called up to serve as Medical Officer with an armoured regiment, then returned to his practice in Lombez following the armistice in June 1940.

In 1941, the Mayor of Lombez was replaced by a "*Délégué nommé par Vichy*", who was a Pétainiste and of whom Raynaud did not approve. It was then that he started to form a resistance group. In 1943, when an attack was made on the house of the *délégué,* Raynaud was suspected, although nothing could be proved against him.

Raynaud died with his *maquisards* at Meilhan on 7 July 1944.

2. 'Mimosa': Xavier Laborde. A baker and *patissier* by trade, he was killed together with his younger brother, Paul (aged 17½), at Meilhan on 7 July 1944.

3. Julien Bedouch. A fierce argument developed between him and Lieutenant Colonel Fuller, with Bedouch saying "If you are captured, you will be made a prisoner but I will be executed." A neighbouring farmer provided a team of oxen to pull the car out of the ditch and drag it *"cahin-caha"* (with difficulty) as far as Tachoires. (Témoinage de Julien Bedouch, Musée de la Résistance, Toulouse.)

CHAPTER XVIII (PP 189–199)

1. The Meilhan *maquis* was created in May 1944 at the instigation of Dr Raynaud and comprised about 95 men. Its principal activities were sabotage and general military training. It was badly supplied with weapons and ammunition. The group had, for some weeks, been based at two farms, de Priou and de Larée, near Meilhan, and had received orders to move from these positions. They chose instead to remain *in situ* as they were awaiting a *parachutage* which was said to be arriving imminently. This was to prove a fatal mistake as, during the night of 6/7th July 1944, a strongly armed German company, consisting of the 116th Grenadier Battalion and the 28th Wehrmacht Regiment, attacked the position and killed 76 *maquisards.*

2. 'Captain Conte': Capitaine Raymond Le Conte of the French Colonial Artillery. He was dropped near Sarlat on 10 June 1944 with the JEDBURGH team AMMONIA. They were met by Arnault, who took them to Philippe de Gunzbourg. The team's mission was "the destruction of communications and the harassing of enemy troops between Brive, Montauban and Bordeaux." (HS 6/476 AMMONIA team report.)

3. Château de Valmirande, two kilometres west of Montréjeau. It has been the family home of the Barons de Lassus since its construction around 1880. (Interview with Madame Luce Porthé, Montréjeau, November 2006.)

CHAPTER XIX (PP 200–209)

1. In the Quartier Espagne, the former home of the 2ᵉ Régiment de Dragons.

2. The building, close to the church, bears a plaque recording that it was used by Starr and Parisot as their HQ.

3. André Bonnay (his real name) was later killed on the Atlantic Front, while serving with the Bataillon d'Armagnac.

4. Château de Castelmore, near Lupiac. During the war the château belonged to the Siame family. (Architectes des Bâtiments de France, Auch, May 2009.) Its most famous owner was Charles de Batz, Comte d'Artagnan (1611–1673), on whose life-story Alexandre Dumas loosely based his novel *The Three Musketeers*.

CHAPTER XX (PP 210–220)

1. The garrison commander at Tarbes was General Mayr, with his Kommandantur based in the Hotel Moderne on the northwest corner of the place de Verdun.

2. Henry Wonsink. (HS 9/339/2 Report by Anne-Marie Walters, 18 September 1944.)

3. In fact, Anne-Marie returned to the Gers after the war and bought a ruined house in Castelnau, which she restored. The Comert and Castagnos families still remain in close contact.

4. At a house belonging to André Coulom: Maison Françoise Annette, rue du Collège, Vic-en-Bigorre.

5. Château de Valmirande. The château is easily visible across the valley from the site of the *maquis* camp on a hill near Izaut.

CHAPTER XXI (PP 221–228)

1. In 2007, 63 years after Anne-Marie walked over the Pyrenees, a group of 20 members of the FANY retraced her steps as part of the Corps' 100ᵗʰ

anniversary celebrations. "The group had trained for 18 months in preparation for the trip. Anne-Marie would have had little more than 18 hours to prepare... The group of 20 FANYs had trained, researched, prepared, made risk assessments, lists and checklists. They had the right kit, plenty of food and water and a shelter each night. Weather forecasts had been checked, local residents' advice had been sought and professional, experienced mountain guides were employed. However, the walk had been tough and difficult and neither for the faint-hearted nor the unfit. All those that completed the walk, in the warm September sunshine, could not help but be humbled at the thought of Anne-Marie, in her tweed skirt, crossing these imposing mountains." (FANY Centenary Journal 2007.)

POSTSCRIPT (PP 229–236)

1. HS 9/339/2 Report by Anne-Marie Walters, 18 September 1944.

2. In an interview for the Imperial War Museum Sound Archive recorded in 1978, Starr stated: "When I got back to England, I faced a court of enquiry for ill-treating German prisoners. Anne-Marie Walters had started it because she hated my guts because I threw her out of France and sent her home for indiscipline. Very lucky I didn't have her shot. She never forgave me, and when she got back she started these stories." (IWMSA interview with G R Starr, 24613, Reel 2.)

"Yes, by Christ, I was a martinet. I had to be. I laughed and joked, but if anybody made a mistake, I'd cuss them, if it was serious out they went. Anne-Marie Walters, eg, for complete disobedience to orders. I felt like shooting her." (IWMSA interview with G R Starr in France, 24613.)

3. Originally an officer with the French Intelligence Services, General André Pommiès (*Chainette*) refused to accept the surrender of June 1940 and thereafter developed his contacts with the army. He received instructions to mobilise a secret army to cover the Gers, Landes, Hautes-Pyrénées and Pyrénées-Atlantiques. His Corps Franc Pommiès (CFP) became one of the largest elements of the Organisation de Résistance de l'Armée (ORA). For two years it was used to transport arms and materiel from *parachutages* and in the destruction of main lines of communication and power stations. At the end of 1943 the group comprised over 30,000 men. Warned by messages from the BBC on 6 June 1944, Pommiès mobilised 12,000 men and became

active in the Pau and Tarbes areas. In addition to normal resistance activities, he received special orders to prevent collaborators and members of the Gestapo and Wehrmacht from escaping to Spain. During its existence the CFP carried out 900 military operations, suffering 387 casualties and 156 members deported to Germany.

4. HS 9/339/2 Report by Anne-Marie Walters, 18 September 1944.

5. HS 9/1407/1 Letter marked 'Very Private and Confidential' from Lieutenant Colonel S H C Woolrych, Commandant, Group B, to Air Commodore A R Boyle. SF/5595, 2 November 1944.

6. The junior member of the Court of Enquiry was Major F A Soskice, a scholar of Balliol College Oxford and at the time serving with the Oxfordshire and Buckinghamshire Light Infantry (Frank Walters' old regiment). Soskice went on to become Solicitor General and Home Secretary.

7. Rates of pay for members of the Bataillon d'Armagnac ranged from FF10 per day for a single man up to FF100 for a married man with five children.

SELECT BIBLIOGRAPHY

UNPUBLISHED SOURCES

The National Archives (TNA), Kew Gardens, Surrey.
Records of the Special Operations Executive (SOE):
    HS 6 (Western Europe);
    HS 7 (Histories and War Diaries);
    HS 8 (Headquarters Records);
    HS 9 (Personnel Files).
Archives Départementales du Gers, Auch.
Archives Départementales de la Haute-Garonne, Toulouse.
Archives Départementales des Hautes-Pyrénées, Tarbes.
Archives Départementales de Lot-et-Garonne, Agen.
Archives Communales de Condom.
GUNZBOURG, Baron Philippe de *Souvenirs du Sud Ouest*.

INTERVIEWS

Sound Archive, Imperial War Museum, Lambeth Road, London:
    Yvonne Cormeau, Catalogue no. 7369.
    G R Starr, Catalogue no. 24613.

PUBLISHED SOURCES

BINNEY, Marcus *The Women Who Lived for Danger* (Hodder & Stoughton, 2003).
BULFONI, Hélène & les élèves de 3ᵉ du Collège Jules-Ferry de Gabarret *La vertu est la plus belle parure de la jeune fille* (L'Atelier des Brisants, 2009).
CAVE BROWN, Anthony *The Secret Servant: The Life of Sir Stewart Menzies* (Michael Joseph, 1987).
CHATEL, Nicole *Des Femmes dans la Résistance* (Julliard, 1972).

CHEVIGNÉ, François *La Tragédie de Meilhan* (Imprimerie Moderne, Toulouse, 1947).

CLARK, Freddie *Agents by Moonlight* (Tempus, 1999).

CLOAKE, John *Templer, Tiger of Malaya* (Harrap, 1985).

COOKRIDGE, E H *Inside SOE* (Arthur Barker, 1966).

COURVOISIER, André *Le Réseau Heckler* (Editions France-Empire, 1984).

ESCHOLIER, Raymond *Maquis de Gascogne* (Les Editions du Bastion, 2004).

FOOT, M R D *SOE in France* (HMSO, 1966 & Routledge, 2006).

GAUJAC, Paul *Special Forces in the Invasion of France* (Histoire & Selections, 1999).

GILLOIS, André *Histoire Secrète des Français à Londres de 1940–1944* (Hachette, 1973).

HELM, Sarah *A Life in Secrets* (Little, Brown, 2005).

JONES, Liane *A Quiet Courage* (Bantam Press, 1990).

MACKENZIE, William J M *The Secret History of SOE, 1940–1945* (St Ermin's Press, 2000).

PEARSON, Judith L *The Wolves at the Door* (The Lyons Press, 2005).

PÉRÉ, Pierre *Bataillon de Guérilla: Demi-Brigade de l'Armagnac, 1er Régiment du Gers, Régiment Parisot, 188e R I* (Imprimerie Dauba, Nogaro, 1987).

POIRIER, Jacques R E *The Giraffe Has a Long Neck* (Leo Cooper, 1995).

RICHARDS, Brooks *Secret Flotillas* (Frank Cass, 2004).

RIGDEN, Denis (Intro) *SOE Syllabus: Lessons in Ungentlemanly Warfare* (The National Archives, 2001).

ROBERT, Jeanne & Michèle *Le Réseau Victoire dans le Gers* (Alan Sutton, 2003).

RUBY, Marcel *F Section SOE* (Leo Cooper, 1985).

SAWARD, Joe *The Grand Prix Saboteurs* (Morienval Press, 2006).

VERITY, Hugh *We Landed by Moonlight* (Crecy Publishing, 1998).

VOMÉCOURT, Philippe de *Who Lived to See the Day* (Hutchinson, 1961).

WALTERS, Anne-Marie *Le Temps du Maquis* (Basil Blackwell, 1949).

WEST, Nigel (Editor) *The Guy Liddell Diaries* Vol II 1942–45 (Routledge, 2005).

ACKNOWLEDGEMENTS

Many people have helped me both here in France and abroad. Howard Davies at The National Archives, Kew, has been more than generous with his time, answering numerous questions and "bending the rules" as far as his pension prospects will allow. Monsieur Pierre Péré, Monsieur Alain Geay, Monsieur Albert Cantal and Monsieur Jean St-Avit have all helped enormously with local research and contacts. Madame Chantal Pagès at the Archives Départmentales de la Haute-Garonne has proved to be a fountain of knowledge about events that occurred in Toulouse and the wider area. Arthur Burland at Lectoure, who has over the years made a study of WHEELWRIGHT and the people concerned, has been a good source of freely-given information. Madame Luce Porthé from Montréjeau, herself a courier for PRUNUS and WHEELWRIGHT, has been another mine of information, many photographs and anecdotes. Madame Jeanne Robert has been a most willing contributor of background details and photographs concerning *réseau* VICTOIRE, which were included in her work *Le Réseau Victoire dans le Gers*. Mrs Yvette Pitt has been more than helpful in talking to me about her mother, Yvonne Cormeau (*Annette*), and also in providing photographs and her mother's treasured railway timetable from 1943.

Madame Josette Durrieu, Senator, showed me the house at Mazères where her parents, Paul and Marie Dufazza, had lived and the barn where they sheltered escapees waiting to cross the Pyrenees. In Tarbes, Madame Campardon (Françoise Coulom) – the young girl suffering from the measles in 1944 – introduced me to her mother, the widow of André Coulom, who told me much about life in Tarbes before and during its liberation in August 1944.

There have been many visits made on my behalf to The National Archives and the British Library in London by Brian and Annabel Karoly, Clare Hewson, George Hewson and Elspeth Forbes-Robertson. It was the latter who introduced me to *Moondrop to Gascony* and got me so hooked on the story. Jean-Pierre Comert and his sister Sophie Dubois (Anne-Marie's children) have been entirely forthcoming in answering my many questions about their mother and providing photographs – and also generous with their hospitality.

Susan Coe at *The Times*, Katharine Ramsay at *The Daily Telegraph*, Mary Bone and Sue Franks at The Royal Institute of International Affairs (Chatham House) and John Montgomery at The Royal United Services Institute have all produced much useful information about SOE and those people whose obituaries they have published.

Jackie Tarrant-Barton at Eton; Dr Robin Darwall-Jones at University College Oxford; Michael Rowe at Ecole Internationale in Geneva; and Mary Keller, at the League of Nations' Archive, have all helped me to a clearer picture of the Walters family.

I am also grateful to Simon Mawer, whose mother served with Anne-Marie in the WAAF at Bentley Priory, and others who have provided further thoughts and information since the first printing of this new edition of *Moondrop to Gascony*.

Without the patience, skill and enthusiasm of Jan Dodd and Moho Books, the encouragement of Professor M R D Foot and my wife's acceptance of a house littered with books, files and papers on SOE, this new edition would never have surfaced. Thank you one and all – and all those not mentioned by name.

David Hewson
Gers
Spring 2011

ILLUSTRATIONS

Acknowledgements and copyright information
Grateful acknowledgement is made for permission to reproduce the following: 1, 3, 7, 26, 30–33, the Comert family; 2, Ecole Internationale, Geneva (from the private collection of Marianne Wilmersdorfer); 4, 25 Pierre Péré, Comité d'Histoire de la Résistance pour la 2ᵉ Guerre Mondiale, Gers; 5, Georgina Cochu; 6, 9, 23, 24, Président de l'Amicale du réseau HILAIRE/BUCKMASTER; 8, Mairie de Castelnau-sur-l'Auvignon; 10, 11, 13, 16–22 Jeanne Robert (From *Le Réseau Victoire dans le Gers*, Jeanne et Michèle Robert © Editions Alan Sutton, February 2003); 12, 14, Yvette Pitt; 15, Monique Feyry-Miannay; 27, 28 Musée de la Résistance, Auch; 29, Architectes des Bâtiments de France, Auch; 34, 35, 37, Archives Départmentales du Gers, Auch; 36, The National Archives, Kew; 38, 39, Archives Départmentales de la Haute-Garonne, Toulouse. Also to Michelin for permission to use their map of southwest France for the cover illustration (© Michelin et Cie, 2009, Authorisation No. GB0908001; Michelin Map 99 – edition 1941.)

INDEX

People are indexed under their real names, and cross-referenced from their field names. Field names are given in italics, eg. *Colette*. Pseudonyms used by Anne-Marie are given in single quotes, eg. 'Jean-Claude'.